# TEACHING CREATIVITY
# THROUGH METAPHOR

**Contemporary Topics for Teachers Series**
SERIES EDITOR
James M. Cooper
University of Houston

# Teaching Creativity Through Metaphor

## An Integrated Brain Approach

Donald A. Sanders
Judith A. Sanders

Longman
New York & London

Pages 116, 121, 124, 217, 232, 264, 275, 307.
By permission. From Webster's Ninth New Collegiate
Dictionary © 1983 by Merriam-Webster, Inc., Publishers
of the Merriam-Webster® Dictionaries.

**Teaching Creativity through Metaphor**

Longman Inc., 1560 Broadway, New York, N.Y. 10036
Associated companies, branches, and representatives
throughout the world.

Developmental Editor: Lane Akers
Editorial Supervisor: Barbara Lombardo
Production/Manufacturing: Ferne Y. Kawahara
Composition: ComCom
Printing and Binding: Malloy Lithographing Inc.

Library of Congress Cataloging in Publication Data

Sanders, Donald A.
   Teaching creativity through metaphor.

   Bibliography: p.
   Includes index.
   1. Creative thinking (Education) 2. Educational
innovations. 3. Motivation in education. 4. Teaching.
5. Brain—Research. I. Sanders, Judith A. II. Title.
LB1062.S312 1984        370.15′7        83-25604
ISBN 0-582-28185-7

Manufactured in the United States of America
Printing: 9 8 7 6 5 4 3 2 1     Year: 92 91 90 89 88 87 86 85 84

*To Priscilla and Rosemary*

# Contents

*Preface  ix*

**PART I: Creativity, the Metaphor,
and the Integrated Brain: Past and Present**          1
   The Heritage  1
   The Present  2

**Chapter 1  Creativity, The Right Brain,
and the Metaphor—The Underlying Theory**          5
   A Look Forward  5
   What Is Creativity?  24
   Bibliography  46

**Chapter 2  Teaching through Metaphors**          48
   A Look Forward  48
   Model Lesson 1: *The Change/Butterfly Exercise*  57
   An Introduction to the Method  57
   Using the Metaphoric Method  59
   The Butterfly Guided Fantasy  63
   Model Lesson 2: *The "Time Movie" Exercise*  70
   The Time Movie  70
   The "Time Movie" Fantasy  78
   Bibliography  87

**Chapter 3  Ancient to Modern:
The Rich Tradition of Metaphoric Teaching**          88
   A Look Forward  88
   Ancient to Modern—The Rich Tradition of Metaphoric
     Teaching  89
   The Metaphoric Method—Recent Contributions  97
   Bibliography  106

**Chapter 4  Creativity, Concept Attainment,
and Metaphoric Teaching**          107
   A Look Forward  107
   Variations on the Theme—Concept Attainment  113
   Bibliography  126

**Chapter 5  The Experiential Learning Model**          127
   A Look Forward  127
   The Experiential Learning Model  128
   Bibliography  146

**Part I—A Summary: The Metaphor as a Measuring Tool**  147
    Bibliography  151

**PART II  Creativity, The Right Brain,
and the Metaphor: Classroom Application**  153

**Chapter 6  The Long Form:
The Metaphoric Lesson as an Instructional Unit**  155
    A Look Forward  155
    The Long Form—Or Planning a Complete Metaphoric
      Lesson  156
    Metaphoric Teaching Lesson Plan:
      *The Change/Butterfly Lesson Revisited*  177
    Summary  194

**Chapter 7  The Short Form:
Planning for an Abbreviated Metaphoric Lesson**  195
    A Look Forward  195
    How Do I Prepare My First Lesson?  202
    Planning the Metaphoric Lesson: A Summary  208

**Chapter 8  Complete (Long Form) Lessons
and Sample Format**  211
    Metaphoric Teaching Lesson Plan: *The Shoes/Empathy
      Lesson*  213
    Metaphoric Teaching Lesson Plan: *The Rainbow/
      Perspective Lesson*  229
    Metaphoric Teaching Lesson Plan: *The Balloon/
      Goal-Setting Lesson*  241
    Metaphoric Teaching Lesson Plan: *The Rock/Security
      Lesson*  261
    Metaphoric Teaching Lesson Plan: Design Format  278

**Chapter 9  Condensed (Short Form) Lessons
and Sample Format**  280
    Metaphoric Teaching Lesson Plan: *Diversity as a Value:
      The Leaf*  281
    Metaphoric Teaching Lesson Plan: *Values Clarification,
      Personal and Historical: The Perfect Day*  289
    Metaphoric Teaching Lesson Plan: *Film Developing/Print
      Processing—A Technical Lesson*  293
    Metaphoric Teaching Lesson Plan:
      *Relationships: Journey to the Planets*  299
    Metaphoric Teaching Lesson Plan: Design Format  306

**Part II—A Summary: The Metaphor as a Measuring Tool**  307
    What Keeps Creativity in the Classroom?  310

# *Preface*

## The Rat, the Seahorse, and the Creative Brain

"But . . . there has to be more!" This thought passed through many of our minds hundreds of times while we wrestled with the findings of certain psychologists during our days in "Psychology 101" and "Ed Psych 433." Indeed, what if they were wrong; for, while this is not a technical book, the findings of recent research in "left/right brain," in motivation, and in the educational potential of images cannot be ignored when developing a new perspective on teaching content, concept, and creativity in the classroom. Thus, if only for a few minutes of reading, we want to take you "back to the basics" (of Psych 101) in order to reacquaint you with something you may have questioned even then . . .

Place: A psychology lab in a major university.

The lab is starkly white, a lone psychologist sits watching a lone rat in a specially designed cage—the "Skinner box." After exploring every inch of the cage, the rat discovers a bar that, when pushed, yields a pellet of food. The rat begins to push the lever and receive his reward—food. The rat continues to push the lever until satiation sets in; then he retires to a corner to rest. Obviously another proof of the validity of the "stimulus" (food) "response" (press the bar) theory of behavior—but is it?

It could be argued that the most significant influence in American education during the past twenty-five years has been RATTUS NORVEGICUS—the common laboratory rat. The behavior of this ubiquitous psychology lab volunteer has been studied and restudied. The results of these studies have been given national attention; an entire school of psychology—behaviorism—relies heavily on the data derived from RATTUS NORVEGICUS. Behaviorism, as a school of psychology, has significantly affected the management of business and education in this country. Entire school districts have adopted the behavioristic model and initiated programs featuring token reward systems, punishment, and the disassembling of subject matter into pieces small enough for classroom "bar pushing."

Place: Another lab, another univeristy.

A psychologist places a rat in a maze and offers the rat two possible paths to food, one direct and known, the other less direct and novel. As often as not, the rat takes the less known path.

Another psychologist places a mouse in a different "Skinner box". Here there is no food as a reward, but if the mouse presses the bar, there is a clicking sound or a distinct change in lighting. The mouse develops the bar pressing behavior in the same way as when food is the reward.

Indeed, rats removed from cages and set on tables will randomly but predictably examine every inch of that table; when placed at the end of a "Y" maze, rats will examine first one "leg" of the Y, then the other. Perhaps food is not the most powerful motivator, perhaps, novelty is!

In fact, psychologists have now been able to "read" the response in the brains of rats and mice and have been able technically to record the response of a single cell using EEG's (electroencephalograms). The results of their work are astonishing; the cellular readings in the areas of the brain called the hippocampus (Greek for seahorse because its shape resembles just that) indicate that the cells are selectively responding to the presentation of novelty in the rat's world—in other words, according to Richard Restak, "single, one cell recordings of the hippocampus enabled psychologists to isolate novelty rather than reward as the factor that 'turns on' the hippocampus." Additional studies have found that, when the hippocampus (located on each lateral ventricle in the brain) is removed from laboratory animals, these animals return repetitiously to areas already explored. The hippocampus, the part of the brain that responds to novelty, is not only excited by the new, but is critical to memory formation and thus to learning.

Indeed, what this research suggests is that, while the behavior of the rat (or mouse) in the classic Skinner box experiment (pushing the bar to receive food), is undeniable, the interpretation of why it was done has perhaps been erroneous. Rats stop pushing the bar perhaps not because they are satiated, but perhaps because they are bored! This "boredom factor," this "novelty need," is presently one of the least understood and most exciting discoveries of recent psychology! It is what teachers know intuitively about their students and themselves; when the tasks get too routine, too unrelated, too unimaginative, teacher and student burnout is often the result. We need hippocampal stimulation, we thrive on it, and, we submit, it is a key ingredient in successful teaching. The search for novel and creative strategies (the use of affect and insight in the mastery of subject matter) is essential. We further suggest that through the use of metaphoric teaching strategies (which naturally expand conceptual understanding), teachers can make regular classroom instruction respond to the human need for "the new." Teachers can, in fact, expand learning by appealing not just to the small pieces of grey matter called the hippocampus, but to the entire "creative brain."

This book, then, links creativity and mental imagery with cognitive and affective insight through specific teaching strategies—the metaphoric method. This is a practical book with a theoretical underpinning, a book to integrate the discoveries of recent brain research with the affective teaching strategies of the past (the fable and parable) and with the creative training exercises of the present (brainstorming and conceptual analogies). It is an introduction to a new methodology that is fast evolving in our country—the conscious use of the metaphor to synthesize all these elements into a highly effective, multiple-use teaching process.

This book owes a large part of its development to those who worked on extending and implementing the original idea of metaphoric teaching into a practical and effective teaching strategy. Specifically, we wish to acknowledge the valuable assistance of our students in the Affective/Generic Teaching Strategies classes we taught at the University of Houston. Among these students, Jan Simonton, Frances Smith, Parvin Khoshnevis, Margaret Coward, Adelaide White, and Joy Smith made especially helpful contributions to the book. Also, we would particularly like to acknowledge the countless hours of proofreading, indexing, and production assistance, as well as unfailing support, of Priscilla Roth. We were encouraged by Jim Cooper at the University of Houston, inspired by John Curtis Gowan, guided by Bob Samples and W.J.J. Gordon, and nurtured by the many masters of the metaphor mentioned throughout the book.

# Creativity, the Metaphor, and the Integrated Brain: Past and Present

## THE HERITAGE

A Public Broadcasting System program called "The Art of Life" recently featured the noted South African author Laurens Van Der Post who told the tale of a man he had befriended many years back. The man was an elderly South African black who, in Van Der Post's words, "was thrown into prison for stealing a sheep from the man who stole his land." This man was later released to work on a small estate as a trustee; the estate was a considerable distance from his original homeland. One day Van Der Post asked the man if this life were not preferable to being in prison.

The man replied that he was, in fact, still in a kind of prison, and, that every time the moon would rise full in the sky, he was reminded of the thing he missed the most. "And what is that?" asked the famous author. The man replied that when he was young and the moon was full, his people would gather around the fire to tell stories, and the stories, well, the best way to explain them was to relate his favorite:

There once was a famous hunter in my tribe. A man of immense strength, steady eye and unmatched sense awareness. He could shoot the bow well, and he could track any animal. He was so accurate with the spear that no man would challenge him. The tribe depended on the man for its survival, such a hunter was he. Then, one day while he was many miles in the forest drinking from a deep pond, the hunter saw the reflection of a great white bird in the water. He looked up almost immediately, but the bird was gone. The hunter set down his spear and traveled in the direction of the great bird.

The hunter travelled for months, then years; at each village he came to, he asked, "Has the great white bird been seen by your people?" Always he was told enough to let him know that the bird indeed existed. The Kyu would say, "We have not seen the bird, but our brothers the Ygono have," and the hunter would travel to the place of the Ygono.

The hunter travelled for years; finally, when he was an old man, and he was many, many miles from his home and his family, he came to the place of a tribe he did not know. He asked these people if they knew of the bird. "Yes, we know of the great white bird," they responded. "He lives on the top of that high mountain, but no man can climb that mountain."

1

The hunter was determined to find the bird. He began to climb the mountain. Day after day, he climbed the mountain until he came to a smooth and sheer rockface that truly no man could climb. Then he saw the great bird itself nesting at the top of this rockface. Just then, the bird flew off and a single feather drifted out of the nest and fluttered down to the hunter who clutched it in his hand as he died. But, the hunter died peacefully; for the great bird is called truth and every man must spend his life pursuing it.*

What Van Der Post's friend missed most was not the family and friends he had left behind, nor the trees and grasslands that were his heritage; what the man missed most were the stories woven around the campfires, the living metaphors that determined his life's course—the stories that preserved tribal wisdom and elicited true understanding.

It seems, however, that in our pursuit of lineal knowledge we have forgotten the simplicity and effectiveness of strategies that teach through devices that are creative, metaphoric, and (as we shall examine) "right-brain." Nevertheless, in some of our schools, in some classrooms these strategies are beginning to be rediscovered.

## THE PRESENT

Switch now to a scene in a fifth-grade classroom in Houston, Texas. The children are in their seats in rows; their heads down, their eyes closed. The room is silent except for the measured, rhythmic voice of the teacher . . .

And, now you are inside a body, you are so small that you can only be seen with the most powerful of microscopes, you are multiplying rapidly, first one, then two, then four, eight, sixteen, thirty-two, sixty-four . . . quickly, your numbers mount. As your numbers grow, you know you are searching, searching through the veins, those long, blue-red canals, and searching along the cell walls, transparent, absorbing gateways appear all around you . . . you are seeking a nerve, a nerve that will lead to a muscle. . . . Nerves are your food—and your enemy. They carry messages to the muscles from the brain and spinal cord. . . . You keep searching, looking for the nerve, and then, suddenly, you see it. There are nerve endings on the outside of the cell body up ahead; you attack and are caught up in the nerve fibers, they are like a net . . . You are trapped, and there is only one escape—you must grow very quickly . . . you feel yourself expanding . . . overcoming and capturing . . .

This teacher is taking the students on a guided imagery experience, an imaginative, yet accurate, mental journey in which each student actively, but silently, experiences the learning moment. In this case,

---

*Fictitious names have been used for the tribes mentioned in the above story; the account itself is true.

the students are learning what it is like to be a virus. Taking this imaginative journey as a virus in the human body is so realistic and such a powerful teaching tool that the process allows and encourages the experiencing of something otherwise impossible to experience—the metaphor bridges that difference between having an ice cream cone explained to you and actually tasting the real thing.

But, let's go back to the classroom and to the teacher who has just completed the fifteen-minute guided journey into the world of the virus. The students' eyes are opening, they are startled by the light as their heads come up from their desks.

TEACHER: I want to talk briefly about what it is like to be a virus. Our guided journey took us on a trip into the human body, a trip much like the one you would experience if you were a polio virus. How was it to be a virus? What did you sense?

ANTHONY: I was, I was in the army; I was on a river in a jungle of nerve fibers; I was in a . . . well, like a search and destroy mission.

CARMEN: I was gooey, but I was bad. They were all scared of me.

RONALD: I felt sorry for the nerve cell, it couldn't defend itself.

VANESSA: It was weird to be that small, but we kept getting bigger 'cause there were more and more of us, we just kept doubling.

SANDY: I knew my job was to paralyze that nerve cell; I didn't care about nothin' else, I didn't even care when I got caught in those fibers at the end of the cell, I just had to get through.

TEACHER: Now think back to when you were inside the body; which of the things we talked about are you like? The virus? The nerve cell? The muscle? The antibodies? Which one is most like you and why? Take a minute or so to think of your answer. (After sixty seconds.) Is there anyone who has not yet thought of an answer? (Three hands go up.) Okay, we'll wait a little longer . . . All right; now which one are you like and why?

FELICIA: I would be the antibodies. I'd just wait for those bad guys to come along. I like to protect kids who can't take care of themselves, but nobody but me knows it.

RANDY: I would be the virus. I'd be so small nobody could see me, sneaking up on the nerves. I'd really zap 'em. I'd get 'em and get into the nerve net and then I'd paralyze the muscles.

FORREST: Sometimes I think I'm just like a nerve cell. There I sit doing nothing while the viruses and antibodies fight over me; but if they get caught in my trap, if they did, they'd be stuck—but sometimes so am I . . .

The students are developing an understanding of concept in a manner not unlike the one used by the tribesman Laurens Van Der Post befriended. The teaching target is the right brain; the teaching vehicle is the metaphor.

The metaphor is a bridge. It is the likening of one word or concept to another, the birth of a thought with a word or a string of words.

Thinking in metaphors links concept and imagination; it expresses thoughts otherwise unexpressed; thinking in metaphors is a teachable skill—a skill that can motivate students to learn multiplication tables or value the principles of social interdependence. Metaphoric thought provides an understanding of concepts not possible in the more passive activities of reading or writing. Indeed, metaphors are tools for insight, for creativity, for concept development, for learning, for true understanding. It is with the metaphor that we can unlock the part of our minds that schools have traditionally left closed and untapped, the part of our minds where conceptual imagery resides, the right hemisphere.*

Metaphoric learning is appropriate for second graders, for fifth graders, for ninth graders, for twelfth graders, for advanced training in corporations, and for undergraduate and graduate education; it is a powerful and efficient teaching tool. Metaphoric teaching prompts the affective insight that enhances cognitive knowledge-building. It is a process that is both creative and experiential. As teachers (and learners) we face ongoing, daily frustration over forgotten facts and misunderstood concepts; metaphoric teaching responds to this frustration and offers exciting new possibilities for encouraging student learning.

In the following pages you will journey through a discussion of creativity and examine its relationship to new learning models and new discoveries in brain functions. You will experience the potential of experiential learning and metaphoric teaching, and you will develop strategies for using these methods in your life and your classroom. Finally, you will examine the metaphor itself; you will explore the various levels of the metaphoric method, and you will learn to use the metaphor to teach and to learn. Along the way, you will meet some of history's greatest teachers and discover for yourself the feeling of mastering the metaphor.

---

*Growing out of research relating to hemispheric specialization in the brain, the terms "right brain" and "left brain" are useful designations. We do not wish in any way to oversimplify the complex interactions that occur constantly and with incredible speed in our brains by ascribing specialized functions that are not yet proven. We have approached the entire area of right/left brain research with enthusiastic, yet cautious, consideration. A detailed discussion of right/left brain research as it applies to the classroom is included in Chapter 3.

# CHAPTER 1

# Creativity, the Right Brain, and the Metaphor— The Underlying Theory

## A LOOK FORWARD

*All advances of scientific understanding, at every level, begin with a speculative adventure, an imaginative preconception of what might be true—a preconception that always, and necessarily, goes a little way (sometimes a long way) beyond anything which we have logical or factual authority to believe in . . . scientific reasoning is therefore at all levels . . . a dialogue between two voices, the one imaginative and the other critical.*

Peter Medawar
*Plato's Republic*

An operating room in a hospital in Northern California. A team of surgeons and nurses probes the mysterious band of fibers that connects the two halves of nature's most intricate, most advanced, controlling mechanism. This mechanism houses the potential for $10^{800}$ synaptic interconnections (Samuels, 1976); it allows us to read, to compute, to remember, to cry, to create—and these surgeons, these highly trained scientists, are tampering with it.

This team is tampering with this brain because this brain has been malfunctioning—because it has been throwing its entire biological entity into such violent seizures that both the life of the body and the life of the brain are threatened. And this is a first. It is the first time that a surgical team has intentionally severed this band of fibers in order to physically inhibit or terminate the processes that cause the epileptic seizures.

True, the procedure has been successfully performed on cats and dogs and even on some primates, but will it work on humans? And there is an additional question. If it does work, will it then relegate this intricate band of fibers to the same realm as the appendix or the tail —an evolutionary postscript—a once necessary item no longer serving the needs of its owner?

One of these questions will be immediately answered: yes, the patient will recover and the seizures will stop. But the answer to the second question—is the band of fibers (the corpus callosum) essential

5

to normal functioning?— will not be found until twenty-one severely suffering epileptic patients have undergone this same operation and, as an unanticipated consequence, have begun to show behavior abnormalities that demand an end to this procedure.

Some of these resultant behavioral abnormalities, however (which are discussed in this chapter), will provide a clue to a mystery that philosophers and scientists have tried to unravel for millennia—the mystery of man's duality of thought. Then, like the serendipitous discovery of the X-ray, this clue will spark a rash of investigations that will produce more and more evidence. The evidence will continue to accumulate until the solution to the mystery, while by no means complete, will become defined, delineated, directed. And out of this operating room will come the initial hint of an answer to one of twentieth-century education's major questions—namely, what is the nature of creativity, and if we know what this is, can we then teach it? The distance from that operating room to today's classroom is now closer than we realize. This chapter explores this narrowing distance and explains why, for teachers, trainers, and researchers, it is no longer acceptable to listen to only half of our thinking brain.

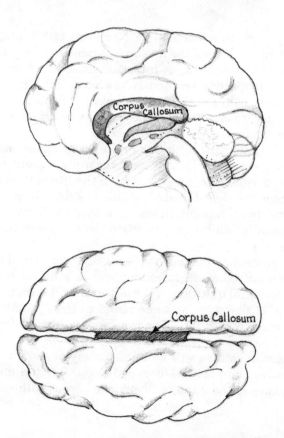

## "1 ÷ 2 = 3"—The Application of New Brain Research

The improbable equation of 1 ÷ 2 = 3 contains, for teachers, the essential message emerging from the most recent research on hemispheric specialization in the human brain. Recent examinations of the functions of the brain's two sides (often called left and right hemispheres) indicate that there are undeniable implications for education, implications that suggest we can now actively and consciously encourage students to intuit novel, creative connections, to enjoy the process of discovery by combining logic with imagery, and to develop a highly effective, natural conceptual tool—the metaphor.

The question is: is there a need for teachers to help develop conscious creativity skills in students? Yes, says Hideki Yukawa, the Nobel laureate in physics (1949), who warns that, in today's world, creative discovery occurs far too infrequently when compared to the number of scientists actually engaged in creative investigation. One reason, Yukawa suggests, is that everybody has become too "digital," too statistically and computer oriented. Yukawa urges the scientific community to look for mental stimulation in either metaphysics or moments of intuition. Likewise, Fritjof Capra in the celebrated *Tao of Physics* (1975) challenges that much is to be learned by relating the study of the world of quantum mechanics (with its inherent left-brain orientation) to the concepts of Eastern metaphysics (with its inherent right-brain orientation). We are, in fact, living in a world fast discovering that to approach only the digital side of a subject is to choose to utilize only half the cerebrum—the left hemisphere. The other half, the right hemisphere, seems to be all too often unobtrusively awaiting an opportunity to contribute—a chance to be consciously recognized!

Is this awareness of the "two" brains in each of us, the existence of dual approaches for information-processing, a new perspective? We suggest that it is not. The two complementary sides of the human condition (and, by extension, of the human mind), a rational, logical side and a creative, intuitive side, have been continually identified in the themes and stories of great teachers and writers for thousands of years.

For example, this dichotomy (reason versus insight) has emerged over and over in recorded folklore. Consider the *Saga of Gilgamesh,* a folktale inscribed in cuneiform characters in the ancient Semitic language of Akkadian some four thousand years ago. This story, passed down orally for hundreds of years from generation to generation before being written on tablets, describes Gilgamesh's search for immortality. A long and intricate tale used by Akkadian sages to instruct listeners on the futility of such an enervating search, the saga teaches the wisdom of accepting one's destiny. The two main characters in the story are Gilgamesh, rational, proud, almost linear in his logical search for everlasting life, and his brother, Enkidu, primitive, animal like, intuitive. Classic profiles are drawn; the ordered reason of Gilgamesh contrasts widely with the spontaneous resourcefulness of Enkidu. The duality of human nature is clearly exposed; the two perspectives are portrayed rather than explained.

Similarly, in the classic modern short story, "Heart of Darkness," Joseph Conrad depicts Marlow, the Western intellectual, as the epitome of rational, logical, goal-oriented behavior; however, Marlow's personal conflict with the savage, untempered, primitive nature of his own mind lifts the frightening journey to find the degenerate Kurtz from the level of a good story to that of great literature. The conflict is eternal, universal. To be human is to be both rational and spontaneous, both logical and intuitive.

Intimations of this duality, the dichotomous nature of our being, extend far beyond ancient sagas and modern literature; the parallel is continually found throughout Western and Eastern writings. G. K. Chesterton, for example, writes of the great thirteenth-century debate between St. Thomas Aquinas and Siger of Brabant. This debate was caused in no small part by Aquinas's assertion that there might be a dual path to truth. In an age of theological purity, Aquinas dared to state that both the scientific exploration of knowledge (as long as the investigator did not declare himself infallible) and the clerical pursuit of supernatural knowledge (as long as this pursuit did not contradict the "deposit of faith") were acceptable modes for discovering the "truth."

The Chinese have long noted this basic dichotomy by visually representing the two complementary sides of human nature. In the *I Ching* long broken lines are used to symbolize the active, strong, rational side of humanness; short, broken lines are used to denote the dark, receptive, nonrational aspect of our being.

What these classics intuitively describe (in fact, one of the qualities that makes them "classic") is presently being proven in experiments carried out at the California Institute of Technology and the Langley Porter Neuropsychiatric Institute in Palo Alto. A new understanding of brain specialization is evolving: the special abilities of the right brain (intuitive leaps, moments of insight, creative imagination) and of the left brain (highly sophisticated hypothesis testing, statistical analysis, technological reasoning) have been the subject of several research studies. The results of the research leave no doubt that there are, indeed, two specialized halves to the cerebrum, the thinking brain, and that each half functions in a separate mode.

The left hemisphere of our brain is logical, analytical, verbal and sequential; the right hemisphere is intuitive, conceptual, nonverbal,

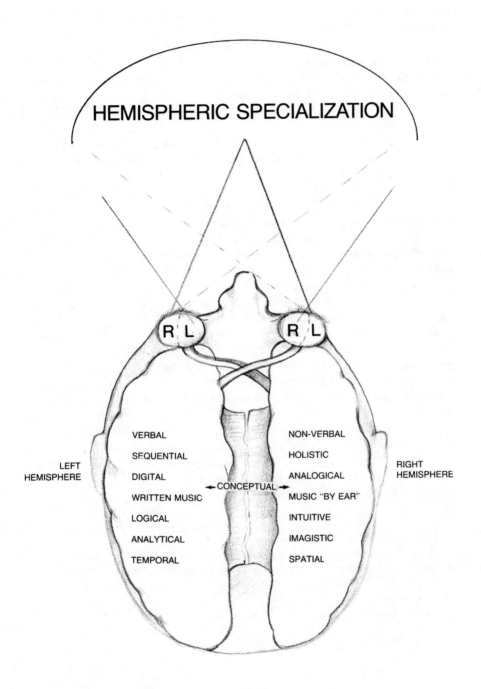

HEMISPHERIC SPECIALIZATION

| LEFT HEMISPHERE | RIGHT HEMISPHERE |
| --- | --- |
| VERBAL | NON-VERBAL |
| SEQUENTIAL | HOLISTIC |
| DIGITAL | ANALOGICAL |
| WRITTEN MUSIC | MUSIC "BY EAR" |
| LOGICAL | INTUITIVE |
| ANALYTICAL | IMAGISTIC |
| TEMPORAL | SPATIAL |

←CONCEPTUAL→

and pattern-seeking. The hemispheres themselves are connected by a band of neural fibers (the corpus callosum) which carries messages back and forth from one side of the brain to the other, almost like a river flowing in two directions. In most people,* the left hemisphere controls language, rational cognition, the sense of time, and the right physical side of the body; the right hemisphere controls spatial relationships, intuitive thinking, imagery, and left physical side of the body. Critical to our design of teaching strategies is knowing that both hemispheres operate continuously—that they function independently and in conjunction with one another at all times. For example, dreams are primarily a right hemisphere "imaging" activity (and we "dream" when we are awake), but our left hemisphere contributes the dialogue of our dreams and controls sequencing. In contrast, during daily "awake" interactions, the left brain monitors our behavior in a logical, rational manner, often consciously obscuring the input of the right hemisphere. Sleeping reduces the dominance of left hemisphere and limits the intake of data; it is, therefore, usually only in the sleeping dream state that the right hemisphere actively exerts dominance over the left. Then, as Carl Sagan suggests in *The Dragons of Eden,* "the dragons can be heard hissing and rasping and the dinosaurs thunder still."

How can we become aware of the input of these two hemispheres in daily life? Interestingly, one of the most common times that we can perceive ongoing interaction between the two hemispheres occurs while we listen to a lecture or read a book. Those moments of guilty mind-wandering are actually examples of the two brains alternating conscious control or acting in partnership. During moments of what we call daydreaming, of sinking into a sort of internal reverie while exhibiting exterior concentration, we selectively tune down (or out) the words of the speaker or printed words of the book (left hemisphere) and test the truth of the message with an array of patterns and images created in our right hemisphere.


From a teacher's classroom journal:
    "I watched intently as fifteen-year-old Juan 'tuned out' the student teacher; oh, he maintained eye contact, but his expression changed from intense interest to passive acceptance (almost boredom). Where was he? Why did he 'turn off'—or did he?

    "Later, I talked to Juan. 'No,' he said, 'I wasn't exactly daydreaming. I was thinking. I was thinking about what Mrs. Grant was saying, and how her life had been so different from mine—that's all!' "

---

*This specialization is reversed in some people (notably some of the left-handed population). In this case the left brain functions as the right; the right brain as the left. Specialization is maintained—the hemispheres are reversed in their functions.

We can tune out in such a way that we are unaware of the flow of words, the actual happenings around us; in fact, we can even feel ourselves "snap out" of a right-hemisphere reverie and return to left-brain information processing. In the classroom, we notice this experience happening with our students, but often we conclude that such daydreaming departures simply mean a lack of interest or unwillingness to pay attention to the subject at hand—and sometimes it does. At other times, however, the blank stare means that the right brain is interested in the concept being taught, that it is seeking a holistic, conceptual understanding. The student's mind could be envisioning how the topic at hand works in real life situations. Abrupt, noticeable body changes (the nodding head snapping up, the dream-like expression replaced by alertness and tautness around the eyes) may be signalling a return to conscious analysis from a state of intuitive expansion.

As teachers, we spend considerable time designing and implementing activities to impact our students' minds; as we have noted, left/right brain research has tremendous implications for teachers, implications that extend the sphere of learning as we currently define it. This brain research began as an isolated scientific quest to discover surgical remedies for brain-related dysfunctions. The fact that the discovery and definition of bicameral functioning serendipitously occurred as the results of this research is one of the most exciting and important stories of our time.

## Basic Research Findings in Hemispheric Specialization

The basic research conducted in hemispheric specialization falls into three groups: first, experiments conducted with epileptics who had their corpus collosa (the nerve fibers connecting both hemispheres) severed to minimize or eliminate the transfer of electrical impulses from one side of the brain to the other; second, research with patients who suffered massive strokes to one hemisphere or the other; third, research with "normals," individuals with no observable neurological damage to the brain. Each of these research areas contributes significantly to the growing data bank on how the brain functions; each contributes information which, linked with the others, is critical to the planning of curriculum, the identification of special student programs (gifted, learning-disabled, hyperactive) or the examination of instructional alternatives (direct instruction versus inquiry).

Foremost in this research are the pioneering studies of left brain/right brain functions by Dr. Roger Sperry. Winner of the 1981 Nobel Prize in Medicine for his work, Sperry's research began in 1958; his research provided the impetus for the growing tide of left brain/right brain efforts now emerging in psychology, neurology, and education.

Sperry's initial work (and the later work of Bogen, Gazzaniga, and Hillyard) on split-brain functions has extensive import for education, the private sector, and each of us individually. It causes us to view the brain differently, to question the assumptions we have held previously.

Let us again return to that Northern California Hospital. It is now two months later. Twenty-two patients have now undergone the severing of their corpus callosa. Our attention is drawn to one patient, who, in order to protect her privacy, is known as "N.G." N.G. is a housewife, and, from all outward appearances, she has fully recovered from the surgery. She has been experiencing no physical ill effects.

Now, N.G. is in a very different hospital room. The room is stark in its simplicity; its purpose is to test what, if any, changes have occurred in N.G.'s mental processes as a result of the operation. The room is fitted with a chair and table—on the table sits a small screen with a tachistoscope behind it. The tachistoscope can project images on to the screen so that they are solely visible in N.G.'s left visual field or her right visual field. An "experimenter" is in the room with N.G.

The experiments begin. The experimenter asks N.G. to fix her eyes on the small black dot in the middle of the screen. Next, a picture of a cup is flashed onto the screen where it can only be "seen" by N.G.'s left hemisphere. When asked what she sees, N.G. replies, "A cup." This picture is followed by one of a spoon; it can only be "seen" by N.G.'s right hemisphere.* Then, N.G. is asked to reach under the screen with her left hand (controlled by the right brain) and to find the object that has been flashed on the screen. She responds by touching all four objects under the screen, and then, confidently, she selects the spoon.

N.G. is cautioned not to look at the object in her hand. (Looking at the spoon would "cue" in the left brain, the brain that is verbal and "talks.") Nevertheless, the experimenter asks N.G. to identify what she has touched; she answers, "A pencil?" (The pencil comment is an attempt by her left brain to guess what it does not know.) Amazingly, the experimenter has discovered that N.G.'s right brain does, in fact, "know" the image it has seen; it has tactically identified that object—but, because the right brain does not "name" objects and lacks the speech function of the left brain, N.G. is unable to verbally identify the spoon she so obviously recognizes.

This discovery (the inability of the right brain to verbally "tell" what it obviously knows) pales with the one that follows. In the next set of experiments, a picture of a nude woman is flashed to the part of the screen "seen" only by N.G.'s right hemisphere. She blushes and giggles, but she can not relate what she is seeing; "Just a flash of light" is all she answers when the experimenter asks what image has been flashed.

---

*Remember, N.G., as a "split-brain" patient, has no easy route through which the right and left cerebral hemispheres can exchange information. Quite literally, objects can be flashed (through the use of the tachistoscope) to appear only within the visual field of one hemisphere or the other.

"Why did you laugh?" questions the experimenter.

"Oh, Doctor, you have some machine here!" she answers with a smile. N.G.'s left brain knows something has happened, but it can not identify what. With partial cues from physical responses in the body, her left brain has offered a reasonable, "face-saving" answer—"You have some machine!"*

It is not a far leap from these experiments with N.G. to the student in the elementary school classroom who honestly says, "I get it," but cannot explain "it," or the algebra student who knows the answer but cannot explain the process by which it was derived. The right side of our brain, in most people, cannot verbalize, but it does "know"; the problem is that we too often ask that "I know" be explained logically rather than metaphorically. The right brain can provide the left brain with an image, a metaphoric perception; the right brain cannot provide logical, detailed, verbal analysis.

Further support for the differentiation of the bicameral functions of the brain was later developed in and from a very different group of research studies. These studies were conducted with hospital patients

---

*When faced with its own lack of knowledge, N.G.'s left brain has, nevertheless, taken inventory of what it does know and has offered a reasonable explanation. It must be an unusual machine that it can cause her body to respond so emotionally.

who had suffered massive strokes.* Stroke patients become essentially unicameral instead of bicameral; legislated control becomes either "left-brain" or "right-brain." Because the left hemisphere controls the physical right half of the body and the right hemisphere the physical left side of the body, observing the effect of paralysis can sufficiently indicate which side of the brain has been damaged by the stroke. Generally speaking, patients who suffer left-hemisphere strokes lose the ability to speak; patients who suffer right-hemisphere strokes lose the ability to function spatially and musically. These are common results. In fact, the initial research on these effects precedes the research with split-brain patients by over one hundred years.

In the late 1800s Broca and Wernicke, the original stroke researchers, began conducting follow-up autopsies of stroke victims. Today, we use their names to indicate specific parts of the brain. Broca's area is located between the frontal and temporal lobes in the left hemisphere; it is a very small area that primarily controls speech. Wernicke's area is in the anterior part of the temporal lobe; damage to this part of the brain results in severely reduced ability to understand speech. These early researchers pioneered in mapping brain functions; their findings, along with those of Dax (1830s), Jackson (1860s) and Liepmann (1870s) were critical in establishing the base from which modern brain research evolved.

Modern research studies conducted with recovering stroke patients substantiate the notion of bicameral specialization—people with left-brain damage have difficulty completing verbal tasks and people with right-brain damage have difficulty handling nonverbal, spatial tasks. Weisenberg and McBride found this to be true in 1935 when they worked with over 200 stroke patients. Curiously (and unfortunately) the results of their research remained unused until the early 1960s. At that time, research concerning the effects of the commisurotomy procedure ("splitting" the brain by severing the corpus callosum) prompted new interest in the Weisenberg/McBride findings. Essentially, it was discovered that effects of strokes had a high degree of correlation with the effects of split-brain operations.

Thus, the evidence of the specific functions of the two hemispheres mounted. But what if the subjects were normal? What if the individuals being tested had never had a stroke or had never undergone a commisurotomy? Would the findings hold? Would we still find hemisphere specialization? Two ingenious tests, one the Wada test, the other the electroencephalogram, provided additional evidence.

---

*When an individual has a "stroke," the blood supply to a specific part of the brain is impeded; the resultant damage to that part of the brain renders the affected hemisphere virtually useless.

Broca's Area

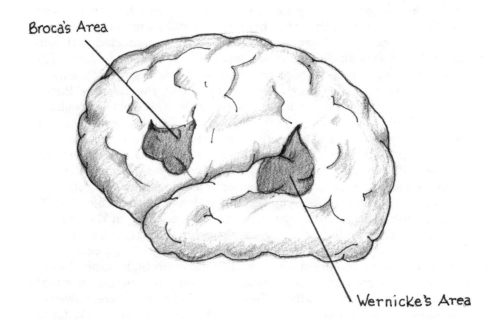

Wernicke's Area

The Wada test is a procedure for anesthetizing an entire hemisphere. In this procedure, a solution of the drug sodium amytal is injected through a tube into a patient's carotid artery on one side of the neck or the other. (The carotid artery on the right side of the neck flows into the right hemisphere, and the carotid artery on the left side of the neck flows into the left hemisphere.) Thus, using the Wada procedure, a physician can literally put half the brain to sleep. The results of experiments conducted with the Wada test confirm the effects noted with stroke and split-brain patients.*

One of the interesting findings of research with the Wada procedure is that 95% of the patients tested who had not suffered any type of brain damage in early childhood and who were right handed, definitely had speech and language functions centered in their left hemisphere.** In cases where there had been damage to the left (speech) hemisphere during early childhood, researchers found higher incidences of bilat-

---

*It should be noted that the Wada test is normally used only with patients who have suffered possible brain damage or physical injury; nevertheless, many of these patients possessed normal intellectual ability.

**Additionally it was found that the majority of left-handed individuals, assuming no early childhood damage to the left brain, also had speech and language in the left hemisphere.

eral or right-hemisphere speech and language. It appears that if the brain damage occurs early enough in the patient's life, there is an excellent chance that the other hemisphere will assume the function!

The electroencephalogram (EEG) studies were conducted with normal subjects as well; these studies support the Wada test findings. The initial research on EEG hemispheric processing began with experiments by David Galin and Robert Ornstein at the Langley Porter Neuropsychiatric Institute in the early 1970s. The electroencephalogram, as its name implies, is a reading of the electrical activity of the brain. In essence, the EEG provides a record of electrical output during different activities and states. For example, an EEG will provide an entirely different wave pattern during a subject's rest than it will when the individual is experiencing stress or intellectual stimulation.

When a subject was tested by Galin and Ornstein, the subject's EEG was monitored from electrodes placed symmetrically on the individual's head. The results of these studies support the research with split-brain and stroke patients. For example, when a subject is given a verbal task to complete, the brain wave pattern indicates high "alpha" wave output in the right hemisphere. (High alpha wave output indicates that the hemisphere is essentially on "idle.") The left hemisphere, however, produces "beta" waves when confronted with a verbal task. (Beta waves indicate "active processing" in the brain hemisphere.) In contrast, when a spatial task is introduced, the left hemisphere emits alpha waves, and the right hemisphere produces beta waves. By noting the change in brain waves, we can determine which brain is actually doing the work!

Yet, the evidence of hemispheric specialization in normals is not limited to studies using the Wada test or the EEG. Other extremely sophisticated and highly controlled experiments have been conducted with normal subjects using the eyes and ears as variables. In normal people, there is a brief fraction of a second when information flashed to the right eye proceeds directly to the left hemisphere before it is transferred to the right. Using the tachistoscope (page 13), researchers are able to flash images or words to one side of the brain or the other and measure that fraction of a second response. The results again support the original findings noted with split-brain patients. Subjects in these tests demonstrated an advantage in completing verbal tasks when the right visual areas are tested (the right visual area is controlled by the left hemisphere) and an advantage in completing spatial tasks when the left visual areas are tested (the left visual area is controlled by the right hemisphere).

In summarizing the work involving normal subjects in testing bicameral specialization of the brain hemispheres, Springer and Deutsch state:

In tracing the history of behavioral investigations of laterality in normal subjects, we have seen an increasingly complex picture unfold. . . . As in the research with split brain patients, we see that basic differences lie in the processing strategies of each hemisphere. . . . Overall, the data (on normals) fit well with the picture of hemispheric differences that emerged from studies of brain damage and split-brain patients. (p. 84)

## The Importance of Left/Right Brain Research to Education

The relevant question for teachers is, of course, what does this mean for the classroom? What does it mean in terms of the way we teach children? What does it mean in terms of the way people learn? How does it impact the way we view creativity? These questions have far-ranging implications—implications that educators must consider. It is time to teach to both brains—to the left brain and to the right.

As research on hemispheric specialization continues, classroom strategies (such as metaphoric teaching) need to be consciously developed; it is becoming increasingly clear that a balance of right/left brain information-processing is critical for efficient, effective classroom learning. How can this balance be achieved? We begin with what we know. We now know, for example, that the left hemisphere takes in data logically and analyzes for details; the right hemisphere, on the other hand, takes in data holistically—as in a picture—and uses life experiences (images and metaphors) to create conceptual (or common-sense) understanding of the data.

How do the two brains work together? Insight is sparked in the patterns of the right brain (the pictures we see before we can express them in words); reasonable explanation emanates from the left. When we make a tremendous intuitive leap such as Einstein did when he suggested that the Riemann-Christoffel tensor be set equal to zero to understand gravity, we use the right brain's ability to perceive holistically, to envision; when we design intricate experiments to test the validity of such a vision, we employ the left brain's ability for logic and sequential analysis. To discover the calculus required a right-hemisphere conceptual leap; to develop the calculus for others to use required a left-hemisphere mapping of the step-by-step process.

How does this process apply to the classroom? When a student looks at a problem and says, "I got it!" the student needs to be given credit for perceiving a relationship among the parts of the problem that may not be easily articulated in the moment (the perception of the relationship is a right-hemisphere activity); the student also needs to be made aware that understanding the "why" of the immediate solution helps him or her apply this knowledge to other problem-solving situations (logical "whys" involve left hemisphere activity). Thus, creating healthy respect for the natural reciprocity of both brains is essential; neither hemisphere provides answers alone. The problem is that today's schools are almost entirely left hemisphere-oriented, that is, oriented toward the verbal, the analytical, and the logical. We are missing the valuable input of the right hemisphere's perceptions and insights. All too often, the facts are learned and the concepts are lost.

How pervasive is left-brain orientation in our schools? There are not many studies that have investigated the utilization of time in the elementary schools (and certainly none that have taken alpha wave counts during different activities), but in one study of Oregon teachers in 1977–1978, the teachers involved in the study were asked to identify time spent on various subject areas and the primary mode of instruction used. The teachers responded that sixty-seven percent of their

### Abbreviated Summary of Specialized Cerebral Hemisphere Functions

| Left | Right |
| --- | --- |
| recognizing/remembering names | recognizing/remembering faces |
| responding to verbal instructions | responding to visual and kinesthetic instructions |
| systematic and controlled in experimenting | playful and loose in experimenting |
| inhibited in responding emotionally | responds with emotion/feeling |
| dependent upon words for meaning | interprets body language |
| produces logical ideas | produces humorous ideas |
| processes verbal stimuli | processes kinesthetic stimuli |
| objective processing of information | subjective processing of information |
| serious, systematic in solving problems | playful in solving problems |
| receptive; abstract thinking | self-acting; concrete thinking |
| dislikes improvising | likes improvising |
| not psychic | highly psychic |
| little use of metaphors and analogies | high use of metaphors and analogies |
| responsive to logical, verbal appeals | responsive to emotional appeals |
| deals with one problem at a time, sequentially | deals simultaneously with several problems at same time |
| critical and analytical in reading | creative, synthesizing, associating in reading |
| logical in solving problems | intuitive in solving problems |
| gives instructions verbally | gives information through movement, gesture, etc. |
| uses language in remembering | uses images in remembering |
| grasps certain, established truths | grasps uncertain truths |

SOURCE: E. Paul Torrance, Cecil Reynolds, Theodore Riegel, and Paul Orlow, *Your Style of Learning and Thinking,* 1980. Mimeograph.

teaching time went to instruction in the "3 R's," and another fifteen percent involved "administrivia," the modes of instruction most frequently used were lecture/discussion, drill/practice, and recitation. Most of these activities tend to involve left-brain verbalization and detailed factual recall. Reading, writing, arithmetic, even a lot of what is called creative writing, emphasize left-hemisphere thought processes. We are not saying that these activities should not occur; they are essential to become a functioning adult in our society. But with slight modification, right-hemisphere imagery could be added; the use of metaphors, open-ended questions and creative paradox would prompt a new dimension of learning for the conventional classroom.

It is not just what is taught but how it is taught that determines the left/right brain balance in the learning process. Repeated instruction geared to facts and details, sequential ordering, and predetermined answers (the common results of lecture, structured discussion, textbook reading, drill and practice; and demonstration teaching) forces a left-hemisphere dominance that tends to ignore right-brain creativity and conceptual ability. The result may just be the continued development of an adult population that is highly competent in left-brain information assimilation and is handicapped in right-brain intuitive perception and holistic understanding.

Further, as we consider the implications of these findings, one salient factor continually emerges: the right brain perceives relationships—it specializes in holistic, conceptual understanding. In other words, if we are to teach concepts as opposed to merely encouraging students to memorize definitions, one very good strategy is to offer students a familiar image that demonstrates how a given concept actually works—a real-life model that shows how the concept can be applied.

The metaphor provides this model, a model that people naturally perceive. Derived from familiar examples of everyday living, the metaphor aids the learner in internalizing the new knowledge, new theory, or new information. It is, perhaps, the fastest and most effective route we have to link the right brain with the left. With the metaphor, the sequential, factual, verbal knowledge of the left brain becomes "real" to the right brain, which assumes a pattern, an image of what the "big picture" means). As such, the metaphor provides a bridge between the two separate thought processes of the brain, a bridge that allows imagery to be verbalized and creates imagery for specific facts. This bridge connects the literal and the figurative, the factual and the imaginative, the proven and the intuitive.

The metaphor, as we might predict, has a long history as an effective teaching tool. The more we sought to apply recent research on the left/right brain, the more we found ourselves returning to one of society's oldest teaching methods—the use of the metaphor. For it is the metaphor that has the power and posture to link the right brain to creativity, to negotiate bursts of insight, and to allow original ideas to take form. This vital role that natural imagery plays in the creative process is the concern of the remainder of this chapter.

## The Metaphor and the Right Brain

Many of history's great teachers have recognized the power of the metaphor and have intuitively perceived that the rational, verbal part of the mind requires more than rules and guidelines. When we review the teachings of these past masters, we find they seemed to know instinctively that directing the mind means capturing the creative insight of the mind—the part of us that grasps the implications of a concept and remembers essential relationships over the long term. Over and over, these teachers used "right-brain" images and metaphors to teach their followers sophisticated social and political concepts.

For example, think of Plato's *Republic*. Of all the profound teachings of this masterpiece of political theory, many of us remember the "Allegory of the Cave" best:

*"And now," I said, "let me show in a figure\* how far our nature is enlightened or unenlightened. Behold! Human beings living in an underground den, which has a mouth open towards the light and reaching all along the den; here they have been from their childhood, and have their legs and necks chained so that they cannot move, and can only see before them, being prevented by the chains from turning round their heads. Above and behind them a fire is blazing at a distance, and between the fire and the prisoners there is a raised way; and you will see, if you look, a low wall built along the way, like the screen which marionette players have in front of them, over which they show the puppets."*

In this famous parable, Plato contrasts the teachings of Socrates (a world of light and true image) with the blind, shadowy perceptions of the material world of everyday experience (the world of the cave). Dwellers in the cave see only imitations of real, living things—shadow appearances of material things, not their true nature. Plato likens this condition to our normal perception of the world; he exposes the difficulty of explaining a new awareness of the world (one of sunlight and personal freedom) to those who are still chained in the cave. Cave referents are always approximations, possibilities for what

---

\*In this case "figure" means metaphor or picture.

the shadows could be. Prizes awarded to the cave's "quick shadow-recognizers" (or in the classroom to the quick rote-memorizers) are meaningless in the outside world. The freed prisoner (the enlightened explorer or the questioning student) transcends this world and experiences the clear light of reality. But this person will find anger and fear when returning to the cave with this new information about the outside world; people prefer the fictions of the familiar to the truth of an unfamiliar world.

Plato further suggests that those who spend their lives in caves cannot understand the sunlight, the trees, the sky; and they are afraid of those who have lived in this outside world—so afraid that, as cave dwellers, they demand the death of those who tell of a world beyond the cave. Plato's cave explains the execution of Socrates, the fate of Jesus, the fates of countless enlightened martyrs throughout the ages. To cave dwellers, the shadow world is preferable to the open, inexplicable, enlightened world that can explode accepted "truths" and offer unfamiliar images of reality.

Eastern teachings reveal a perceptive use of metaphors as well; Confucius, one of the best-known masters of the metaphor, provided continual examples for his followers. His messages were both political and social in nature—image guidelines for his people to follow. Take, for example, this situation where the Baron of Lu has asked Confucius whether or not the people who break the law deserve to be executed. Confucius responded:

*The virtue of the prince is like the wind; that of the people is like the grass. For it is the nature of the grass to bend when the wind blows upon it.*

Awareness of interdependent relationships is critical; whose law should or should not be broken is not the issue.

This wisdom is familiar; we have heard this message in the metaphoric teachings of Jesus of Nazareth. He, too, answered his followers with parables and images. When asked whether or not the people should pay taxes, Jesus asked to see a coin and then answered with:

*"Whose likeness and inscription is this?" They said, "Caesar's." Then he said to them, "Render therefore unto Caesar the things that are Caesar's, and unto God the things that are God's."*
(Matt. 22)

Philosophically, these leaders recognized that inner peace and good being are qualities that transcend secular issues of who should govern and be governed. The ability to govern oneself (to seek the "kingdom within oneself"), is primary to contentment with life itself. Like the prisoner released from the cave, the enlightened leader seeks to stimulate awareness of personal identity and personal responsibility.

In similar fashion, Sakyamuni Gautama (the first Buddha)* taught his disciples to question the usefulness of details independent of concept:

*It is as if a man had been wounded by an arrow thickly smeared with poison, and his friends and kinsmen were to get a surgeon to heal him, and he were to say, "I will not have this arrow pulled out until I know by what man I was wounded, whether he is of the warrior caste, or a brahmin, or of the agricultural, or the lowest caste."*

*Or he were to say, "I will not have this arrow pulled out until I know of what name or family the man is—or whether he is tall, or short, or middle height; or whether he is black, or dark or yellowish; or whether he comes from such and such a village, town or city; or until I know whether the bow from which I was wounded was a chapa or a kodanda, or until I know whether the bow string was of swallow-wort, or bamboo fiber, or sinew, or hemp, or of milksap tree, or until I know whether the shaft was from a wild or cultivated plant; or whether it was feathered from a vulture's wing or a heron's or a hawk's, or a peacock's; or whether it was wrapped around with the sinew of an ox, or of a buffalo, or of a ruru-deer, or of a monkey; or until I know whether it was an ordinary arrow, or a razor arrow, or an iron arrow, or a calf-tooth arrow." Before knowing all this, that man would die.*

*Therefore, my disciples, consider as unexplained what I have not explained, and consider as explained what I have explained.*

Interestingly, in each situation real life problems are presented for the "master's" interpretation. The world of shadows (the world of unexamined belief systems) is exposed: who has the legal right to punish? Who determines taxation? Who manufactured the arrow? The enlightened leader must challenge people to be aware of interrelationships, aware of the issues that are truly critical to their happiness. These issues center around self-awareness, perception, and seeing the "bigger picture."

The problems of living in the cave (of coping with the daily problems of material possessions, political pressure, and strife) obscure the real problems of life—the necessity of learning how to be open to experience, the sense of self-determination and personal freedom of choice, the expanding of self-identity and awareness with the Creator. To live in the cave is to accept the interpretations of cave dwellers (the rules of the past, the regulations that have become traditions); to live outside

---

*Buddha means the "enlightened one," or "awakened one." Sakyamuni Gautama or Siddhartha lived in the sixth century B.C. and was the first of many great religious leaders of Buddhism—all known as Buddha or "master." This system of religion focuses upon internal awareness of self-governance and the paradoxical nature of all TRUTH.

the cave is to accept personal responsibility for the beliefs and values we live by. The message is profound and powerful; the medium for delivery lies in the imagery of each metaphor.

Why do these teachings demonstrate this metaphoric power so vividly? The answer lies in the way the metaphor allows the listener to experience the overall concept being introduced. Each story, each living example, suggests rather than demands; it creates an image that expands rather than a definition that limits; it leads to possible conclusions rather than specifies a given answer; it appeals directly to the right brain's holistic perception rather than the left brain's memorization.

Indeed, the metaphor taps the potential of the right brain—a potential essential to the complexity of human relationships and the world we now face, a potential we can no longer ignore in our schools. In fact, the metaphor, and the many other right brain teaching strategies that are just now emerging, actively court the duality of the brain and create a synergy of information that dwarfs the contribution of either alone. Recognizing that the brain is divided into two parts with very different functions does increase learning dramatically; it is, indeed, as if one divided by two equals the power of three.

## Creativity, the Right Brain, and Concept Attainment in the Classroom

But what about creativity as related to the right hemisphere and the metaphor? Can creativity affect concept learning? In a word, yes; creativity is supportive of all classroom activities and skills; it is a process that utilizes right-brain imagery.* Creativity is a critical skill for conceptualizing new ideas, and it can be taught either with or apart from other academic skills. In the same way that we do not expect the violin to carry the entire symphony, but we do appreciate an outstanding violin solo, creativity has an enhancing, vital role in developing intellect and perception. Creativity is synergistic; it makes the parts greater than the whole; it touches cognition, affect, and behavior and enriches them all. As educators, feeling pressure from both school boards and administrators to produce academic achievement for normative measurement, we can now defend the critical role of creativity in developing the measurable "product." Further, we can now identify the integral role of creativity in developing a process awareness—an awareness that can result in products of high academic quality.

---

*Given the level of present left/right brain research, it is definitely an oversimplification to say that creativity is only a product of the right cerebral hemisphere; nevertheless, imagery, spatial relationships, and intuition (qualities so critical to creativity) are primarily right-brain.

Many of us have learned painfully what happens if our students simply memorize the concepts we teach them; they create personal "Potemkin Villages" of conceptual understanding. The spectre of their own conceptual confusion is hidden behind a facade of recall definitions and rote memorization. We test them with open-ended questions and discover they cannot apply the new knowledge they have learned (the "right" answers) without an understanding of what the lesson was all about. Today, we are discovering that concept attainment requires more than the memorization of attributes—it requires a working knowledge of how the concept works in many settings—an ability to generate analogous metaphors for the concepts—metaphors that "show" how the concept works. The right brain is holistic; when involved through the use of creativity and metaphoric exercises, concept attainment becomes a mutually interactive experience, a product of both the left and right brains.

This hemispheric interaction is critical for teaching students to rely on their own thinking and to apply newly learned concepts to new situations. If we are to avoid producing an entire generation of "cognitive cripples" (people who depend solely upon the "left brain" or upon thinking of others), we must introduce creative methods as well as methods to enhance creativity within the classroom. We must teach our students how to think for themselves.

In the remainder of this chapter, we will review some of the prevailing definitions of creativity (defined both conventionally and metaphorically), relate some of the experiential moments that have contributed to our cultural concept of creativity, examine some of the most recently developed strategies for prompting creativity, and look at one of our culture's most detrimental artifacts of the development of creativity.

## WHAT IS CREATIVITY?

The idea of the "creative individual" has been around for a long time. But while we recognize the creative individual when we encounter him or her, we are often at a loss for explaining what makes this person "creative." In recent years there have been many operational definitions of creativity set forth in the literature.

George Prince in *The Practice of Creativity* defines creativity's spontaneity coupled with ordering and pattern:

*Creativity:* An arbitrary harmony, an unexpected astonishment, a habitual revelation, a familiar surprise, a generous selfishness, an unexpected certainty, a formable stubbornness, a vital triviality, a disciplined freedom, an intoxicating steadiness, a repeated initiation, a difficult delight, a predictable gamble, an ephemeral solidity, a unifying difference, a demanding satisfier, a miraculous expectation, an accustomed amazement.

In this highly paradoxical definition, Prince captures the very merger of left- and right-brain perspectives, for, as we will discover, creativity is both the conscious thinking of the left brain and the spontaneous patterning and imaging of the right brain. Creativity is the product of their merger, the product of loosening the bonds of order and predictability, the result of valuing the unusual connections and alternative images the right brain offers while utilizing the left brain's ability to order and sequence these connections and images into a logical perspective. Many other educators have also tried to capture in words this conceptual leap that occurs when both brains actively exchange the information they have gathered.*

| | |
|---|---|
| Paul Torrance | "Creativity is a process that *involves sensing gaps or disturbing missing elements,* hypotheses, communicating the results and possibly modifying and retesting these hypotheses." |
| Robert Samples | *"New Know"* |
| Jerome Bruner | "*'Effective surprise'*—An act that the hallmark of a creative enterprise . . . I could not care less about the person's intention, whether or not he intended to create. The road to banality is paved with creative intentions." |
| Jean Piaget | "If you want to be creative, *stay in part a child,* with the creativity and invention that characterizes children before they are deformed by adult society." |
| Arthur Koestler | "*The combination of previously unrelated structures* in such a way that you get more out of the emergent whole then you have put in." |
| S. J. Parnes | "Let us start with the premise that *the essence of creativity is the fundamental notion of the 'aha'*—meaning the fresh and relevant association of thoughts, facts, ideas, etc., into a new configuration . . . one which pleases, which has meaning beyond the sum of the parts." |

*We have added the italics to demonstrate the commonality emerging in these definitions. Without the spontaneous input of the right brain's images and perceptions, the left brain analyzes old information; it does not allow new patterns to come forth. Creativity, then, requires being aware of the information emerging from both hemispheres—being open to the unusual moment of new connection and new ordering.

| J. P. Guilford | "*Divergent thinking* in problem solving." |
| Abraham Maslow | "Primary creativity comes out of the unconscious . . . is the source of new discovery (or real novelty) of *ideas which depart from what exists at this point.*" |
| Clark Moustakas | "Creativity is an *abstraction that attains a concrete form only in a particular and unique relation.* The branches of a tree stretch out expansive and free, maintaining a basic identity, an essential uniqueness in color, form, and pattern. They stand out in contrast to the fixed nature of the trunk. Yet, one cannot see a tree without recognizing its essential harmony, its wholeness, and its unity. (Creativity, like the branch, as meaning only in relation to the larger system.)" |
| Carl Sagan | "Mere critical thinking without the search for new patterns is sterile and doomed. To solve complex problems in changing circumstances requires *the activity of both cerebral hemispheres: the path to the future lies through the corpus callosum.*" |

Indeed, in our search for definitions of creativity, we found two basic kinds of information: the careful *systematic prescriptions* of researchers in the field of creativity and the *spontaneous descriptions* of people who have made outstanding creative contributions to the world. It is as though both the left-brain organizer and the right-brain practitioner supply only half the picture.

First, let's look at the highly ordered (and most quoted) classic research study on creativity, the research that stands behind most of the educational inquiry in the field of creativity—Graham Wallas's 1926 *Study of Creativity*. Wallas identified four sequential stages critical to the development of creativity in the individual: preparation, incubation, illumination (inspiration or insight), and verification.

The names of Wallas's stages convey a meaning close to their usage in normal discourse; that is, *preparation* is the "getting ready" for an investigation or new knowledge—learning of a given subject area's language or studying a specific topic like quantum mechanics. Preparation also means taking time to collect information, listening to the opinions of others, searching for data. *Incubation* is simply that—a gestation period, a time (perhaps a few hours, perhaps a few years) that divides the preparation period from the moment of illumination. It involves a "time-out" in which the brain sorts things unconsciously, tries out a myriad of possible combinations, "plays" with the available information and potential patterns.* *Illumination* (originally referred to as an "inspiration") is often called the "light bulb moment," that time so familiar from cartoon strips when the character makes a sudden connection and says, "I get it!" Illumination cannot be demanded; it is a time when hunches, intuition, and insights—sometimes even solutions—emerge suddenly without intense effort. It is a moment of renewed energy and new perspective, and it must be followed by intellectual *verification,* a longer, more disciplined period of time during which the process of negotiating the image into a logical, verbal mode occurs. Verification examines the illumination in the clear light of reason to determine if, in fact, the insight, hunch, or new perspective can sustain the effect of left hemisphere inspection, rationality, and order.

But does Wallas's paradigm for creative discovery really explain the processes of invention and aesthetic originality? Let's look at two separate examples of creative discovery and how these moments were consciously perceived by their creators. The first of these is the familiar story of Mendeleev's discovery of the periodic table of the elements; the second, the less familiar report of Kekule's discovery of the formula for the benzene ring.

Mendeleev reports (in his journal) that one night in late 1869 he went to bed absolutely exhausted from a day-long struggle to conceptualize a system in which the basic elements could be arranged by atomic weight. That night he "saw in a dream a table where all the elements fell into place as required." When he awoke, he quickly wrote the vision down on a piece of paper. Amazingly, Mendeleev had even anticipated the vacant spot needed for helium. We now know this vision as the Periodic Table of Elements.

In the case of the Dutch chemist Kekule, it was a formula for the benzene ring (the movement of the atoms in benzene) that haunted and eluded him—Kekule had been struggling with this chemical formula for months. Arthur Koestler, in his book, *The Act of Creation,* quotes from Kekule's diary:

I turned my chair to the fire and dozed. Again, the atoms were gamboling before my eyes. The smaller groups kept modestly in the background. My mental eye, rendered more acute by visions of this kind, could now distinguish larger structures of manifold conformations, long rows sometimes more closely fitted

---

*Although Wallas did not have the recent brain research findings on the left/right brain, he is describing the period of time when the left brain relaxes and does not try to order and sequence the information, a time when the right brain mulls over the information and arranges it into clusters of patterns and images.

together, all twining and twisting in snake-like motion. But look! What was
that? One of the snakes had seized hold of its own tail and the form whirled
mockingly before my eyes. As if by a flash of lightning I awoke. (p. 118)

Both Mendeleev and Kekule, were, in Pasteur's phrase, "well prepared minds"; they had studied the subjects of their discoveries for
many years, had gathered data, had both sought out and listened to the
opinions of others in their field. The "incubation" time likely stretched
over many years as each scientist searched for new patterns, new
arrangements for the information received from both hemispheres.
The time of the "illumination"—that moment when the pattern or
image allowed them a new conceptualization, a new insight on the
problem at hand, occurred in less than an hour; in terms of the time
already spent in preparation and incubation, it was almost instantaneous. The verification process, however, the fourth stage in Wallas's
model, again required considerable time—time for the illumination to
be ordered, tested, evaluated, and refined.

Although verification is occasionally a short process, it can also be
quite a lengthy one. In the case of Gregor Mendel, the creative discov-
erer of the modern science of genetics, the process lasted almost a
lifetime. At the completion of Mendel's initial genetic investigations
with plants, he sent the results of his experiments to a respected German biologist of the time, Karl Nageli. Nageli reviewed Mendel's work
and promptly rejected it. Not for over thirty years were the brilliant
insights of Gregor Mendel fully accepted by the scientific community.
Mendel, who carefully recorded observations on almost thirteen-thou-
sand hybrid specimens, was not a trained biologist; although he had the
well-prepared mind, Mendel did not have scientific credentials to prove
it.* The scientific community, therefore, demanded highly rigorous
proof of Mendel's discoveries before his work would be accepted. Part
of the verification process, it seems, is the test of time and the acceptance of colleagues who will further probe, test, and expand the
insight.

This process of preparing one's mind, of allowing the struggle to
abate and incubate, of later experiencing a moment of clear vision or
image, and then of verifying the new configuration through refine-
ment, evaluation, and ordering provides a sequential (left brain-ori-
ented) overview of the highly complex process of creativity. However,
with examples such as Kekule, Mendel, and Mendeleev, Wallas makes
a persuasive argument for the validity of the four stages he outlines as
being the essential steps of the creative process.

---

*Interestingly, Mendel was an Augustinian monk who had originally wanted only to
be a teacher, but he failed the Austrian state examination for teachers in 1846.

Yet, there are gaps in this four-stage conceptualization of creativity. For instance, knowing that the process exists does not assure that it will occur. Take the case of the discovery of X-rays, a situation where having a prepared mind, a lengthy period of incubation, and ample opportunity for illumination did not assure the discovery of a creative solution.

In fact, there is a dual story in tracing the discovery of X-rays. The first story, the classic story that lends credence to the Wallas model, is that of Wilhelm Roentgen's discovery of the X-ray. This story is a common part of the elementary and junior high school science curriculum: Roentgen perceived a relationship between fogged, useless photographic plates and the action of a Crookes' tube, a vacuum tube invented some years before Roentgen's remarkable discovery. This perception led to the discovery of the X-ray and a means for using it.

There is a second story, however, a story as important to the process of creativity as Roentgen's. This story is seldom included in the curriculum: it is the story of the frustrations of William Crookes. Crookes developed an apparatus known (appropriately) as Crookes' tube (a vacuum tube) which we now know gives off X-rays. This function of the Crookes' tube, however, was unknown to Crookes. Crookes himself had noticed that the unexposed photographic plates left in boxes around his laboratory sometimes became fogged, but he blamed the manufacturer and his shippers. Only later, after Roentgen's discovery of the X-ray did Crookes make a connection between his fogged film and his own Crookes' tube. This failure to make the connection, to discover the principles of the X-ray, was a source of frustration and annoyance to Crookes for the remainder of his life. Roentgen and Crookes—both prepared minds, both with the opportunity for unconscious incubation to occur over a long period of time, yet only one experienced the moment of illumination, only one identified the X-ray and found the key to his creative effort. What separated these two men? What missing factors are not included in Wallas' paradigm?

We would suggest that a vital, missing element in the Wallas model is that Wallas does not include a step for imagery and curiosity, a step where there is a sense of "playing" with existing variables, where the anticipation of accidental patterns can trigger new connections and possibilities for the information at hand. A keen awareness of imagery, independent of logic and sequence, may be a critical link in our ability to perceive creative relationships.

Mendeleev and Kekule both described patterns they glimpsed in dreams, patterns that gave clues to the new ordering of their research; Mendeleev's dream table became the Periodic Table of Elements, Kekule's atomic snakes twisted into a ring—a ring that solved the formula for benzene. And Mendel found a new ordering for genetics, in no small part because he did not have the academic biases of his contemporaries: he was not sufficiently schooled to know that his arrangements could not possibly be right. Roentgen found the X-ray because he wanted to know why his film was fogged—he didn't blame someone; he became curious. What these people all have in common is a sense of trusting in their own intuitive perceptions—they were willing to investigate images that were not appreciated by rational academic preparation (left-brain skills)—images that deviated from the accepted norms. They were willing to look at alternative patterns and to seek out the implications of an improbable arrangement—a perception normally discounted as illogical by the left brain.

There is, then, an attitude essential to creative discovery, an attitude the artist, architect, musician, and creative writer naturally possess. That attitude must be one of allowing curiosity, images, unpredictability, and chance combinations to be possible guides in the process. By overlooking new patterns and relying upon the left brain's prejudice that existing theories are proven beyond doubt, we often miss vital clues—the new connections of our own right brains. The artist, the recognized creative professional, knows the need to be open to this process; artistic creations thrive upon new combinations. The creative scientist, weighted down by the empirical proofs demanded by the given science or discipline, needs also to be open to new images, new connections, new combinations—open to renewed inquiry into old theories and ready to value the preconscious visions and metaphors available from the right brain.

How critical for creative perspective is this need for *curious irreverance* towards what is established as proven? Let's examine the discovery of Alexander Fleming. Fleming observed that one of his bacteriological cultures had become contaminated by a penicillin mold, but he did not throw the culture out (which had always been done in such cases). Instead, he waited, watched, and discovered that the culture did not grow back. It's important to note that Fleming was not the first to notice this phenomenon, since a report in 1875 predated him. He was, however, the first to become intrigued and curious about the implications of penicillin's impact, so curious that he proposed and tested a hypothetical explanation. His "well-prepared" mind, coupled with his natural curiosity, allowed him to produce a creative new idea—the use of penicillin for treating bacterial infection, a breakthrough that came years before the systematic study of antibiotics.

Scientists are not the only "creators" who describe the process of creating as allowing for chance combinations or unusual connections. Leo Tolstoy described the following scene to his wife Sonia who, in turn, recorded it in her diary. Tolstoy was struggling with the development of a new chapter of *Anna Karenina*. In his own words,

I am sitting downstairs in my study and examining the white silk piping on the sleeve of my dressing gown, which is very beautiful. And I begin to wonder how people came to invent all those intricate designs . . . and all of a sudden this silk piping gives me an idea for a whole chapter.

## And Brewster Ghiselin quotes from a letter from Mozart:

When I am, as it were completely myself, entirely alone, and of good cheer— say, travelling in a carriage, or walking after a good meal, or during the night when I cannot sleep; it is on such occasions that my ideas flow best and most abundantly. Whence and how they come, I know not; nor can I force them. All this fires my soul, and, provided I am not disturbed, my subject enlarges itself, so that I can survey it, like a fine picture or a beautiful statue, at a glance. Nor do I hear in my imagination the parts successively, but I hear them, as it were, all at once!

Creative change often requires experiential risk and willing acceptance of new patterns, pathways, and unproven possibilities. In "The Nature of Science" (1972), Kuslan and Stone point out that the scientific method is "a guide that can point out the road but cannot guarantee safe passage." The creative scientist, like the creative artist, must stay aware of "likeness in unlikeness," "order in disorder." It is the same quality that William Coleridge defined when describing beauty as "unity in variety" and that Melville captured so aptly in his poem, "Art":*

> *What unlike things must meet and mate:*
> *A flame to melt—a wind to freeze;*
> *Sad patience—joyous energies;*
> *Humility—yet pride and scorn;*
> *Instinct and study; love and hate;*
> *Audacity—reverence. They must mate,*
> *and fuse with Jacob's mystic heart,*
> *To wrestle with the Angel—Art.*

Sciences, like the arts, require the burst of conceptual insight that the right brain provides—the alternative, heretofore unaccepted, novel image.

Charles Nicolle, who first recognized how typhus was spread, wrote about this burst as a "sudden flash of creative imagination, this sudden illumination, this instantaneous certainty of a new fact"—"I know of it," he wrote, "I have experienced it in my life." In fact, a careful study of creative breakthroughs in a variety of disciplines reaffirms the importance of this process; originators frequently speak about "the role

---

*The Works of Herman Melville,* Vol. XVI Poems, New York, Russell & Russell, Inc., 1963, p. 270.

of intuition, hunches, chance thoughts, and lucky accidents" in their research and work (Kuslan and Stone, 1972). Illumination, by whatever name, intuition, hunch, "Eureka" experience, inspiration, gestalt, metaphoric insight, is the crux of creativity; not surprisingly, it is also the core of metaphoric teaching. And although Wallas did not include curiosity and image awareness as factors critical to creativity, he nevertheless made a major contribution to the study of creativity when he identified the illumination moment—the moment of insight. Mendeleev, Kekule, Mendel, Crookes, Roentgen, and Nicolle—all share in their own way a common experience, a moment when image and illumination combined to produce a new creative solution.

There are, however, other drawbacks with the Wallas model; for example, Wallas essentially described scientific problem solving rather than the creative process; and the model does not explain the creative process of the artist—where illumination is an ongoing process, not merely the sudden glimpse of a possible product. Further, Wallas's approach is biased toward rational inquiry; Wallas described sequenced stages, but these stages do not automatically generate creative products. There is a need to expand the orderly structure of Wallas's paradigm, to develop an awareness of the creative simultaneity of "right brain thinking," the thoughts that come in images not words.

As we discussed earlier, the right brain is a brain of process rather than a brain of defined, tested products. The right brain thrives upon spontaneity, upon the simultaneous appreciation of countless options, and upon experiential process rather than finished concrete products. In science, where empirical proof and investigation are critical validations of well-defined disciplines of thought, creative moments can appear sequential in their occurrence. The creative process of science often begins with the left brain's investigation of what is known. Later, new combinations and connections will begin to emerge as "right-brain" perceptions are noted; these images and connections occur in countless possibilities; finally, a moment of insight causes the investigator to notice a combination that fits—a potential creative solution. This solution, then, must be pursued with disciplined ordering and redefinition of existing theory. Such a description of the creative process fits the logical, sequential orientation of sciences well.

Another dimension is needed, however, when we look at the artistic experience—when the medium itself is, by nature, "right brain"-oriented and dependent upon uniqueness of perception and combination. In music, literature, art, and architecture, the emphasis on illumination shifts from "the moment of" to the "ongoing struggle and process of." When the subject is primarily "right brain" in its orientation, there is considerably more time spent in the right brain and considerably more attention needed to the actual process of creativity itself.

Children (who naturally view the world as "process" not "product") need an environment for creativity, not just orderly prescriptions. Yes, we seek "to prepare" their minds, "to incubate" their ideas, "to allow illumination" to occur, and to teach them skills "to verify"; yet, experiencing creative thinking means much more than a four-step formula. Creative thinking—experiencing the fun, play, curiosity, and excitement of being creative—requires a climate where spontaneity, simultaneous alternatives, and process itself are valued and fostered, where products are not the "raison d'être" for the experience.

In the search to identify approaches to creativity that stress process rather than product, educational researchers have prescribed several models; but perhaps no model has been more widely accepted or more quantitatively defined than Frank Williams' *A Total Creativity Program for Individualizing and Humanizing the Learning Process* (1972). In this model, Williams set forth six basic premises—derived from research findings:

1. Creativity is made up of a large number of skills and talents—both cognitive and affective.
2. Creativity is found to some degree in each individual, yet, some children and adults appear to have more creative potential than others.
3. There are vast differences in the ways creativity is expressed. Some may express it in art, another in science or literature—or athletics. Yet, this creativeness, wherever it is found, has common attributes.
4. Because creativity is a mix of many talents, attitudes, and abilities, no single test or method is sufficient to measure it or to nurture it in all students.
5. Each child has to be assessed for a present level of creativity and then encouraged to become more creative from that point.
6. A difference exists between teaching creatively and teaching for creativity. The former consists of using novel strategies, techniques, and approaches. The latter is a way of teaching designed to enhance creative behavior in the classroom.

Williams makes a convincing argument for viewing creativity as a teachable quality, a quality found in everyone, a quality to be encouraged and appreciated for its diversity in form, behavior, and given talent.

In exploring the phenomenon of creativity, Williams defines eight observable classroom behaviors that are indicative of a child's basic level of creativity. The first four of these are based upon Guilford's Structure of the Intellect model and his principles of divergent thinking: *fluent thinking* (the child with many thoughts), *flexible thinking* (the child who takes many different approaches), *original thinking* (the child who has novel or unique ways of thinking), *elaborative thinking* (the child who can add on to the ideas of others—take them a step further than the originator). In addition to these four cognitive behaviors, Williams cites four feeling behaviors that are essential to the creative individual: *risk-taking, complexity, curiosity,* and *imagination.*

To bring children into the creative mode, Williams suggests eighteen specific strategies (including the skills of *search, creative writing, asking provocative questions,* and skill in the *use of discrepancies and analogies*); these strategies are used to implement a total creative process—a program often referred to as Cognitive-Affective Interchange (CAI), which is packaged in kit form for teachers. The kit includes two introductory volumes on *identifying, measuring,* and *encouraging creative potential,* and another volume of almost four hundred ideas for implementing the eighteen teaching strategies as well as posters and workbooks to further utilize the program.

Wallas and Williams are not, of course, the only creativity researchers to develop a classroom model. Whereas Wallas noted four components of creativity and Williams suggested eight, the team of Mitchell, Stueckle, and Wilkens identified fourteen separate elements of creative behavior including the four from Guilford's model *(fluency, flexibility, originality,* and *elaboration)* as well as *sensitivity to problems, humor, tolerance for ambiguity,* and *synergy.* Numerous lesson plans are included in their book *Conceptual Planning for Creative Learning* (1976), and there are plans outlined within this text to teach the fourteen identifiable behaviors they have specified.

As with the Wallas model, one of the major problems of all these approaches is the assumption that creativity can be approached not just as a process, but as a sequenced, step-by-step process—that, in fact, each observable skill can be taught independently and then made part of the whole. The truth is, that while this can sometimes be done, it is analogous to teaching people to swim or play tennis by the "piecemeal" approach. Yes, people do eventually learn to swim or play tennis by learning the "steps," but recent research in physical education is showing us that there is a faster, more effective way to learn the basics of a sport (Gallway, 1975). This research indicates that people actually learn motor skills more quickly and more holistically if they are taught to focus upon the total motor behavior involved—to look at the image as a whole—what it means to swim or to play tennis.

We believe that this learning occurs because the right brain is the dominant brain for these experiential activities—it is not a sequential, detail-oriented brain; rather the right brain is conceptual and image-aware. It learns perceptively, not logically.

There is further research to substantiate this viewpoint: Knapp (1978) has discovered that nonverbal actions are not taught well in sequence or separately; people who learn how to move their hands, bodies, legs, eyes, or face muscles find coordinating these new skills to be clumsy and to be perceived as "put on." However, Knapp has had remarkable success in teaching people to perceive the nonverbal messages of others—and immediately, his subjects begin to imitate that behavior they like best in the other person. Nonverbal behavior, it appears, is better taught holistically as perception than sequentially as a series of independent actions.

What does all this imply for creativity? Basically, that although creativity can be perceived as being made up of several, sequential, observable skills (like the serve in tennis or the mastery of facial responses in nonverbal behavior), this is not really what creativity is— nor is it how creativity should be taught. Actually, creativity is a continuous process, which can disappear if analyzed too scrupulously. Creativity needs to be taught holistically.

When we take a creative moment apart and teach it as a series of separate skills, we are essentially assigning an integrated process totally over to the left brain; the left brain will, indeed, make things orderly, but it will not consider the unfamiliar connections, the novel images or the unsequenced simultaneity of creative insight. In the same way that it is helpful for the tennis coach to be able to analyze the tennis serve as a series of sequential moves and correct the one subtle flaw that destroys the perfect serve, so it is appropriate for the teacher to analyze the creative process in the classroom and correct for "flaws" in preparation or verification. But in the same way that the perfect serve is truly fluidity of motion, so creativity is truly fluidity of thought.

Creativity is not sequencing "A" to be followed by "B" to be followed by "C"; it is the "aha!" moment. It is not "If I do this, then that, then the other, I'll have a creative product"; it is "I wonder what would happen if . . ." Ask the creative contributer, the artist or the composer, if creativity is sequence or is it simultaneous perception? Is creativity a primary "left brain" prescription or a primary "right brain" happening?

Yes, as teachers, we can greatly benefit from understanding the individual skills of creative thinking; but we must remember that our students will benefit more from moments of creative experiences (moments in which the basic medium is explored, in which images and alternatives are "played with," allowed to emerge from the individual's preconscious, are prompted and enhanced by the images available within the environment and life experiences they have had).

Creativity can be a daily, ongoing, teachable experience—an experience of novel perceptions and holistic understandings; students can learn to use the creative process the rest of their lives, an ability that will help them whenever they need alternatives and original solutions. We have found that creative moments beget more creative moments, and that when insight and image responses become the norm, creativity expands enormously. Allowing for an atmosphere where creative responses to real-life situations are encouraged increases each individual's potential for original thinking, for independent learning. Using right-brain teaching strategies (such as metaphoric teaching, brainstorming, musical background to testing, and visual images with lectures) encourages an attitude that accepts alternatives as "correct" responses to instructional inquiry. In return, this attitude increases the creative perspectives of each student in the classroom.

This need for ongoing creative thinking, for merging the information of both brain hemispheres, is critical in the 1980s. We are increasingly becoming challenged to develop innovative thinkers; our nation has dropped from first place worldwide in patented inventions to third place; our productivity is seriously challenged by smaller nations; our artists are sorely in need of public support. We believe that seldom in the history of our country has it been more important to establish that "creativity-inducing" atmosphere than now—a time when imagery is being subconsciously structured by electronic media, and when American children are being bombarded by the television and the video game package.

## Creativity and the Metaphoric Brain

The question now is: how is the crative moment linked to the metaphor? Why can't left brain in its own way provide the creative moment? Interestingly, the recognition that the metaphoric (right) brain and creative potential, that the process of imaging and creativity, are linked is not new; great artists, philosophers, scientists, and discoverers have shared this perception throughout the ages. In fact, recent efforts to better understand creativity and individual creative potential have prompted renewed investigation of the creative process in all areas of the sciences and the arts. Journals, diaries, and other personal descriptions and accounts reveal amazing parallels between the creative processes of diverse creative individuals; and there is an immediate relevance of these reports in terms of what we are now learning about how the brain functions and specializes.

Again, whereas researchers into the field of creativity have successfully identified sequential patterns, detailed skills, and parts of the whole that result in creative products; the creative producer, the creative artist, and creative scientist have often identified creativity as a process of expanding on moments of insight or imagery. E. S. Ferguson, for example, describes this relation of metaphoric imagery to the creative process in science:

Many features and qualities of the objects that the technologist thinks about cannot be reduced to unambiguous verbal descriptions; they can only be dealt with in his mind by a visual, non-verbal process. His mind's eye is a well developed organ that not only reviews the contents of his visual memory, but also forms such new or modified images as his thoughts require.

This imagery experience is also critical to the artist's creativity. Consider these words from Brahms when asked about the creative invention of his music:

To realize that we are one with the Creator as Beethoven did is a wonderful and awe-inspiring experience. Very few human beings ever come into the realization, and that is why there are so few great composers or creative geniuses . . . I always contemplate on all this before commencing to compose. This is the first step. When I feel the urge I begin by appealing directly to my Maker . . . I immediately feel vibrations which thrill my whole being . . . In this exalted state I see clearly what is obscure in my ordinary moods; then I feel capable of drawing inspiration from above as Beethoven did.

These vibrations assume the form of distinct mental images . . . Straightaway the ideas flow in upon me, directly from God, and not only do I see distinct themes in the mind's eye, but they are clothed in the right forms, harmonies, and orchestration. Measure by measure the finished product is revealed to me when I am in those rare, inspired moods . . . I have to be in a semi-trance condition to get such results—a condition when the conscious mind is in temporary abeyance, and the subconscious is in control, for it is through the subconscious mind, which is a part of Omnipotence, that the inspiration comes.
(Quoted in Abell, 1964)

Indeed, a review of historical personal descriptions produces many such examples where the metaphoric imagery moment appears to be essential to the development of a unique product, theory, or discovery:

| | |
|---|---|
| Archimedes | shouting from the bath tub "Eureka" as he connected the problem of density and displacement with the image of the water and his own body and solved the dilemma of measuring the weight of the king's crown. |
| Newton | staring at the apple that fell on his head and then devising the law of gravity. |
| Michelangelo | describing how he sculptured his masterpieces: "What I desire I must first sense. |

What I sense I create." Then, he explained that he would first envision in raw marble the image of the work he conceived in his mind; his work meant painstakingly revealing that image entrapped in the stone.

**Michael Faraday** speaking of the way he visualized narrow tubes carving their way through space as he struggled to conceptualize a breakthrough in the field of electrochemistry; a discovery that culminated in the "Faraday Effect"—the effect of magnetism on polarized light.

**James Clark Maxwell** reporting that he had developed the habit of making a mental picture of every problem related to the definition of the relationships governing electric and magnetic fields.

**Albert Einstein** stating quite definitely that he rarely thought in words at all, that it was the use of imagery that produced the background for his contributions to the scientific community.

**Picasso** commenting that the initial vision of a work remained almost totally intact even after the painting upon which the image was based was complete.

The examples can be found everywhere—wherever the actual words and descriptions of the artists, scientists, and philosophers are being discussed. For the creative genius, creativity and imagery are one and the same. Creative problem solving, it seems, is thus a subset of this experience. Creativity itself is not the end product of preparation, incubation, illumination and verification, nor is it merely the happy combination of cognitive (frequency, flexibility, originality, and elaboration) with affective (risk-taking, complexity, curiosity, and imagination). It is encouraged by active acceptance of these steps and qualities; but, creativity itself is much more.

For at the heart of creativity lies a different way to think—an alternative thought process—the thinking structure of the right brain. This structure is not sequential, nor expressed in words and language. This thought process is simultaneous, spontaneous, metaphoric, and expressed in images. Its energy is overwhelming; its ability to thrill, motivate, excite, and captivate seem limitless. Knowing that the right brain does, in fact, exist and "think" differently (in image messages not words), we can begin to envision what teaching creativity could be. We can help students value the pictures they create in their minds to explain the experiences they are having; we can cause creative connections to be stimulated. We can, for example, place a familiar image in juxtaposition with an unfamiliar one (to walk in someone else's shoes is to be empathetic), or we can place the unfamiliar concept in juxtaposition with the familiar (co-opting a foreign government is like learning how to leave room for the mouse when baiting the mousetrap with cheese). We can teach students to value "playing" with potential, simultaneous alternatives for a given situation or task—to spot the pleasing images that make new, intriguing patterns. We can teach students to find metaphors to "show" us that they do, in fact, really understand the concepts we are teaching:

| | |
|---|---|
| "federalism" | It's like the animals in the wolf pack who let the leader have the power, so long as they still can make important decisions about their daily activities and their own wolf cubs. |
| "procrastination" | The problem is not "being as fast as the hare"; the problem is that most of the time only the turtles finish the race. |
| "antibodies" | They're like having white knights in your bloodstream who have found the green dragons of that particular disease before. |
| "management systems" | They are a necessary function of living together—like the rules by which the lion pride, the dolphin school, the chimpanzee colony, and the flock of wild geese live; without the system, the animals could not accomplish their basic tasks of living together. |
| "courtesy" | The gentle dew we drop on "people flowers" to watch the petals open and embrace the sunshine of the day. |
| "insight" | The "rainbow" alternatives inside each of us that await a moment of seeing the color and experiencing the energy. |
| "desire to change" | The decision to enter a cocoon when you are not sure what kind of a butterfly you'll be when you emerge. |

The potential expands with each concept; the images are all around us. There are countless possibilities for each concept, for each new thought we would have students grasp and understand.

Look at the myriad possibilities when considering the concept of "being fair." We can look at the "scale of justice," Solomon's baby, the role of the umpire or referee, the way the rain waters a garden, the story of the little red hen. Being fair means choosing to be impartial, choosing to treat equally despite personal favorites, controlling emotional reactions and considering all alternatives. How much easier it becomes to teach this definition with the aid of images and stories— with the focus of the right brain as well as the left.

Robert Pirsig, in his intriguing book, *Zen and the Art of Motorcycle Maintenance,* takes the reader on a journey into the realm of quality. Pirsig's search for the meaning of this common yet elusive concept is clarified for the reader as we accompany him on the journey; the exercises throughout this book are intended to have a similar effect for you—they are designed to expand your understanding of creativity and its critical process of thought—IMAGERY. By participating in these exercises, you will not only have an increased understanding of metaphoric teaching, but you will begin to think and speak this alternate language—the language of half your cerebrum—the language of the right brain. The metaphor is your Rosetta stone; it will unlock the ciphers and allow countless insights to pour forth. Before we enter into these exercises, however, we would like to briefly pause and examine a double-edged sword that both enriches imagery in our culture and limits its conscious use. Television has become this paradoxical resource—a resource that expands and simultaneously limits the image world of our children.

## The Dilemma of Modern Imagery

> *Television captures the imagination, but it does not liberate it. A good book at once stimulates and frees the mind.*
>
> Marie Winn, *The Plug-In Drug*

Today's young people have an incredible mental bank of images. They can easily picture what it is like to be under the ocean, in a space ship, standing in Moscow's Red Square, or falling from an airplane. All these images, and many more, have been readily supplied by television. This phenomenon has immediate benefits in terms of using guided imagery in the classroom; in fact, television has linked cultures, customs, and ideas around the world. But there is another side to this controlled and controlling, highly structured, external source of imagery; namely that, because of television, we may be losing much of our natural propensity and ability to create images.

While the evidence as to the importance of the process of imagery formation in both creativity and concept development is rapidly accumulating, there is a simultaneous accumulation of evidence to suggest that in our visual-media society, children have fewer and fewer opportunities to develop the "muscles" of the imagination.

For example, most of our students will watch over fifteen thousand hours of television before they graduate from high school (compared to the approximately eleven thousand hours they will have spent in classrooms). They will also have attended numerous motion pictures, read hundreds of illustrated comic books, and attended various visual media events. When they do listen to the radio (often while completing a homework assignment), they will listen to the sounds of popular music sounds that distract the right brain, but not to stories that captivate its imagery. They will spend countless hundreds of hours listening to sophisticated stereo systems that amplify, both in volume and message, the sounds of the youth culture. Even the highly popular video games define and limit their individual imaginative responses; video game solutions must be within the linear, programmed formats of the game itself. Technological advances can, in fact, limit, as well as expand, the development of independent imagination in our students.

Television in particular is a major offender; it is both prescriptive and descriptive. There is little imaginative leeway while watching "LaVerne and Shirley," "Happy Days," or "Real People"—even the "surprises" of the Saturday morning cartoon shows become predictable after a short period of viewing. The characters on television shows are defined for us. Would we imagine "The Fonz" to look like Henry Winkler if "Happy Days" were a radio program? Would our imaginations create Mork, Alice, or Archie to look like the characters who play them in the television series? Strangely enough, television creates its own stereotypes—stereotypes that prevent alternative, personal images of the stories and characters it portrays.

Not only does the endless succession of new TV series reduce the development of imagery by delineating the physical characteristics of both the characters, the story, and the situation for the viewer, but the technique of television itself is designed to keep our entire attention focused on the small box with the bright screen no matter what else is happening in the immediate vicinity. (If you have ever had the experience of visiting a friend who greets you warmly at the door, takes you back into the living room, sits back down in the easy chair and neglects to turn off the television, you know that it is almost impossible to carry on a conversation while competing with the TV.)

Television is designed to keep our attention by attracting our "orienting reflex"; thus, there are quick shifts in material, rapid movement of plot and characters, and distortion of time. All of these processes impede the comprehension of words and the creation of personal images. Even the well-intentioned Sesame Street, with its rapidly switching focus and continual barrage of information, has been found by some researchers to hinder learning in some students.*

Regrettably, many of us have been sidetracked from the goal of attacking television itself, because we have been so busy attempting to deal with the quality of what our children watch. *Thus, many of us have missed the central point, which is that they watch so much.* The TV problem is not merely a question of inappropriate role models, poor grammar, too much sex or too much violence, too little that has any social value, and too much that glorifies the undesirable; *it is also a problem of what is not happening every time that little screen shines forth.* When children are watching television they are not reading, because most children cannot really read and watch TV at the same time; they are not dreaming, fantasizing, or building their own internal worlds while the flashing shapes scream for their attention. These activities require that the left hemisphere be at rest; children are not playing, because they might miss something important in the program. In short, they are not developing the right-brain potential for personal images, stories, ideas, and imagination. On the contrary, they are becoming external-image addicts, losing the conscious interplay of either the right or left hemisphere. Internal imagery stops; reasoning is unnecessary. Television provides both images and logic; the viewer's role is one of passive acceptance.

Marie Winn points out in her book, *The Plug-In Drug,* that before the typical American youngster reaches the age for admission into first grade, he or she will have spent at least five-thousand hours in front of the television set; each one of those hours is an hour that might, in past generations, have been spent in developing individual, imaginative, creative ability. Many teachers who have been in the classroom for thirty years or more assert that there is a noticeable difference between the generations before television and the generations of the television years: the latter are comparatively lacking in spontaneity and imagination; they have a different way of communicating, of speaking their thoughts—they imitate the homogenized world of television. This truncated world of the television generation is confined to the world that they have seen, and often not understood, while sitting in front of the Great Tube. And indeed, the process of bringing all images to the student in prepackaged, easily digested, non-imagination-inducing formats seems to be snowballing.

---

*Thomas D. Cook et al., *"Sesame Street" Revisited* (New York: Russell Sage Foundation, 1975). Two factors emerged: (1) although the program is superior in design, it is, nonetheless, fixed—not adjustable to the individual child; (2) it is so engrossing that children will not choose to do anything else in its place (becoming far more passive an experience than we would suppose).

Recently, classic children's stories such as Madeline L'Engle's *Wrinkle in Time,* Jean Lee Latham's *Carry on Mr. Bowditch,* Marguerite Henry's *King of the Wind,* and Carol Ryrie Brink's *Caddie Woodlawn* have been made available in a cassette tape/filmstrip format. Older students can read illustrated (that is, cartoon-like) versions of *Kidnapped, Call of the Wild,* and *Moby Dick.* Regrettably, as teachers and as parents, we consciously or unconsciously contribute to this trend. We often use the justification that it is better that children see the cassette/filmstrip version of *King of the Wind* than never come in contact with the story at all—and perhaps, in a very few cases, this is true. But in the long run, the students pay a price, the price of losing flexibility and strength in controlling their own personal resources of imagery and imagination.

How big a price are our students paying? We suggest it is higher than most of us suspect, and this suggestion comes both from personal experience and from the decline in creative, original thinking that is presently limiting our nation as a whole. To illustrate the dilemma facing today's would-be innovators, we cite the years between 1967 and 1978, when we both were actively involved in public school education. Between the two of us, we taught every grade level in elementary school as well as junior and senior high school.* During this decade, it was generally expected that students in the elementary classes would participate in approximately twenty minutes per day of Super Sustained Silent Reading Time (always known by mid-October as SSSRT). There was an additional expectation at the elementary level of approximately twenty additional minutes per day for storytime (depending on the grade level, these times varied slightly), a time when books were read to the students. Books were chosen for their content and their illustrations and books with occasional illustrations (which suggested rather than defined images) were preferred. Younger children, of course, needed both more illustration and more complete illustrations than did the older students.

In March 1977, while reading to a third grade class from the Laura Ingalls Wilder's book, *Little House in the Big Woods,* we noticed that the same students who normally could not get enough of other illustrations seemed not particularly interested in Garth Williams' intriguing and understated pen drawings. When asked about this, the students

---

*Dr. Judy Sanders's experience in the public schools included five years of teaching German and English in consolidated school systems (7–12) and half a year in a kindergarten classroom (in graduate school). Dr. Don Sanders taught extensively in elementary schools for a period of ten years—all levels and many differing ability groups. Their combined background also includes eight years of working with student teachers and graduate students (returning teachers); their research has always included a heavy emphasis on field experience and actual practice within the public school classroom.

replied, "Oh, we already know what Ma and Pa and Laura look like."
The TV series "Little House on the Prairie" was at its peak at this time
and the Ingalls family was probably better known than the "first"
family. Television had clearly defined the images made by the words
of the "Little House" books. Marie Winn quotes a ten-year-old on the
effects of TV representations of what he has read in books:

The TV people have a stronger impression. Once you've seen a character on
TV, he'll always look that way in your mind, when you read the book yourself
. . . The thing about a book is that you have so much freedom. You can make
each character look exactly the way you want him to look.

At the same time that television is limiting the development of
imagery in our students, there is mounting evidence to suggest the
importance of increasing imagery. Imagery not only helps produce
insights that prompt us to link the familiar with the unfamiliar, but
imagery also enables students to remember what they have already
learned (Pressley, 1976), facilitates the learning of basic memory tasks
(Levin, 1976), and provides assistance in remembering prose content
(Anderson and Kulhavey, 1972). According to Steingart and Glock
(1979), imagery formation results in significantly higher levels of infer-
ence-making as well as improving recall; additionally, in the Steingart
and Glock study, the use of imagery markedly facilitated the comprehension of text relationships. The impact of the image brain on the
analytical brain is both profound and inescapable, yet the opportunities for children to engage in fantasy, to create their own images, to fill
in "mental blanks" with their own creations, are becoming fewer and
fewer.

Alan McLeod describes the passing of one such method no longer
available to students, a method that encouraged the incidental formation of imagery in him:

As a youngster during and after World War II, I recall sitting on our living
room rug, my ear pressed to the speaker of our floor model radio, one hand
adjusting the tuning knob, and a world of imagination at my finger tips. I could
'see' Clark Kent's change to Superman, Jack Benny counting his money,
Franklin Roosevelt's funeral . . . and a host of other characters and events. My
mind was forced to construct mental pictures from words and other sounds. I
was compelled to participate in creating and visualizing setting, plot and character.

Indeed, we can remember sitting by the old "Philco" listening to
"The Whistler," "Bull Dog Drummond" and "Boston Blackie." But this
time has passed; today, our students have few opportunities to hear
anything other than music, news, and sports on the radio. Their lives

are dominated not by the printed word or the imageless sound, but by the visual images of television; images that define and restrict their world.

It is ironic that in a time when so much of both our leisure and school time is devoted to activities that require little or no imagination that we are simultaneously uncovering the critical nature of this activity. As Eugene S. Ferguson notes in the conclusion of his article, "The Mind's Eye, Non-Verbal Thought in Technology":

Much of the creative thought of the designers of our technological world is non-verbal; its language is an object of a picture or a visual image in the mind. It is out of this kind of thinking that the clock, printing press and snowmobile have arisen. Technologists, converting their non-verbal knowledge into objects directly or into drawings that have enabled others to build what was in their minds, have chosen the shape and structured the qualities of our man-made surroundings.

The evidence continues to accumulate: studies of the great teachers, scientists, artists, and statesmen point to the human need for internal imagery; recent research in brain development, and especially hemispheric specialization, support this need—people are, indeed, more than the verbal, rational, logical beings they are often portrayed as being; people are also intuitive, spatial, pattern-creating, imaginative, and image-making.

"All right," you say, "I will agree that the 'right brain' processes information differently from the 'left brain.' I will agree that we need more creativity in our classrooms and that most subject matter is taught from a 'left brain' orientation. I will even agree that the metaphor is an obvious and relatively simple tool to produce right brain stimulation; the question for me as a teacher is: 'How do I implement metaphoric teaching approaches in my classroom?' "

Chapter 2 offers specific answers to this question. Couched along with some of the more illuminating metaphors of great teachers and political leaders of the past are two complete classroom metaphoric exercises in creative metaphoric thinking that can be used immediately. These lessons are designed to provide you with a basic strategy, a simple, efficient technique, for bringing the rational/verbal and the intuitive/imaginative into creative synthesis. The two lessons in this chapter, therefore, are models (an additional eight lessons are found in the second half of this book); you will find that the method can be adapted to fit any subject matter area.

It may be only in school that our students still have the opportunity for a defined time to create personal imaginative connections; we, as teachers, can help our students experience the pleasure and advantage of such "aha!" experiences, and we can assure this creative development through classroom practice. Metaphoric teaching offers a doorway into a world filled with new moments of expanding awareness— a world not dependent upon the shadows of the cave, rather a world that sparks new ideas, new solutions, and new inquiry.

## BIBLIOGRAPHY

Abell, Arthur M. Talks with the great composers. Quoted in *Creativity—Its Educational Implications* (2nd edition) by J.C. Gowan, J. Khatena, E.P. Torrance. Dubuque, Iowa: Kendall/Hunt, 1981.

Anderson, R.C., and R.W. Kulhavy. "Imagery and Prose Learning." *Journal of Educational Psychology* 63 (1972): 242–243.

Capra, Fritjof. *The Tao of Physics*. Boulder, Colo.: Shambala, 1975.

Chesteron, G.K. *St. Thomas Aquinas*. Garden City, N.J.: Image Books, 1956.

Cook, Thomas D. et al. *"Sesame Street" Revisited*, New York: Russell Sage Foundation, 1975.

Ferguson, Eugene S. "The Mind's Eye, Non-Verbal Thought in Technology." *Science* 197 (1977): 827–836.

Galan, D., and R. Ornstein. "Individual Differences in Cognitive Style, I: Reflective Eye Movements." *Neuropsychologica* 12, (1974): 367–376.

Gallaway, W. Timothy. *The Inner Game of Tennis*. New York: Random House, 1974.

Ghiselin, Brewster. *The Creative Process*. Berkeley, Calif.: University of California Press, 1952.

Knapp, Mark L. *Nonverbal Communication in Human Interaction*. New York: Holt, Rinehart and Winston, 1978.

Koestler, Arthur. *The Act of Creation*. New York: Macmillan, 1964.

Kuslan, Louis, and A. Harris Stone. "The Nature of Science." *Teaching Children Science*. Belmont, Calif.: Wadsworth, 1972.

Levin, J.R., and V.L. Allen, (eds.) *Cognitive Learning in Children: Theories and Strategies*. New York: Academic Press, 1976.

Levy, J., C. Trevarthen, and R.W. Sperry. "Perceptions of Bilateral Chimeric Figures Following Hemispheric Disconnection." *Brain* 95 (1972): 61–78.

McLeod, Alan. "Listening, Writing and the Realm of Imagination." *Clearinghouse* 53 (1979): 8–10.

Medawar, Peter. *Plato's Republic*. London: Oxford University Press, 1982.

Mitchell, Bruce, Arnold Stueckle, and Robert F. Wilkens. *Conceptual Planning for Creative Learning*. Dubuque, Iowa: Kendall/Hunt, 1976.

Pirsig, Robert. *Zen and the Art of Motorcycle Maintenance*. New York: William Morrow, 1974.

Pressley, G. Michael. "Mental Imagery Helps Eight-Year-Olds Remember What They Read." *Journal of Educational Psychology* 63 (1972): 242–243.

Prince, George. *The Practice of Creativity*. New York: Macmillan, 1970.

Restak, Richard. *The Brain: The Last Frontier*. New York: Doubleday, 1979.

Sagan, Carl. *The Dragons of Eden*. New York: Random House, 1977.

Samuels, David. "Your Mind Is Better than You Think." In Buzan, Tony, ed. *Use Both Sides of Your Brain.* New York: E.P. Dutton, 1976.

Smith, Houston. *The Religions of Man.* New York: Harper and Brothers, 1958.

Springer, Sally, and George Deutsch. *Left Brain, Right Brain.* San Francisco: D.H. Freeman and Co., 1981.

Steingart, Sandra, and Marvin Glock. "Imagery and the Recall of Connected Discourse." *Reading Research Quarterly* XV (1979): 66–81.

Tolstoy, Leo. *Anna Karenina.* Translated and with an introduction by David Magarshack. New York: Signet Books, 1961.

Wallas, Graham. *The Art of Thought.* London: C. Watts, 1926.

Weisenberg, T., and K. McBride. *Aphasia: A Clinical and Psychological Study.* New York: Commonwealth Fund, 1935.

Williams, Frank. *A Total Creativity Program for Individualizing and Humanizing the Learning Process.* Englewood Cliffs, N.J.: Educational Technology Publications, 1972.

Winn, Marie. *The Plug-In Drug.* New York: Viking, 1977.

# CHAPTER 2

# *Teaching through Metaphors*

## A LOOK FORWARD

An eighth-grade teacher was attempting to explain the concept of states' rights to her class of inner-city students. Having exhausted the traditional textbook explanations of the topic, she finally said in exasperation,

Look, I am certain that all of you have seen movies or TV shows about the life of a hunting animal—like the wolf or coyote. One animal becomes the leader; he takes care of the others; he makes the decisions about when to hunt, when to hide, when to stalk, when to make the kill. But, he only leads because the other animals have, through fights or facedowns, approved him as the leader.

If we were to put it in human terms, we would say that the animals have banded together and said to the leader of the pack, "We have agreed to give you the power to lead us, but your power comes from us and, without our consent, you cannot lead. We will make some decisions for ourselves, such as how to make the kill and where to make our dens, and if you try to take these decisions away from us, we will replace you."

Well, this is what states' rights are all about—some things the central government can do, and some things it cannot do. The states have not given up all decision making. The central government, like the leader of the pack, will stay in charge *as long as the states themselves are willing to follow. If they can make only limited decisions for themselves, the states will usually not question the central government's leadership.*

Suddenly, the students "get it." They understand what the lesson is all about. In surprise and delight, the teacher has discovered the power of the metaphor, in this case, for teaching the concept of states' rights versus federal control.

Later in the week, this teacher returned to the same metaphor to provide her students with insights about themselves and the political climate that preceded the American Civil War. She first referred to the discussion of states' rights and the metaphor of the wolf pack:

Today, I want you to think back to our discussion on Monday and how hunting animals agree to give leadership power to the head of the pack. Now, think of yourself in such a hunting pack. Who are you in the pack; what are you doing? And, how do you feel? . . . Now quickly jot down on the paper before you any of the thoughts that come to your mind. Write down as many ideas as you can about who you are, what you do in the pack, and how you feel about all the others. There are no right or wrong answers—just write down what it is like to be part of that group.

(MINUTES LATER) . . . Now, look at your comments and decide—are you someone who has been given the leadership power or have you chosen to assign that power to someone else and to be part of the group. What happens if the leader does not stick to the agreements? How would you feel if no one would follow?

(AFTER CONSIDERABLE DISCUSSION) . . . Today, we're going to look at something very similar that happened about a hundred years ago in our country—we're going to look at the political climate in the United States just before the Civil War broke out.

The teacher is using a metaphoric bridge to help her students link the overall concept to be learned (states' rights versus federal control) with the subject matter at hand (the American Civil War). She is teaching history, a cognitive topic, but she is also encouraging personal insight—a natural, affective motivator. In this case, she has used a consistent metaphoric image to link concept with the information to be learned; in doing so, she encourages students to understand the concept of states' rights—both logically and personally. When facts and feelings are combined, the students' concept mastery is greatly increased. Rapid, exciting, critical understanding results. Students suddenly know not only *what* they are really learning, but they often also know *why.*

In Chapter 2, we will examine the metaphor as both an ancient and a modern teaching strategy. We will see its teaching power used by well-known statesmen and great teachers; then, we will see the metaphor in new guises in teaching strategies ready for your classroom. Metaphoric teaching has a solid and ancient foundation; this chapter and the next will help you identify, explain, and understand the nature of the foundation and the learning structures it naturally supports.

## What Is Metaphoric Teaching?

Metaphoric teaching is exciting, stimulating, insight-generating, and a powerful tool for learning. As a classroom strategy, metaphoric teaching has been nurtured by the intriguing discoveries from recent educational, neurologic, and psychological research; research related not only to the unsuspected discoveries of the importance of the hippocampus, but also to: how people learn skills (the experiential learning model), how the brain works (studies on hemispheric specialization), and how affective instruction can impact concept attainment (the instructional benefits of role-playing, simulations, and synectics).

The roots of metaphoric teaching, however, are not to be found in recent research, rather these roots can be found in the recorded and oral histories of almost all cultures. In fact, recent findings merely support the intuitive approach shared by great historical leaders and teachers throughout the ages, an intuitive approach that emerges and re-emerges in the artifacts of many cultures and the writings of many world leaders. Traditionally and historically, the metaphor has captured human imagination and channeled this energy into teaching the most valued concepts of human interaction, the most sophisticated concepts of the pursuit of knowledge. The fables of Aesop, the parables of Jesus of Nazareth, the ancient African tales of Anansi the Spider, the homespun prose of Abraham Lincoln, the homilies of Ben Franklin, and the lessons of the Sufi masters—all demonstrate the timeless universality of teaching concepts with metaphors. Our greatest, most valued lessons have almost always had metaphorical roots!

When Thomas Henry Huxley first defined "The Method by which the Causes of the Present and the Past Conditions of Organic Nature Are to be Discovered" (that is, the definition of the scientific method), he explained this scientific process with a series of metaphors. For example, Huxley described "induction" using the following apple metaphor:

Suppose you go into a fruiterer's shop, wanting an apple,—you take up one, and on biting it, you find it is sour; you look at it, and see that it is hard and green. You take up another one, and that, too, is hard, green, and sour. The shopman offers you a third; but, before biting it, you examine it, and find that it is hard and green, and you immediately say that you will not have it, as it must be sour, like those you have already tried.

Observing that the two apples that are hard and green are also sour leads the scientist to "induce" that a third, hard and green apple will quite likely also be sour. Thus, the principle of induction in the scientific method is one of projecting proven characteristics of a given experiment onto similar instances of the same phenomenon. The scientist then concludes that his or her generalization will hold in all similar circumstances, and new knowledge is born.

Political as well as scientific concepts have often been clarified through metaphoric interpretation. In 1939, when Franklin Delano Roosevelt sought to warn the people of the United States of the dangers of Nazi expansion, he used this long remembered metaphor:

When an epidemic of physical disease starts to spread, the community approves and joins in a quarantine of the patients in order to protect the health of the community against the spread of the disease.

Such imagery helped people see Nazism as a plague to be stopped, as an affliction that could cripple the community, create untold suffering, and result in national mortality.

In 1961 in John F. Kennedy's memorable Inaugural Address, a metaphor dramatized Kennedy's firm resolve as world leader and suggested an historical pattern that the nation should avoid:

. . .in the past, those who foolishly sought power by riding on the back of the tiger ended up inside.

The image of ignorantly (or foolishly) courting the speed of the dangerous tiger and thereby becoming the tiger's meal challenged people to question their attitudes toward the Soviet Union. The "meal" was far too real to those listening; the metaphor left no doubt—the contemporary tiger was innocently, but clearly, exposed.

This book, however, journeys beyond using metaphors in speaking and writing, because metaphoric teaching is more than a new version of mastering the analogies, metaphors, and similes we struggled to learn in high school. Metaphoric teaching is a universal approach for all subjects and all age groups; it is a method that actively stimulates concept mastery in the mind.

Why does this work? One reason is that the discovery of a metaphor to represent what we already know is an exciting discovery; it therefore responds to our basic need for "novelty"; another reason is that students are able to associate intellectually the "big picture" (the concept) with the details to be learned (the information or facts of the lesson at hand). Emotionally, students are experientially involved; the new knowledge fits into the experiences of their lives, and self-motivation naturally results.

Teaching with the metaphor, as we have suggested, is not new. Using a suggested or implied likeness (a metaphor) to compare something familiar with something unfamiliar is basic in human communication. Analogies to clarify, to simplify, and to explain are found in all written records throughout the ages. However, recent new research on how the brain processes information suggests that the power of the metaphor is awesome—that the metaphor is, by far, our most informal and most effective instructional tool.

## Taking the Leap Forward—
## Creating the Unsuspected Connection

One of the clearest, most articulate examinations of the metaphor and its impact is found in the pioneering, now classic, study of the process by which human reality is conceptualized—Jerome Bruner's *On*

*Knowing: Essays for the Left Hand* (1976). In this daring monograph, Bruner provides a basic intuitive leap that was later "piggybacked" by several other writers, teachers, and psychologists who also sought to explain the nature of creative thinking. Bruner asserts in this manuscript that "(The) metaphoric combination leaps beyond systematic placement; (it) explores connections that were before unsuspected." Bruner reveals a basic quality of creative thinking; the magical, unreasonable leap that imagination willingly makes—allowing new, original ideas to be born. At the heart of this process, Bruner finds the metaphor. The metaphor challenges logic, introduces expanding imagery, suggests new awarenesses.

How does this work? What is the nature of the creative leap prompted by the metaphor? What is meant by new connections that expand? Consider the examples of metaphors in our lives, metaphors familiar to us all; note your own imagery and expanded awareness that result when you allow them to be visualized in your mind.

In the poetry of Yeats, we encounter these lines:

> *O body swayed to music, O brightening glance*
> *How can we know the dancer from the dance?*

If we think of our own life as being a dance and ourselves as being its dancer, we find the beauty of Yeats's poem quickly expanding in our mind. We begin to look for our own source of music, to sense the rhythm of our life, to see the way we approach and dance out the activities of our days. As we explore the dance metaphor, we can glimpse the tempo of our own music, the audience for whom we perform, perhaps even those with whom we dance. The pattern of our life flashes before us; we can see our own choreography, our options for dancing to different music in different settings. Are we square dancing our way through life, are we driven by the fast tempo of disco, or do we seek out the slow, once highly prized, Viennese waltz? For some of us, it's often a solitary dance of improvisation; for others, we want (or need) the partners, the group and the conventional steps that everyone knows are "right."

Or consider this more popular example of the metaphor from the well-known song, "El Condor Pasa" ("If I Could"):

> *I'd rather be a sparrow than a snail,*
> *I'd rather be a hammer than a nail,*
> *--I'd rather sail away*
> *Like a swan, that's here and gone. . .*

This refrain again causes us to examine our own motives for how we live our lives. Some of us want to fly like the sparrow, or to be the prime power like the hammer, or to wander the world like the swan. Others recognize the beauty in the snail's secure home or in the nail's strength and crucial function—for them, the song suggests only the yearning of someone who sees the world differently, who is restless, who is not at peace with the world as it is.

When we ponder the Belgian proverb:

> *Experience is the comb*
> *that nature gives us*
> *When we are bald.*

We wonder at its innate wisdom; how painfully we have learned that experience is what you get right after you need it. But the metaphor says more than the age-old message of "Wait, you'll learn it, and then you won't need it." It also captures the pathos, the frustration, and the dubious usefulness of the gift experience will provide us. The comb may be pretty, but we miss the hair. As older, wiser people, we simultaneously understand the lessons of our lives, and miss the beauty that came with youthful energy, innocence, and spontaneity.

Irony can be captured with the metaphor; consider this admonition from Will Rogers:

> *I tell you, folks*
> *All politics*
> *Is applesauce.*

We smile inwardly at the comparison and the universal truth expressed; applesauce may have the taste of apples, but you can't bite off a chunk and see where you have marked the apple. Unlike the shape and color of the apple, applesauce is blandly mushed together, has often lost its original color, and, more often than not, needs sugar. How truly this analogy fits political compromise where original ideas seem lost, and the "MacIntosh" becomes mashed to a pablum even babies can eat. It may provide the meal, even taste like an apple, but the essence has been lost.

It is in the nature of the metaphor to cause us to stop, pause, and reflect on the expanding implications of its image; we read Emerson:

> *When it is dark enough*
> *You can see the stars*

and are comforted in our own search for meaning. Perhaps, it is only in extreme contrast that true stars can be seen. We read Voltaire:

> *We are on this globe*
> *Like insects in a garden.*
> *Those who live on an oak*
> *Seldom meet those*
> *Who pass their short*
> *Lives on an ash.*

and we see the isolation of our little worlds in the garden of total humanity. The metaphoric moment of insight causes us to reread the passage, to pause, and to put our own lives in perspective with those around us, to examine the tree we live on and reflect on the different trees around us. We make a connection between the known and the unknown, the familiar and the unfamiliar. This process is the essential core of the metaphoric mode; we can use its impact consciously to teach concepts—but to teach them with a difference. That difference lies in the student's understanding, which happens more quickly, more holistically, and more personally.

## Fostering the Conceptual Leap in the Classroom

Appreciating the unique power of the metaphor is only a beginning. As teachers we seek a specific approach, a set of steps to encourage students to use metaphoric thinking to solve problems, to generate creative insight, to master complex concepts in the classroom—concepts in science, social studies, mathematics, and language. To develop these steps (to be used by teachers working with students from kindergarten to college to adult education classes), we explored the nature of metaphoric imagery and its role in concept mastery. We visited classrooms, we taught lessons to all ages, we mapped out the metaphoric experience, and from all of this a pattern emerged—a pattern that arranged the metaphoric parts into steps for classroom use. Next, using this pattern, we designed a series of exercises to demonstrate how the metaphoric process can work in most teacher/learner relationships. In time, these exercises divided into two basic instructional groups: concept-related metaphoric lessons and personal growth-related metaphoric lessons.*

The following two lessons, then, are examples of the overall metaphoric modes ("The Change/Butterfly Lesson" and "Perspective/The Time Movie Lesson"). In both of these lessons, the instructional focus is primarily concept-related (although personal growth insights will certainly accompany the classroom experience). Both the "Change" lesson and the "Perspective" lesson are complete instructional units in themselves; they can be included in classroom units on metamorphosis, change, geologic time, historical records, and a host of other topics. Wherever the concept of change and natural growth is the focus of the classroom lesson, the butterfly metaphor will prompt new associations,

---

*Personal growth-related metaphors involve quick-association exercises: "How are you like a badger?" "Think of a system in nature that describes your school, your day, your home, your friends." "If you could be any form of transportation what would you be and why?"

new interest, new understanding, and new motivation to venture forth. Likewise, wherever the history of people, the nature of the planet, or the fleeting essence of time is central to a lesson, the "Time Movie" will cause new awareness, new desire to explore what is known, new appreciation for the fantasy and fact of historical record.

How is this conceptual leap possible? The answer lies in the very nature of reality as we perceive it. Words, the primary mortar of concepts, are learned in a cultural context. Each word's meaning is more than the dictionary's definition; it is the sum of total experiences we have had in learning and using the word. Consequently, underlying each word (each concept) is a host of images obtained in the moments when we have used the word with family, friends, and teachers. In fact, new research in linguistics (Lakoff, 1981) is now discovering that our entire language can be seen as an extension of countless metaphorical associations resulting from personal and cultural experiences—each word is caught up in its own family of images—the juxtaposition of any one word with another offers several metaphorical possibilities.*

How does this work? Take, for example, the concept of "change." The dictionary defines "change" as: "To alter, to make different, to pass from one phase to another, to be in transition." Yet, from our lives, we have discovered that "change" is much more—it is difficult, risky, unknown, and anxiety-producing. In daily interactions, therefore, we tend to use "change" as it is culturally defined rather than literally defined.** Change tends to mean *"the fixing or repairing of something."* Experientially, we teach our children that "change" often stands for the process of "making something better" or "if something isn't working, get something that will!"

As teachers, we have also learned (through experience) that change can be a process of growth, expansion, even evolution. It can be positive without criticizing what has been changed. It can mean achieving one's own potential. The problem lies in helping our students understand this perspective for changing; they are (understandably) caught up in the cultural definition they've learned at home: *"Change it!—means make it better!"* We want students to learn a new context for changing; we want them to learn that changing can be the growth of skills and self-awareness, not the need for correcting a present inadequacy.

This new context can be taught, but not by conventional instructional methods. Cultural definitions are not altered by logical discus-

---

*This idea of the metaphoric concept behind the literal definition of a word is explored more fully in Chapter 4.

**Please turn to Chapter 4 for a more detailed explanation of conventional and cultural definitions of words and concepts. Conventional definitions tend to be logical and literal (left brain); cultural definitions tend to be holistic and experiential (right brain).

sion or by new definitions that are learned and memorized; to change a cultural definition, in effect to alter the concept's metaphorical definition, a new life experience must occur.

Suppose you wish your students to see the conceptual change in skill that will occur when the ability to add and subtract is complemented with the ability to multiply and divide. Or suppose you want your students to understand the nature of political change that occurs when nations progress from feudalism to social democracy. In both cases, the emphasis is on the growing potential of accepting new alternatives.

The following lesson provides this psychological transition for the learner; it allows a new life experience. It reveals a new meaning for the concept *change*. To begin, just read the lesson and enjoy it. When you finish, we'll further examine its implications and then move on to experience the same basic phenomenon in the "Time Movie" lesson that explores the concept of *time* as historical perspective.

# The Change/Butterfly Exercise
*The Concept of CHANGE as Growth,
Evolution, and Expanded Potential*

## AN INTRODUCTION TO THE METHOD

In order to make these lessons work, try actively imagining you are the teacher and that there are students, young or old, in the situation with you. Choose your topic—why would you be teaching *change* as a concept in your classroom? Then imagine that it is your students who will be experiencing this lesson and responding to its questions.

If you allow your imagination to enhance this experience, you will discover that the whole process will seem quite natural and less "foreign." Later, when you actually try the lesson with your own classes, you will find that the metaphoric method can be as natural and effective as directive teaching, recitation, or the discussion method.

### The Butterfly Exercise—The Concept of Change

The following lesson is divided into these parts:

| | |
|---|---|
| *Context:* | The metaphorical definition of the concept the teacher wishes to introduce. |
| *Method:* | The actual process of the METAPHORIC MODEL<br>Level I—The Focus Level<br>Level II—The Personal Comparison<br>Level III—The Metaphoric Interaction<br>Level IV—The Insight Moment for Concept Mastery |
| *Implications:* | Application to specific content areas. |

*Context*

Inherent in the nature of *change* is risking, being vulnerable, and a moment of uncertainty when the "die is cast" but the course is uncharted. People often fear change for this reason; they do not know where the change will take them: the new skills, the new knowledge, and the new obstacles that will result. Rather than venture forth to explore the potential, to create the new opportunity, people often cling to what is given, what is familiar. Exploring these feelings and looking at the benefits that come with daring a new approach is basic to most classroom lessons.

Consider the history lesson on Columbus sailing to the New World, the second grader learning to count without his fingers, the junior high class practicing democratic group process; consider the first yearbook, the new play, the first day of a new P.E. unit, the examination of values —the possibilities for teaching students to value change are limitless. They occur every day in the classroom. Change, however, involves a leap of faith, a willingness to patiently plough forward without immediate dividends. But change is also the nature of life; it is one of the certain elements of our existence. Change provides the excitement that keeps boredom, dull predictability, and tasteless sameness from being the norm. History, literature, the arts, science, math, sports—all share the challenge to grow and change perception, skill, and attitude. The following lesson brings a new context for viewing change in your classroom; it introduces the *impact* of change with honest, positive clarity for students of all ages.*

## The Method

The metaphoric lesson has four parts: the focus, the personal comparison, the metaphoric interaction, and the insight moment. The first three stages are designed to lead up to the final stage of concept mastery and insight. Beginning with a brief focus on the concept to be learned and the metaphoric image to be used, the lesson actively engages the attention of both brain hemispheres (see Chapter 1 for an in-depth discussion of how these hemispheres interact); finally, the lesson concludes with imagery and feelings that combine and enhance subject matter mastery and concept formation. Level IV thus becomes a moment of self-discovery, of conceptual insight, and of increased curiosity. As such, it produces a personal motivation to learn more—a sense of "the best is yet to come."

## USING THE METAPHORIC METHOD

### Level I: The Focus Level

In this first level, students associate the concept to be taught (*Change as Growth, Evolution, and Expanded Potential*) with a metaphoric image (in this case, the butterfly). The lesson begins with a clear advance organizer:

---

*Among the many people to whom we have personally taught this lesson are eight-year-olds, gifted fourth graders, junior high school science students, high school seniors, student teachers, graduate students, and adult education students in a public-speaking class.

Today we're going to think about the change that occurred when the South began its Reconstruction.

or

Today we're going to explore what happens when an animal undergoes metamorphosis.

or

Have you ever thought about the change in you that occurs when you learn to read? (To multiply? To speak a foreign language? To build a new skill?) Today's lesson focuses upon that kind of changing.

It is crucial in this first step of Level I to clearly link the subject matter of the instructional unit with the concept (change) to be explored in the metaphor. Next, expand the concept to introduce the metaphoric image of the lesson:

To look at this change in the South, we are first going to focus on the life and habits of a familiar little creature you all know well . . .

or

To understand the nature of changes in metamorphosis, we're going to look closely at the life of an animal whose very existence depends upon this process.

or

When thinking of the change that will occur in your life when you can read (can multiply, can speak a new language, can build this skill), we will find this change much the same as what happens to a little animal we all know.

At this point, the class will be shown several images of the butterfly. Try to have as many pictures, drawings, and paintings of the butterfly as you can find. Greeting cards, posters, and magazines are good sources for finding these pictures. Provide many examples and leave all of them out in the room. Soon, every "right brain" in the room will be fascinated and "tuned in." The images are patterns, pictures for the right hemisphere to enjoy; the result is almost total attention from the students. Next, write the word "BUTTERFLY" on the chalkboard; point out what this word conjures up in our minds—the images all around the classroom.*

Following these conventional symbols, show the class abstract art objects that represent butterflies, use artistic versions of the symbol. We have used several different media in this phase: pillow butterflies, metal butterfly sculptures, butterfly candles—things that tend to make the butterfly image a little strange. The students will hesitate as the

---

*If you are teaching a foreign language, include its word for "Butterfly" as well: French—"Papillon," German—"Schmetterling," Spanish—"Mariposa."

images become more unusual (two of the best we have used were a batik butterfly and a large stained-glass butterfly). These strange images are, however, of critical importance. They give the learner time and space to realize that categorizing a symbol as a "butterfly" can be a conscious choice, a process that involves both brain hemispheres. We generally say something like:

Did any of you hesitate? Did you finally say in your mind, "Okay, if you want to call THAT a butterfly, I'll let you, but it sure is stretching what a butterfly really is!"

Usually such a comment to the class is quickly followed by the nods of several heads and even surprise that you could guess what they were thinking.

Follow the parade of images with questions about them. These questions help students make a distinction between the real object and representations of the object:

What makes an image a butterfly? Can the image stand for anything else? For several things at the same time? What characteristics are essential?

These questions will prompt insights from the class. Explain that, in exploring metaphors, we naturally gain insights about how we see things—moments when we catch ourselves saying, "Oh, I get it!" or "aha!" In fact, it is through the image that we open a doorway of understanding for our own thoughts, feelings, and motivations. The butterfly will help us learn how it really feels to make a large change in life.

### Level II: The Personal Comparison

In this second level of the metaphoric method, students are asked to compare themselves with the metaphor; in doing so, they begin to identify with the lesson's metaphor. Introduce this level with the comment that it will help each person begin a "new way of thinking," to see himself or herself in a new perspective, to gain more knowledge about personal feelings and values. Next, pose the following questions or something similar:

How are you like the butterfly? Think of one way.
or
If you were to think of a way that you and the butterfly are alike, what would it be?

We have discovered that "How are you like the butterfly?" prompts quicker answers than "How is the butterfly like you?" The first question requires knowing things about themselves; the second question requires more familiarity with the metaphoric image itself.

Be sure to give students plenty of time to think of an answer. We usually ask them to raise their hands if they need more time to think of an answer. When everyone is ready, ask for a volunteer to begin a sharing round-robin session. Answers should be kept brief; explanations are not necessary. Proceed in an orderly fashion around the room —avoid calling only on those with their hands raised—and encourage everyone to contribute when it is his or her turn. Join in by giving your own answer as well when your turn comes. (The imagery that occurs when these answers are shared around the room will be immediate, vivid, and contagious. There is no need to spend time on long, personal, and often overly revealing explanations.)

Sometimes we find it helpful and motivating (especially with older groups) to write a shortened version of their answers on the chalkboard. Seeing the visual pattern of their answers will tend to prompt those who are hesitant. Younger students usually respond best to warm, open eye contact that encourages each person's contribution. Positive, nonverbal reinforcement helps everyone. You will discover that students really enjoy answering a question for which there is no "right" answer.

If someone responds with a very obvious comparison such as, "We're both alive" or "We both breathe" treat the answer with as much respect and encouragement as the more insightful comments like, "We have both changed and have learned to adapt to new homes and new opportunities" or "We're both vulnerable and must learn to fly alone."

When all the responses have been shared, comment generally on some of the insights gained in the process. Be careful of these insights, however; include only those that do not threaten or reveal too much. Here is such an example:

The butterfly is bright, beautiful, and loves flowers; that's just like me.

Clearly, you don't want to judge the comment with "This person probably thinks he/she is beautiful, loving, and bright." Instead, say something like:

Jane/Ted loves bright and beautiful things—especially flowers.

Soon the students will connect their responses with insights about themselves; some may want to share these. To encourage such responses, use your own personal comment as an example:

I thought of the butterfly coming from a cocoon, and I sometimes see my teaching as being a butterfly that came from a cocoon called "college."

One of the most exciting aspects of the Level II Comparison is gaining personal insights about your students; you will see them as distinct individuals with personal hopes, dreams, and fears. In a manner similar to Gestalt* psychology, students will indirectly reveal personal values that motivate and influence their lives. Remember to respect these values. For the student, discovering a personal attitude or value can be a fragile process, a process as fragile as the transformation in the cocoon.

## Level III: The Metaphoric Interaction

This level is designed to give the learner a personal opportunity to interact with the metaphor itself. It could, in this case, involve an actual field trip to a place where students would find both butterflies and caterpillars. It could involve role-playing what it would be like to be a caterpillar and then a new butterfly. However, we have chosen to use the "guided fantasy journey," as an instructional alternative that is immediately accessible and very effective.**

## THE BUTTERFLY GUIDED FANTASY

### Preparation

Make sure the students are sitting comfortably, the room is quiet, and separate from other groups. Dim the lights or turn them off. Ask the class to relax, close their eyes, and begin breathing deeply, to totally relax . . .

Then begin the dialogue. Take time to pause after each specified ". . ." pause moment. These moments help the students better envision the scene you are depicting for their imaginations.

---

*Gestalt psychology explores the use of images and symbols to help clients reveal unconscious motives and conflicting values and feelings. Several excellent counseling books are available on this technique.

**Guided fantasy journeys are imaginary experiences you can provide for your students with internal visualization. Basically, you encourage them to relax, close their eyes, and listen to the sound of your voice. Considerable discussion is given to this teaching technique in Chapter 7 where basic guidelines for design and presentation are outlined.

## The Dialogue

Imagine you are a caterpillar in a far away meadow . . . It is a warm, sunny day, and you are on the far edge of a beautiful, green meadow . . . Looking up at the sky, you see puffy, white clouds in a clear, blue horizon . . . Take a moment to look at yourself carefully . . . What color are you? . . . Are you a fuzzy caterpillar? . . . Are you a sleek, shiny caterpillar?

Now begin your journey across the meadow . . . You are moving slowly but surely across the green, soft grass, toward the distant edge of the meadow where the forest begins . . . Ahead of you are some flowers . . . They smell sweet and fresh in the meadow air . . . Crawl slowly toward them, toward one flower in particular . . . When you are directly under the flower, look up at it . . . What kind of a flower is it? . . . What does it look like? . . . What colors can you see? . . . Is it special?

Now look ahead of you . . . There is a clump of trees in the distance . . . Slowly, begin the long process of making your journey toward them . . . The grass is new and slightly damp from the dew . . . It feels like moss as you crawl over it . . . Soon you come to a rock . . . You know you must crawl up over it and down the other side . . . What does it look like? . . . How does it feel? . . . How big is it? . . . After you crawl past the rock, you encounter only more soft, pleasant grass until you come upon a footprint in your path . . . Move closer to it, and look at it carefully . . . Who or what made this footprint? . . . Now crawl past the footprint and continue your journey.

As you near the edge of the meadow, you can see many trees . . . They are tall, green, and inviting. One of the trees is especially beautiful . . . You decide to go up to that tree . . . When you are really close, you can smell the bark of the tree and feel a difference in the ground underneath you . . . You decide to leave the meadow below and to climb the tree . . . Slowly, start up the trunk of the special tree in front of you . . . You will find the tree easy to climb, exciting to feel . . . As you climb the trunk, you feel a little breeze . . . It ripples across your body, but it doesn't stop you from climbing . . . When you reach the first tree limb, crawl out on the limb and look for a special twig, a twig that will be your home . . . When you see that special twig, crawl onto it, and wait for a moment.

Soon a strange thing is happening . . . You are beginning to spin a beautiful, silky substance around and around you, you are becoming attached to the twig . . . This is something you have never done before, but it feels comfortable and natural.

You know somehow that this little tent is going to be your new home . . . It feels very soft and very safe . . . When your cocoon is all made, close the opening with more of your silky substance.

Now time is going to go by . . . You feel night coming, then day, then other nights, and several days go by . . . Soon, you can feel yourself changing . . . All that is you is still there in the soft, quiet home, but all of you seems to be restructuring, to be transforming . . . It is almost like melting and reforming . . . It is strange, wonderful, and very special . . . The days continue to go by, then weeks, and the outside world seems to cease for you . . . All that there is now is the reorganization, the changing of what is you.

Then, one day you feel the sun . . . It is coming in through the cocoon and seems to be beckoning you to come out and feel its warmth . . . You reach forward with one of your limbs, and you open a hole in the cocoon . . . Damp, and barely strong enough to crawl out, you slowly inch your way out of the cocoon and into the sunshine . . . You find the twig is still there, the sky is still blue above your head, but the weeks have changed the scene . . . It is now late spring, it is warm, and it is beautiful.

You can feel the sun drying you off, and a strange new body seems to be yours . . . There are huge wing-like arms for you, and you look in wonder at them . . . What color are they? . . . What do you look like? . . . Then, slowly, a little breeze comes and lifts you off the tree . . . You are flying out over the meadow, back to where the flowers were, the flowers at the edge of the meadow . . . Down below is one flower, a special flower you want to visit . . . You glide down to this flower, and you smell the sweet nectar within . . . You perch on its petal . . . Look at the meadow, the sky, and back at the trees . . . It is a glorious day . . . It is a moment of splendor . . . It is a moment to remember.

Now, slowly, when you are ready to leave, and not before, return from that meadow and from your flower . . . Come back to this classroom, and when you are truly ready, open your eyes.

## The Debriefing

When the students have all "returned," it is essential to debrief the guided fantasy experience they have just had. The following questions are very helpful; begin with simple hand counts:

1. How many of you were the fuzzy kind of caterpillar? How many of you were the smooth kind?
   *Usually half the class will respond one way, and half the other way.*
2. What color caterpillar were you?
   *This question will prompt many answers—green, brown, gray, many-colored, striped.*
3. I told you the sky was blue and the sun was out—did you feel the sun?
   *Usually this means head nods—even surprise! Many will not be aware that they actually felt warmer.*

4. What did the flower look like—looking up from underneath? Was it a different way to see the flower? Why?
   *This question prompts awareness of perspective; answers include comments like: a large umbrella, seeing the veins of the petals, and realizing that they couldn't see the whole flower, just its inside.*

5. Next, you came to a rock in your pathway—what did the rock look like?
   *Again, there will be many answers; some see brown, rough rocks; others see smooth, white ones. Usually there is a difference in heat as well. Some students encounter cold rocks; others found theirs to be warm.*

6. You continued on and then encountered a footprint—what did you see?
   *Some students will see animal footprints; others see human. Probe to find out which animals were represented. We've heard all kinds.*

7. As you journeyed on, you could feel the grass all around you. What was this experience like?
   *This answer changes from region to region and depends upon whether the students are used to Kentucky Bluegrass or St. Augustine. The bluegrass is soft, like velvet; St. Augustine will seem like a green jungle.*

8. When you neared the trees, what kind of trees did you see?
   *Again, this answer depends upon the geographic regions in which students are or have been living.*

9. You began to climb the tree, and I told you that a breeze rippled across your body. Did you feel the breeze? What happened?
   *Students will report feeling cooler or other pleasant sensations— some may say that, for a moment, they slipped or held on.*

10. What was the bark like? Rough, smooth, sticky? Could you smell it?
    *Some students will be able to smell the bark; most won't.*

11. How did you choose your twig? How did it feel when you began to spin your cocoon?
    *This question prompts a sense of mystery and excitement; twigs are usually chosen for strength—spinning often feels like melting.*

12. What was it like to be inside the cocoon? Did you feel yourself changing?
    *Most students love the cocoon. Older students will describe it as a return to the womb. Younger students will describe it as a safe hiding place. A few may not like the cocoon as much as the rest of the experience; these students sometimes fear moments of change. Be careful not to single them out; just accept their comments.*

13. Then, one day, you felt the sun and knew it was time to emerge. How did it feel to crawl out of the cocoon?

*The sun will be very warm—usually sudden. The emerging experience is exciting—sometimes slow.*

14. What color wings did you have? How did it feel to be so different?
    *There will be many colors, many descriptions; many of the butterflies the students saw in the beginning of the lesson will be the ones they choose. Students enjoy showing you which butterfly they were.*
15. When you flew back across the meadow, how did it feel to see the meadow from such a different viewpoint? What flower did you fly to? Why?
    *Many describe the incredible difference between crawling and seeing very little and flying and seeing the whole scene. Most choose the flowers they saw in the beginning.*
16. When you had to leave the meadow and return to the classroom, how did you feel?
    *Many will answer—sad!, reluctant, did not want to leave, not ready to leave such a restful place.*
17. What was really different about this experience?
    *Students will answer in terms of perspective, point of view, or seeing things as a small creature rather than a human being. Some have reported a sense of fragility—as if their pet kitten could have hurt them; some have reported a sense of soaring and changing that was exciting, inspiring, or like life itself!*

### Results of the Debriefing

As the students answer these questions, they will quickly discover how different each person's guided journey was. The imagination of each student creates personal details of the experience that cause thirty different versions of the experience to emerge. Students who were not sure they wanted to go on the guided fantasy and mentally "sat the experience out" are surprised to discover the enthusiasm and special experiences everyone else had. (They will become involved the next time; the debriefing is an automatic motivator for future metaphoric lessons.) The rest of the students will have enjoyed the process; it was work, it was fun, and it felt good. Older students may want to continue the debriefing with more substantive issues such as:

1. What's involved with feeling vulnerable?
2. Does all change involve an element of risk?
3. What are the benefits of changing? What are the obstacles?
4. When we change ideas, attitudes, life styles, do we have to pause and restructure ourselves like the process of the cocoon?
5. What are (have been) "cocoon times" for you? (Many will see high school or college as such moments—some see marriage or the year after a divorce.)

## Level IV: The Insight Moment for Concept Mastery

This is the culminating level of the metaphoric teaching method. It is the step that almost demands creativity, new perspective, and concept attainment. It is the creative product of the metaphoric lesson, the integration of image with information (right brain with left) to produce personal internalization. It results as the natural product of the other three levels of the model: the focus, the comparison, and the actual experience.

At this level, the teacher poses improbable analogies that relate the metaphoric image, in this case, the basic concept of change, to the subject matter at hand. To do this, simply state the connection to the students as a statement of fact; then, ask them to explain why or to "prove" that the statement could be true. Some examples are listed below. To maximize the impact of Level IV, you will need to tailor these examples to your own instructional lesson or unit.

## Implications

History:
: The Reconstruction period of the South was a cocoon opened too quickly, without a breeze to dry the new butterfly's wings.

    Columbus left Spain as a caterpillar; he returned as a butterfly. Explain.

    Studying the Middle Ages is studying the journey of a caterpillar into its cocoon; the Renaissance was the opening of that cocoon.

Math:
: Counting in your mind (not on your fingers) is spinning a cocoon for the future.

    A word problem is a cocoon about to be opened.

    Multiplying is being able to fly—dividing allows for you to find the individual flower.

English:
: A fable is a cocoon. Why?

    Punctuation is having caterpillar legs; writing paragraphs is having wings.

    The theme of a novel is the type of journey the caterpillar takes.

Science:
: Changing form in nature involves a cocoon phase.

    Metamorphosis means keeping what is really you while you change.

    Science lab is a cocoon; a field trip is a chance to fly.

    Larva to pupa to imago is nature's child to teenager to adult.

Students enjoy brainstorming their "proofs." Their answers will amaze you in their depth, understanding, perception, and wisdom. As the lesson ends, you will find that the basic elements of the concept have been explored and have re-emerged, but not just as carefully memorized responses of information you once presented. Instead, the concept of change will be integrated with the student's own life experience; it will be internalized as a "learned lesson" for which the students have feelings and vivid perspectives—their own ideas on what it means to dare to change, to evolve, to grow and transcend their present limitations.

The following lesson, the Time Movie Exercise, follows the same basic format and Part II of this book details two complete lesson formats for teaching the metaphoric lesson. However, the essential metaphoric elements are briefly summarized here in order to provide clarity regarding the relationship of the parts of the method to the overall purpose of the lesson.

*Level I—The Focus Level.* At this level it is important to link the subject matter you are teaching with the metaphor you want to use to teach the concept. In this unit, the butterfly was chosen as the metaphor to exemplify the concept of change.

*Level II—The Personal Comparison Level.* At this level, students compare themselves with the metaphor in order to initiate the process of generating insights that personally link the concept to be learned with the metaphoric object. The students should already be somewhat familiar with this object and understand that they are going to use it to learn something new.

*Level III—The Metaphoric Interaction Level.* This level is where the student personally interacts with the metaphoric object in order to begin the process of using that object to teach a concept. In the case of the change lesson, a guided fantasy tracing the butterfly from caterpillar to cocoon to butterfly was used to metaphorically represent the process of change.

*Level IV—Insight Moments for Concept Mastery.* At this level the teacher suggests unusual and improbable analogies in order to force concept/metaphor connections. It is from these connections that the learning of the concept emerges.

# MODEL LESSON 2
# The "Time Movie" Exercise
## Looking at Concepts of Time
## and Historical Perspective


### THE TIME MOVIE


### Extending the Metaphor's Potential—
### An Advanced Lesson

Most students will be familiar with the butterfly, many will have seen caterpillars and cocoons; some will have felt the gentleness of the butterfly in the open palm of their hands; a few may have been collectors or observers of this metamorphous insect. But what about the less common image for the more abstract lesson? Can the metaphor work as well when the image is less well defined and the concept to be taught requires students to make abstract connections?

The answer is a qualified yes. Advanced metaphoric lessons cannot take those students who are totally locked into Piaget's concrete operations stage and quickly move them into abstract thinking, although it can help. However, with those students who are in the early stages of abstract thought, the advanced metaphoric lesson is a tool of immense teaching power.

The concepts to be taught in this next lesson revolve around "time" and "perspective." Time, as suggested above, is an extremely abstract concept, very difficult to teach to the average student below age twelve. Even "concrete time" as measured by the clock is a difficult notion to teach; teaching second graders to "tell time" is one of the most difficult elements in the primary curriculum. By the seventh or eighth grade, however, students should begin to realize that conventional time is, like the compass, a human convenience for quantifying and specifying an abstract phenomenon.

The concept of time is pervasive in junior and senior high school curriculum. In English literature, for example, time is a major focus of William Faulkner's *The Sound and the Fury* and Anne Frank's *Diary of Anne Frank.* In biology, time can be the mini-seconds of synaptic connections and cell life, or it can be time as revealed by nature with the change of seasons or growth of trees. Earth science introduces time as it is perceived by geological change over centuries of geologic formations. History attempts to capture historical eras and moments in history that changed the direction of cultures and destiny. In philosophy,

JAN. FEB. MARCH APRIL MAY JUNE JULY AUGUST SEPT. OCT. NOV. DEC.

·ONE YEAR·

time becomes a relative concept—a cultural construct. In anthropology, time concepts can mean a better understanding of a given culture and its artifacts—like Egyptian pyramids or Roman road systems. Political science, too, often requires the understanding of completely different notions of time from country to country. Chinese, for example, has no way to express the complicated verbal tenses of English.

The following metaphoric exercise can be used in many curricular areas; however, integral to this metaphoric exercise are three general and widely applicable instructional objectives:

1. Students will develop an increasingly sophisticated conceptual understanding of the concept of time.
2. Students will gain insight into themselves and their life situation as related to the concept of time.
3. Students will generate creative perceptions concerning the subject matter being presently taught and its relationship to the overall concept of time.*

### The Context

As noted above, elementary, high school, and college curricula are replete with time-related concerns. Science texts often deal with the larger concepts of the age of the earth, the infinity of the universe, the macro and micro effects of the passing of eras and other time-related historical or scientific concepts. Likewise, history, social studies, and elementary social science texts are often concerned with investigating changing populations, historical movements, and the growth and decay of cities and civilizations. While linguists investigate the history of language development and the impact of the passage of time as people create new languages while old languages and old dialects become outdated, mathematics wrestles with the notion of infinity. In fact, all subject areas seem somehow related to the study of time and the ways in which we have recorded its impact on events and happenings.

Time, as a construct, is an all pervasive notion in our society. As a nation, we tend to record what we value and to measure epochs according to those events which we most prize. For example, we assess, often

---

*Note: Some students find the exercise (without adequate preparation) to be controversial because of its portrayal of evolution. We have piloted this exercise with both teachers and students; though some have noted this discrepancy with the creationist version, all were willing to "go along" with the movie if we introduced it as an imaginary experience.

Please note the way we anticipate this viewpoint in the lesson's introduction; this can make the lesson a creative exercise for everyone. The exercise itself can be used with students sixth grade and up. It works best with students who have had some experience with metaphoric teaching exercises.

incorrectly, the historical implications of recent events only in light of our own nation's two-hundred-year history. Our notion of the tumultuous events in China during the last thirty years might better be viewed in light of China's four-thousand-year historical development than from our own brief national life. When George Orwell wrote *1984* in the late 1940s, it was science fiction; what will the perspective on this classic be in the year 2000? Some few accomplishments are even removed from the time dimension by receiving the accolade "timeless." The plays of Shakespeare, the sculpture of Michelangelo, the writings of Confucius, all fall into this category.

All this is to say that "time" as a concept and as a phenomenon is an important topic for all curricular areas. Time is past, present, future; it concerns perspective and it is relative. Time is measurable but ethereal; it is easier to lose than to gain. The following metaphoric lesson is designed to challenge our students' often unexamined notions about time. It will enable them to visualize, in a relatively compact lesson, the fact that their concept of time influences their perspective on almost every facet of their lives and, in fact, determines the very depth of experience they allow themselves to have.

### Level I: The Focus Level

At this level students explore the way they conceptualize the passing of time. We like to begin the lesson with a recording of Judy Collins' "There is a season . . ." Then, for presenting "time" as a conceptual perspective many symbols are available: pictures of clocks and watches (particularly of such famous timepieces as "Big Ben"), water clocks, chronometers, sundials, and hourglasses, sequential pictures of fall, winter, spring, and summer—all suggest ways we record and note the passing of time. After showing your students several representative "time" images, ask the students what these images all have in common —they usually respond that all those images represent ways to view "time," or ways in which people record the passing of time.

Next, write the word "TIME" on the board and ask what this word means to them personally. In our experience with this metaphoric lesson, students first suggest the kind of symbols that were shown previously, next some students will say that the word "time" means "more like history" or "since the age of the dinosaurs" or "the cycle of life." Finally, the students begin to relate personal experiences— "times when . . ."

Once the students have shared their reactions, provide an advance organizer that will help link concept, metaphoric image, and subject matter. For example, if you are teaching a lesson on the effect of time on the monarchical power in Europe, you might want to read Shelley's

"Ozymandias" to the class. Then, show the class more abstract symbols of time—symbols that stretch their imaginations (such as the picture of the "watchdog" from the book *The Phantom Tollbooth,* or a "backwards" clock, or a candle that burns at both ends*).

### OZYMANDIAS

> *I met a traveller from an antique land*
> *Who said: "Two vast and trunkless legs of stone*
> *Stand in the desert. Near them, on the sand,*
> *Half sunk, a shattered visage lies, whose frown,*
> *And wrinkled lip, and sneer of cold command,*
> *Tell that its sculptor well those passions read*
> *Which yet survive, stamped on these lifeless things,*
> *The hand that mocked them and the heart that fed.*
> *And on the pedestal these words appear—*
> *"My name is Ozymandias, king of kings:*
> *Look on my works, ye Mighty, and despair!*
> *Nothing beside remains. Round the decay*
> *Of that colossal wreck, boundless and bare*
> *The lone and level sands stretch far away."***

**Percy Bysshe Shelley**

Next, move quickly from one place in the room to another, and ask the students, "Was that a portrayal of time?" Have them look at a clock with a second hand; then have them watch sixty seconds go by—while they think about what time really is. Raise these questions:

1. Do clocks record time?
2. Do clocks actually measure the minutes of our lives?
3. Are clocks merely symbols for an experience we have in common?

These questions will intrigue your students; they may be confronted with assumptions they have never questioned, never taken time to question. Often they have given very little thought to time except in relation to the way their own lives are patterned; all can identify the role of time in their present worlds: time for bed, time for breakfast, school, lunch, afterschool sports, and doing homework. Some will discern the differences between types of time: vacation time, stress times, rewarding moments, or moments of confusion and high anxiety.

Take a moment to brainstorm with the class an overall definition

---

*Candle shops often stock these candles; those curved like horseshoes provide a dramatic effect for abstract representation.

**Oscar Williams, *The Mentor Book of Major British Poets.* New York, The New American Library, 1963, pp. 166–167.

of *time*. Point out how the American Heritage Dictionary defines time:

"Time is a nonspatial continuum in which events occur in apparently irreversible succession, or an interval separating two points on this continuum."

Ask if this definition meets their definition in any way. Students will immediately note how much more experiential their definitions are. Their definitions include:

"A way to talk about a given experience that begins and ends."
"A period that describes the way people lived or what happened in their lives."
"A way of talking about the ongoing passage of our lives."

The class will note the personal nature of their definitions; time is, in fact, only meaningful to us in terms of the personal value we have assigned to it.

We have found that student-generated definitions usually contain certain elements:

1. First, time is part of a continuum of events.
2. Second, time is nonspatial; it is not physically perceived as an entity separate from the experience.
3. Third, time is apparently irreversible (depending upon the age of your students and their knowledge of relativity, this observation provokes exciting debate and inquiry.)
4. Fourth, time is a measured interval in the ongoing parade of universal events and destiny.*

Link these observations to the conventional dictionary definition to demonstrate the commonality of human perception and the elusiveness of explaining what time really is all about.

At the end of the focus phase, return to your original focus comments; remind the students that time itself is usually understood only in terms of our own experiences, that time as a precisely measured, sequential continuum is a strictly human invention, and that their depth of understanding of time is typically limited by their need to know and understand other concepts.

---

*Lakoff in *Metaphors We Live By* (1980) identifies the prevailing cultural metaphor of time as TIME IS MONEY. "We bank it, spend it, save it, and waste it." This lesson expands student awareness of the concept and offers an alternate understanding of time as a concept—time as being the function of the individual's experience and perspective, the flexible telescope through which we view the world in which we live.

## Level II: The Personal Comparison

The next level of the metaphoric method asks students to compare themselves with the lesson's metaphor; in this case, time symbols. As they compare themselves to these symbols, they will discover personal insights about themselves and their perception of "time" in their lives. Begin with one of the following comparisons (or questions quite similar):

1. If you were to think of a way that you and an hourglass (watch, clock, sundial, monument) are alike, what comes to your mind?
2. Choose the "time object" that most resembles your life and the way you are living it.
3. How is the burning candle (the four seasons, the calendar, the stop watch, the metronome) like you?

It is critical at this juncture to make certain that all your students have a response ready; this may mean waiting two or three minutes until everyone has "answered" the question and made a mental comparison. Be sure to remind the students that there are no "right" or "wrong" answers to your question. Next, ask the class to share these comparisons around the room; move in a predictable, regular pattern so every student has the opportunity to participate. Avoid asking for explanations; this often forces the student to defend his or her response and unfairly probes a spontaneous insight.

If possible, take time to write the responses (in brief, but accurate form) on the board; this visual record will prompt more insights from students and help them feel that their observations are valued. Reviewing this list later will generate more in-depth reflection on the nature of time as a function of experience and personal perspective.

When all have shared their comparisons, select a few (noncontroversial) responses for class discussion; this will allow the students to identify with one another and search for additional insights; "Oh, yeah, I'm like that, too." Typical responses from previous lessons when the question, "Choose the time object that most resembles your life and the way you are living it," has been posed, include:

| | |
|---|---|
| With the calendar | "I seem to always be going from one phase to another." (sixth-grade student) |
| With the clock | "My heart keeps ticking just like a clock, and it scares me to think of when it will run down!" (fourth-grade gifted) |
| With the four seasons | "There is a real regularity to my life; I'm like the seasons: sometimes I'm in a |

|  | mood; sometimes warm; sometimes cold. It depends upon where I am or where I'm at." (tenth-grade student) |
|---|---|
| With a time line | "I keep going in one direction; I can't go backwards—I just keep getting older and older. And, there's nothing I can do about it; just like time just keeps going forward." (eighth-grade student) |
| With minutes in an hour | "We are all like minutes; no two minutes are ever the same—none of us is ever exactly the same as someone else!" (seventh-grade student) |

Teacher sensitivity is the key to the success of the Level II Personal Comparison. Some of the answers will involve a creative juxtaposition that indicates a truly insightful moment for the student, such as the occasion when a tenth-grade student said, "You know, I never thought about it before, but my mom is the clock in our home. She determines everything, she is always ahead of you, and she is as fair to one person as she is to another; I mean time is really impartial." Other responses may reveal problems ("My life is like a time bomb only I don't have control over the timer.") or problems with studies ("I feel like a stop watch—always racing to beat my former best time; there has to be a limit, I just can't do all the things I am supposed to do.")

It is critical that you respect the privacy of each student in this process; be sure to allow the comments to be shared without judgment or interpretation; this will build a strong trust basis within the class and increase the number of personal insights students can gain. The discussion should end only after each student has had an opportunity to share and respond. In our experiences we have discovered that you will often need to facilitate this process by revealing two or three of your own personal insights as well. These discussions tend to generate such enthusiasm that they can run on and on; some students expand their insights verbally, and others withdraw into their own private worlds to deal with the new perspectives that emerge. For everyone, insights are energizing and exciting; expect spontaneity and even profound observations. The right brain is not a censoring brain; it can reveal new relationships that we have not consciously perceived as part of our lives.*

---

*Timing is critical in the metaphoric lesson. To achieve the full power of Levels I and II, do the entire lesson in the same day. You can, however, discuss the context of the concept in the day preceding the metaphoric lesson and further discuss the implications in the day following the lesson.

## Level III: The Metaphoric Interaction

This level provides the learner with an opportunity to interact with the lesson's metaphor—the "time movie." Student interaction will be in the form of a guided fantasy journey through a "calendar" of the earth. One could use slides or a real movie, or a visit to a museum or any of a number of other interactive experiences. The metaphoric interaction included in this unit tested with various grade levels from fourth to twelfth grade is called the "Time Movie." It is important to remember that the time movie is only one of a number of metaphoric interactions that could be included in a time lesson. It would be necessary with third graders to use a different interactive experience.* Remember, the metaphoric interaction level is designed in terms of the life experience level of your students. There are many variations on this overall theme of time that will excite and involve the right brain.

## THE "TIME MOVIE" FANTASY

### Preparation

First, be certain that the students are all comfortable, that the room is quiet and the lights are dimmed. Tell the students that some of them may feel that the movie does not reflect the Biblical version of creation and the earth's history. Reassure these students that the time movie does not use the term evolution and that latitude is allowed for personal interpretation. It is, however, a movie worth seeing and worth experiencing, because it captures in a small period of time a visit to an enormous period of time.

Next, explain that the students will travel in their minds to a theater where they will watch a twenty-four-hour-long film of the history of the planet earth. For the students, it will be like experiencing the kind of "time warp" they have seen on "Star Trek." Time will be compressed and will seem to go by very fast. Also explain that the movie is based upon a scientific study by James C. Rettie (1950) who viewed the passing of earth time in a very creative fashion, and that this guided journey will explore the earth's aging in terms of his research.**

---

*Younger students need more immediate, concrete experiences. A weekly calendar of family events, a yearly calendar of family and friends' birthdays, a recreation of school when their parents were little, a family tree—all are possible metaphoric interactions for Level III.

**It is important to remember when teaching this lesson that the focus is to increase your students' sense of time, not inundate them with a series of ever-changing "facts." Scientific debate continues to rage over the age of the earth. Researchers at the Univer-

Rettie essentially postulated what it would be like if the inhabitants of a nearby planet had used a stop action motion picture camera with a supertelephoto lens to take one picture of the earth every year for the last 757 million years. If the resulting film were to be shown at a normal rate (twenty-four frames per second), it would take just one minute to show 1440 years, only an hour to show 86,000 years, and just a day to show two million years. A year of earth time, however, would be required to show the entire 757 million years of photographed earth history.

To begin Phase III, the room needs to be quiet and outside distractions minimized; darken the room if at all possible. Then, speak in quiet, measured, almost somber tones. Seriousness is essential for the success of this exercise; you will find students will follow your model in this kind of instruction. We always caution people not to laugh and to be as "nonverbally attentive" as possible. It is important, however, for the success of the lesson to follow the script closely and to pause whenever a pause moment is indicated by three successive periods ( . . . )*


## The Journey

"Imagine you have an assignment to sit in the school auditorium to watch a very special movie, a movie that will show continuously for twenty-four hours a day for an entire year. You are going to see a film of the earth, a film taken by people on a nearby planet at the rate of one frame per year for the last 757 million years . . . The movie will be shown to you at the normal rate; twenty-four frames a second. Now in our imaginations, we are all going to see that film together in this classroom today . . . It is important to relax, to get comfortable, and to close your eyes . . . Listen to the sound of my voice . . . Breathe deeply and completely relax. You are in the theater; it is January first, the

---

sity of California at Los Angeles have used radioisotope measures to date recently discovered microfossilized "pond scum." Their results indicate that life forms have existed on this planet for three and a half billion years! Thus, according to this research, Rettie's time frame is incorrect in its estimation of the age of the earth.

An update of these findings might mean rewriting this journey to make it a movie two years in length with life appearing on the planet in the early days of the month of February. For children under the age of twelve, the fantasy is very difficult to conceptualize; for older students, a discussion of the importance of time in examining the origins of the earth could lead to a new, student-generated guided fantasy.

*As you are reading the words to yourself, the impact of the metaphor is lessened. In order to perceive the full potential of this experience, we suggest that you have someone read this part to you while you are in a similar position—with your eyes closed and relaxed. If this is not possible, "tape record" this section of the lesson, then play the tape back to yourself when you are relaxed.

lights are dimming, and the movie begins on the large screen in front
of you . . . You see the earth, a large globe in the dark blue sky—gases
and liquids seem to make up its surface. There are bubbles of steam,
spurts of volcanic fluids, thick liquids over the surface of the earth
. . . All is changing and yet unchanging. The first week passes and then
the first month. There are small changes on the earth . . . The surface
appears cooler but still liquid . . . You see water and more water . . .
Little else changes . . . It is now the middle of the second month; little
is changed. Just the globe and its matter, liquid shapes and solid surfaces . . . The second month ends . . . There is still little change in the
basic appearance of the earth. It merely appears to be gradually solidi-
fying . . . You remained fixed, gazing on the earth before you . . . The
third month comes. . . . You stare at the never-changing image before
you on the film . . . March ends, still no real differences; and then,
slowly, in the early part of the fourth month of watching the film, you
witness a change—indistinct at first, but gradually becoming clearer
. . . A few single-celled organisms emerge . . . April has brought a
significant change to the earth . . . Life has finally appeared on the
planet.

Late in this same month, many-celled organisms appear in the waters of the earth . . . Then a month passes and a new life form can be
seen—the first vertebrates . . . animals with backbones . . . organisms
looking like some types of fish still on the earth today. Look at them
closely . . . What do they look like? Are there different colors? Shapes?
Sizes? . . . Time goes on, May ends, and June comes . . . Things remain
much the same . . . More time passes . . . More land plants appear
. . . It is these land plants that will pave the way for land animals to
develop . . . Look at the plants closely, watch them sway with the winds
of the planet . . . Watch them grow tall and close to one another . . .
Close to the waters from which they emerged . . . Then slowly, very
slowly watch them grow further and further inland. For an entire
month, from July to August, you watch these plants continue to grow
. . . Larger and larger plants cover huge land surfaces on the earth.
Then, late in the month of August, the first land vertebrates come out
of the waters—the amphibians become clearly visible . . . Little animals, breathing both water and air, they emerge from the water and
crawl out onto land . . . They grow and change, becoming larger, changing form and structure. The ancestors of the reptiles have entered the
earth's population.

. . . In the middle of September, the first dinosaurs can be seen
. . . Some are only a foot tall . . . Some grow to be twenty feet, thirty
feet tall. All eat plants and graze on the surface of the planet. . . . They
live on through the tenth month, and continue to dominate the earth
through the first part of the eleventh month. Their period of ascend-

ancy is almost sixty days . . . In mid-November, a new life form appears on the earth . . . The first true birds begin to share occupancy of the earth . . . Soon, the mammals begin to emerge . . . slowly, ever so slowly . . .

Near the end of November, you see the earth shift abruptly and the Rocky Mountains come into being . . . Land masses become covered with water, water surfaces become land. The period of reptilian domination is definitely ending . . . During the beginning of the twelfth month, you see the mammals become dominant on the earth. What kind of mammals are largest and strongest? What kinds are weak and vulnerable?

The earth continues to change ever so slightly. The modern geology is emerging. As the end of the twenty-fifth day of the twelfth month approaches, the Colorado River begins to churn its path through the Grand Canyon, wearing down the rock and slowly carving its imprint upon its surface . . . The movie is almost over . . . And no signs of man . . . Then, suddenly, on the last day of the twelfth month at about noontime, you see the first human being on earth . . . Look closely at this person . . . What does this person look like? Are you looking at a man or a woman? How is the person dressed? What does he or she eat? Where does the person find shelter? . . . At three o'clock in the afternoon, another natural change occurs . . . The first glacier shift slides ice and rocks towards the center of the earth. New parts of the earth are covered with ice and snow. At about 3:30 the glaciers shift again. . . . Parts never touched before by cold are covered with ice and then re-emerge. This happens four times.

Finally, around five o'clock, the glaciers recede permanently, not to leave the polar regions again . . . The hours go by . . . Little changes on the earth . . . Man looks much the same as when the first human being appeared. By 10:00 P.M., after twelve months, on the last day of the last month, almost a full year from when you started watching the film, man is still not much in evidence . . . Another hour passes . . . At 11:00 P.M. the first Stone Age people make their appearance . . . They begin to compete with the other mammals for domination of the earth . . . The minutes go by; you watch them control fire, you see them discover weapons . . . At 11:45 P.M. in the last hour of the film, men appear who can cultivate the soil . . . who can use crude tools and implements . . . The minutes tick on . . . There are only seven minutes left in the film.

During the next five minutes, you witness the building of the great ancient cities of the Near and Far East . . . You see the pyramids being constructed, the cradle of civilization being formed . . . At just one minute and seventeen seconds before the end of the film, the Christian era begins, and you see the great cities of the Mayans and the Incas

... After watching the film for eleven months, thirty days, twenty-three hours, fifty-nine minutes, and forty seconds, you finally see Columbus discover America ... You briefly glimpse the little band of ships on the large Atlantic Ocean. ... Seventeen seconds later the Declaration of Independence is signed ... And you see the rise and fall of Adolf Hitler in a fraction of a second before the Cold War begins ... With less than one second left to the film, you can see four billion human beings on the planet ... In that final fraction of a second, one last event occurs. You see your hometown and ... You are born. ... Now the curtain is dropping, the theater lights are slowly coming on. ... The earth's time movie is at an end ... Slowly, and when you are ready ... Return to this classroom and open your eyes.

*Debriefing Questions*

Debriefing the guided journey is a critical element in the metaphoric lesson. It is a time to prompt and solidify insights—to explore the momentary "aha's" that invariably accompany each individual's guided journey. (Guided journeys without debriefing are trees without leaves—interesting, but incomplete.) The following questions are suggested for the beginning metaphoric teacher; after a few experiences with metaphoric teaching, debriefing questions will come quickly and naturally to you. Not all questions included here, of course, have to be used; choose those you think most appropriate for your class.

1. Describe the earth that you saw at the beginning of the film.
   *Most people today see the world as the astronauts saw it—the space shot from the moon.*
2. Were you in space? Were you close to the surface? What did the molten liquids look like?
   *People describe the sensation of being in space—looking down upon the earth, and seeing the gases and liquids in much the same manner as seeing volcanoes.*
3. How did you feel when it was March and still no change had happened in the world?
   *Surprise! Bored! Where are the life forms? People are amazed at the time involved for the earth to just cool down and solidify.*
4. How did you feel when the first single-celled organism arrived? What did it look like? How did you see it?
   *First, there is relief and excitement when life appears on the planet. The organism resembles an amoeba—people often report the sensation of feeling like they looked through a telescopic lens that could magnify and really "see" the organisms.*
5. Describe the fish that came next. Did you see sharks? Did you see fish you could recognize?

*What surprised us were all the bright-colored fish people see. Some do see sharks, but many see all kinds of beautiful tropical fish.*

6. What did the land plants look like? Where did they first appear? Were you excited to see them?
*People describe cattails, grasses, and ferns. They first ring the water and grow inward.*

7. How did it feel to know that land animals were arriving?
*Good! Land animals are closer to people; it seemed more like the earth we know.*

8. Did you see the amphibians? What did they look like? Where did they go when they left the water?
*People see frogs emerging from the waters and moving into the grasses. Next, they see reptiles—all kinds.*

9. In September, you saw the dinosaurs. What did the first dinosaurs look like? Did they have colors? What did you see them doing? Did you see the Brontosaurus?
*All kinds of dinosaurs—but especially the green, long-necked Brontosaurus, gently eating grasses.*

10. What kind of carnivorous dinosaurs did you see? Were they familiar? Where were you viewing them? Did you see the Tyrannosaurus Rex?
*The viewer is always safe—way out of reach of the dinosaurs; almost everyone will see the Tyrannosaurus Rex.*

11. Did you see the earth shift and the Rocky Mountains come into being? What did it look like?
*For many, it's like an earthquake or a slice in the ground (much like a slice in a large, gigantic cake).*

12. The dinosaurs dominated for two full months—How did you feel when their era was over, and the mammals were coming into their own?
*People are shocked at how long a time the dinosaurs had on the earth; they are usually ready for man to arrive and they start looking for him.*

13. What did the first birds look like? What did the first mammals look like?
*Actually, people usually mention the winged, prehistoric Pterodactyl; they sometimes mention more conventional birds as well. Many see the prehistoric horse, the mammoth, and the saber-toothed tiger.*

14. On the last day of the movie, you finally saw the first human being. What did this person look like? How did this person seek shelter? Food? Other people?
*Some people see the Neanderthal man; most see movie-type images —lots of hair and very primitive behaviors and sounds.*

15. The glaciers came and covered new parts of the earth. What did

they look like? Where did they go? Did they take things with them? Did you feel cold? Were you sad? Angry? Curious?

*Most people are amazed when the glaciers come! Somehow dinosaurs and glaciers go together. They see the rivers of ice, the great rocks and debris, and often report being cold.*

16. At 11:00 P.M. on the last day of the last month, the first Stone Age people can be seen. What were they doing? How did you feel when you saw them?

    *Again, people have the sensation that things are getting pretty late and where's all the action? It's surprising to them that it's 11:00 p.m. and still no modern man.*

17. At 11:45 P.M., you see the first farmers. What did they look like? What did they grow?

    *People report images of primitive people growing corn and a mounting sense of anxiety—where is modern civilization?*

19. Did you see the pyramids? The Incas? The ancient cities?

    *These are seen in a flash—usually text-book images that students have already studied.*

19. Did you see Columbus and the three ships? Where were they? What were they doing?

    *Many people report seeing them out in the Atlantic ocean—braving the storms and winds. One person reported seeing Dali's "Columbus Discovering America" painting.*

20. Where was the Declaration of Independence? Did you see the men signing it?

    *People usually mention the familiar picture so often shown in history books of the signing of the Declaration of Independence.*

21. What did you see of Adolf Hitler? How did you see the rise and fall of the Third Reich?

    *People see swastikas, the image of Hitler in a flash, and lots of flags and bombs. Some may see the concentration camps.*

22. What did four billion human beings look like?

    *Crowded! Too many! Countless faces! Some are reminded of a "Star Trek" episode where the Enterprise crew visits a very overcrowded planet.*

23. What did it feel like to be born?

    *This is usually very hard for people to visualize—just a sense of newness, or the background of a hospital.*

24. How did you feel when the curtain dropped and the movie was over?

    *Worn out! The pace in the last day is accelerated, leaving the viewer exhausted and amazed at how very little time we, as people, have actually had on this planet. Most mention the responsibility we have to keep the earth from blowing up.*

## Extending the Creative Experience

Sometimes student answers indicate a sophistication that can be further probed and expanded. When student enthusiasm is high, answers are quick, and general excitement fills the room, it is often helpful to use these additional questions (sometimes even in place of some of the first twenty-four questions).

1. How did it feel to watch the film? Describe your own experiencing of time as it passed in the movie.
2. As you watched the film, where were you? In space? On earth? Did you change places?
3. Did you have difficulty seeing the whole earth and then a tiny, single-celled organism?
4. As the earth aged, the life forms became more complex. How does the life experience of the earth parallel your life experience?
5. Have you personally experienced different dominating forces in your life? Do you have a "dinosaur" period and then a "mammal" period in your life?
6. Describe the first human being you saw. Was there color? How hairy was the person? What sex? Why do you think you visualized the person as you did?
7. How did it feel to experience 757 million years? What's the difference between this experience and that of looking at a time chart or a description of the earth's evolution?
8. If you could be represented by a grain of sand, how large do you think a pile of sand would have to be to represent all the human life we've had on this planet?

## Level IV: Creative Insight

This level of the metaphoric lesson links the experience of the time metaphors with the overall concept of the lesson—a personal perspective on the passage of time. With insight questions, the student is prompted to merge both image and concept, to allow a creative connection to occur, to view his or her time experiences from a totally new, often quite surprising, viewpoint. The placing in juxtaposition of unlike elements (time/staircase, trees/telling time, cancer/stopwatch) causes a simultaneity of awareness to occur in the mind. This paradoxical tension produces a moment of insightful creativity—a moment of original, new perception.

Continued use of these questions will invite increasingly sophisticated awareness and responses. This is the moment the entire lesson has fostered; be sure to relate the image to the subject matter you are teaching and the conceptual framework for time inherent in that subject matter.

## Insight Problems for Group Discussion

Break the class into small groups and give each group one of the following topics (or similar compressed analogies from your subject area emphasis) to brainstorm and record answers. The groups will need about five to ten minutes to fully explore the possible, creative connections that these insight analogies will stimulate. Then, let each group report their findings to the class as a whole.

1. Time is a staircase for all our successes. Why?
2. If dinosaurs are grandfather clocks and ancient cities are sun dials, what clock symbolizes our present American society? Our classroom? Why?
3. How do trees tell time? Rivers tell time? Rocks tell time? Birds tell time?
4. Death is a sun dial for every generation. Why?
5. Cancer is the twentieth century's stopwatch. Why?
6. History is a self-winding wristwatch. Explain.
7. Society is an alarm clock we need to wake us up. Why?
8. A novel is an hourglass that is ready to be turned over and over. Explain.
9. Science is a process that "tells time" by exploring nature. Show this to be true.
10. Math is having a clock that tells the correct time for any place on earth.

Take time to enjoy your students' insights and their expanded awareness of time's role in their lives, the world, and this point in history. Then, be sure to relate these findings to the subject matter at hand. You will find that any subject area can be enhanced by exploring its relationship to time factors and time concepts; crucial, however, will be the illuminary moment when the metaphor and the subject content merge, expand understanding, and become internalized. This moment produces the creative, conceptual insights that aid the overall learning of new information, skills, and values.

In fact, what these two lessons do is both new and seasoned; they take the essence of the age-old teaching tool we call the metaphor and adapt its power for immediate classroom application. Yes, the process is, on the surface, sequential, but the methodology encourages insight and analysis, creativity and logic, "right-brain" skills and "left-brain" skills—in sum, the simultaneous interaction of both hemispheres.

This ability to prompt simultaneous consideration of both fact and image, of both information and concept, is the essential, creative dimension of the metaphor—a dimension intuitively known to the writers and sages of old. For, as we shall examine in the next chapter, when persuasion was the purpose, metaphor was the method.

## BIBLIOGRAPHY

Bruner, Jerome. *On Knowing: Essays for the Left Hand.* Cambridge, Mass.: Howard University Press, 1962.

Huxley, Thomas Henry. "The Method by which the Causes of the Present and the Past Conditions of Organic Nature Are to Be Discovered." In D. Bryant and K. Wallace, *Fundamentals of Public Speaking.* Englewood Cliffs, N.J.: Prentice-Hall, 1976.

Lakoff, George, and Mark Johnson. *Metaphors We Live By.* Chicago: University of Chicago Press, 1980.

# CHAPTER 3

# Ancient to Modern: The Rich Tradition of Metaphoric Teaching

## A LOOK FORWARD

*The intellect of the wise is like glass; it admits the light of heaven and reflects it.*

Augustus William and
Julius Charles Hare

Confucius, Buddha, Jesus—we remember these great "masters" as outstanding individuals who left their mark upon the world. However, when we look at their teachings, we discover that they were more than "masters," they were also "master teachers," teachers who used the power of the right brain to create images that convinced, taught, and motivated their followers. Their stories, parables, and metaphoric allusions portray vividly the powerful concepts they introduced—concepts that changed both the direction of the civilizations they encountered and the direction of the world in which we now live.

The metaphor is a pervasive, historical teaching tool; in fact, we find that most of the significant messages emerging from the world's many populations (including those cultures without written languages) have been taught with the help of metaphors. Folk wisdom and folk traditions, the mores and epic histories of specific tribes and whole cultures, have been passed down from generation to generation through the use of stories in folk tales, fables, and parables. Why? It is as though these great leaders intuited a basic truth about the human mind; namely, that the image is more powerful than the word, that the story is, in and of itself, an image experience. Each story, in whatever guise, generates a set of active pictures in the mind of the listener; in doing so, the story creates an unforgettable synergy of conceptual insight. The story with its right-brain imagery leads to left-brain application and holistic understanding. Henry Alford summarizes this impact of the metaphoric image when he explains:

Truth does not consist in minute accuracy of detail, but in conveying a right impression; . . . when the Psalmist said, "Rivers of water run down mine eyes, because men keep not thy law," he did not state the fact, but he stated a truth deeper than fact, and truer.

Modern research in this area confirms the efficacy of teaching with images; in fact, imagery is fast emerging as a critical tool for stimulating learning and enhancing content retention. Allen Paivio, in *Imagery and Verbal Processes* (1971), has substantiated this function of imagery in memory research that tests verbal and visual memory retention. Paivio (who, incidentally, is responsible for helping us understand why it is easier to remember faces than names) constructed an experiment where abstract nouns, concrete nouns, and images were flashed on the screen for one-sixteenth of a second at five second intervals. His subjects were then tested for recall after a five minute pause and then again a week later. The results were amazing! Right brain image recognition was significantly more effective than left brain verbal recognition. Paivio found that more images were remembered after a week's lapse of time than words were remembered after a five-minute pause! There was, by this ratio, a 120,000 times greater time-related memory retention for the image than the abstract word—no matter how concrete the word.

How does Paivio's work substantiate the folk tradition of storytelling? It offers additional evidence toward what the sage has always known. Cultural concepts (the moral teachings, acceptable behavior, folk wisdom, historical perspective, and religious beliefs of a given people) are far more likely to be remembered if associated with an image, a fable, or a parable, than if presented as fact or logical argument. Surveying the literature of folklore reveals the consistent utilization of an obviously simple, yet highly effective, instructional medium —the use of the metaphor.

This chapter, then, takes you on a brief tour of classic fables and stories told by peoples separated by thousands of miles and hundreds of years. It explores the metaphoric nature of these stories, introduces the pioneering modern research that has prompted enthusiasm for the use of the metaphor, and suggests ways to adapt right-brain imagery to the teaching of concept attainment. Further, the chapter discusses how recent examinations of ancient writings have contributed to the development of the metaphoric method.

## ANCIENT TO MODERN—THE RICH TRADITION OF METAPHORIC TEACHING

The early "schooling" of our ancestors consisted of diligent memorization of Biblical passages; the Bible provided frontier children with "readin," "writin," and " 'rithmetic." American schools in the

And unto one he gave five talents, to another two, to another one to each according to his several ability: and he went on his journey. Straightway he that received the five talents went and traded with them, and made other five talents ⬦ In like manner he also that received the two gained other two ⬦ But he that received the one went and digged in the earth, and hid his lord's money ⬦ Now after a long time the lord of those servants cometh and maketh a reckoning with them ⬦ And he that received the five talents came and brought other five talents, saying, Lord, thou deliveredst unto me five talents: lo, I have gained other five talents ⬦ His lord said unto him: Thou hast been faithful over a few things, I will set thee over many things: enter thou into the joy of the lord

From Charles Hampden Turner, *Maps of the Mind,* London, Mitchell Beazley Publishers Ltd., 1981. Reprinted with permission.

twentieth century have left this rich source of right-brain images be-hind; we now teach "readin," "writin," and " 'rithmetic" with a highly analytical, left-hemisphere orientation. In fact, even our approach to teaching responsibility and recreation is usually left brained—more logic and sequence than spontaneity and pattern. In our enthusiasm to be more scientific, more systematic in our teaching, more analytical in our pursuit of knowledge, we have lost an important teaching tool—the power of teaching by example and story. For example, the parables of Matthew were more than religious indoctrination; they were cultural lessons essential to the mores of the society that taught them and heard them:

For it will be as when a man going on a journey called his servants and entrusted to them his property; to one he gave five talents, to another two, to another one, to each according to his ability. Then he went away. He who had received the five talents went at once and traded with them; and he made five talents more. So, too, he who had the two talents made two talents more. But he who had received the one talent, went and dug in the ground and hid his master's money. . . .

"Master, I knew you to be a hard man, reaping where you did not sow, and gathering where you did not winnow; so I was afraid, and I went and hid your talent in the ground. Here you have what is yours." But his master answered him, "You wicked and slothful servant! You know I reap where I have not sowed, and gather where I have not winnowed?"

"Then you ought to have invested my money with the bankers, and at my coming, I should have received what was my own with interest. So take the talent from him, and give it to him who has the ten talents. For to every one who has will more be given, and he will have abundance; but from him who has not, even what he has will be taken away."

(Matthew 25: 14–30)

The lesson of the talents thus provided an arithmetic lesson, a litera-ture lesson, a grammar lesson, and a social studies lesson. The value of banking, of investing, of taking what you have and increasing it, was critical to the establishment of new frontier towns, new outposts, and new states. It served society as a whole to teach American capitalism with the Biblical passages long-memorized and internalized as the mandated ethics of a God-fearing nation. Regardless of how many "tal-ents" you had, it was important to invest them and use them—not hide and hoard them. Frontier preachers had ample justification for the system of business and government being developed.

Parables and fables, however, date back thousands of years before the New Testament in terms of their political, social, and moral mes-sages; in fact, history reveals these extended metaphors as central to the oldest, richest traditions of teaching—the primary media through which cultural wisdom was transmitted. Consider this example that comes to us from the words of Phaedrus, a Roman poet in the first century A.D. Phaedrus, the translator of many of Aesop's fables, recorded these fables in Latin, often shortened them, reduced their complex interweaving tales, and added his own satirical notes. The following fable, based on an Aesop fable written around 600 B.C., can be interpreted many ways (an inherent feature of the metaphor) and was used by Phaedrus to lampoon the politics of his day:

*A fox invited a stork to dinner and put before her on a slab of stone some very thin soup which the stork could not find a way to taste even though she was very hungry. Then, the stork invited the fox to dinner and put before him a narrow mouthed jar full of solid food. Into this jar she put her beak and ate her fill while the fox sat tormented with hunger. While the hungry fox was licking the neck of the jar, the stork said, "One who sets an example should be able to bear it in patience when it is returned in kind."*

Phaedrus himself considered these stories to have a quality of "utilitas";* they were meant to teach the obvious as well as the subtle. (Those who would torment others can expect such behavior to be returned in kind.) Fourteen hundred years later, Leonardo da Vinci chided those who governed the Rome of his day; he, too, used a fable—The Fable of the Bell Tower, the Crow, and the Nut.

*A nut was carried by a crow to the top of a tall bell tower where it fell from the crow's beak into a crevice in the tower wall. Having escaped the jaws of fate, the nut asked the wall to give it shelter, praising the strength of its stone and the beauty of its form.*

*The wall, taken in by the false praise and feeling sorrow for the nut, agreed to give the nut shelter where it had fallen. Soon, however, the nut burst open and the roots grew into a tree and destroyed the wall. The wall, realizing that its pride had sealed its fate, lamented the curse of its own destruction. Then, shortly thereafter, it collapsed into ruin.*

Although these two political commentators were separated by over fourteen hundred years of cultural history, the vehicle of instruction was identical. Both urged politicians and people of their day to consider the implications of their actions; both used nature as the source of metaphoric images; both designed stories to teach on two levels: each

---

*Interestingly, the morals at the end of Aesop's fables (the morals that essentially predetermine the focus of the story) were not part of Aesop's original fables; the morals were added in the Middle Ages—a time when acceptance of authoritative interpretation was politically advantageous for both Church and State.

fable offered one message explicitly while it suggested a more subtle message by implication.

Historically, both Phaedrus and da Vinci belong to history's academy of "master teachers"—teachers who, we will find, intuitively used metaphors to bridge political opposition and intrigue, who continually used metaphors to present universal wisdom and truth. The list of such teachers emerges from every culture and every century. From Hesiod (Greek, eighth century B.C.) to Han Fei Tzu (Chinese, second century B.C.), from Aesop (Greek, sixth century B.C.) to the Sufis (age-old teachers of Islam), from Berechiah ha Nakdan (the Jewish Aesop, tenth century A.D.) to the timeless tales of Anansi the Spider (Africa); from the authors of the Panchatantra (Indian, first century A.D.) to the parables of Jesus of Nazareth; from the humorous retelling of Aesop by William Caxton (English, fifteenth century) to the satirical spoofs of Ivan Krylov (Russian, nineteenth century), great teachers throughout the ages have consistently used metaphoric images to entertain, to instruct and to provide insight on the human condition.

There is a timelessness pervading these insights, a timelessness of both content and style. The Sumerians, for example had a proverb which, roughly translated, reads "No one gives away a cow for nothing" —remarkably similar to our own, "There is no such thing as a free lunch." Likewise, an incredible commonality links Japan and Africa, two countries dramatically apart in culture and geography, when we read the following two stories—stories that comment essentially on the uncanny effectiveness of appearing dumb or weak, of catching one's opponent off guard, and of turning the opponents' own strength against each other (the basic "Columbo" approach).

*A Bear was living with a Fox. One day they made a sled and dragged each other back and forth. First the Bear dragged the Fox, but he tired quickly. So the Fox dragged the Bear, but he foolishly ran into a narrow place between some trees.*

*The Bear shouted, "You are really dumb! Where the trees are thick, don't run so fast." But the Fox was angry and did not listen to him. Later they came to a cliff; the Fox turned the sled over and the Bear rolled over the cliff and was killed. The Fox skinned the bear, took him home, and ate the meat. When he had finished eating, he tied the bladder to his tail.*

*A few days later the Fox was hungry again, so he went to the forest to look for food. He saw a herd of reindeer and one of them said, "Listen, Fox! How did you get such a fine thing attached to your tail!" "Let me stand among you," answered the Fox, "and if you butt at me with your antlers, you also will have such things attached to your tails." So two reindeer took the Fox between them, and tried to toss him with their antlers; but the Fox leaped out of the way, and they became tangled, and eventually died of exhaustion. Then the Fox skinned them and carried home their meat.*

The Ainu (Northern Japan)

And, similar in message, is this fable of the Bulu, a tribe located on the
western coast of Africa:

*The Tortoise had just finished building himself a village when a Hippo came
and destroyed it. The Tortoise rebuilt the village, but this time an Elephant
came along and destroyed it. The Tortoise thought, "I am certainly tired of
building villages."*

 *So he took a large rope and went to the place where the Hippo lived in the
river, and said to him: "Let's match our strength by pulling this rope. If you are
able to drag me forward, then you are the victor; if I am able to drag you, then
I am the victor." The Hippo accepted the challenged readily.*

 *Then the Tortoise went to the Elephant, and challenged him: "You have
bothered me long enough—let's have a test of strength with this rope. If you can
move me, then you are the greatest; but if I can move you, then I am the greatest."
The Elephant quickly agreed and said, "We will do it early tomorrow morning."*

 *As the day dawned the Tortoise went to the Hippo and said, "Now, Hippo,
tie this rope around your body. As soon as you feel me tug a little, pull with all
your might." Then the Tortoise hurried to the Elephant and said, "Tie this rope
around you; when you feel me pull, then pull with all your strength."*

 *The Tortoise went to the middle of the rope, and gave little tugs with his
teeth. The Hippo thought, "the Tortoise is starting to pull," and he began to pull.
The Elephant also pulled. The Tortoise sat low between them. The rope tight-
ened around both of them; they bloated, and died.*

The Bulu (Kamerun, West Africa)

 Both of these stories depict the triumph of brain over brawn, of
cleverness over brutishness, of the thinking David over the hulking
Goliath. Both stories use a familiar image from the real world instead
of intellectual discussion. And, although the lessons to be learned from
these stories are fairly obvious, each story leaves room for personal
interpretation. We can focus on the cleverness of the fox and the tortoise, or we can look at the shortsightness of the elephant, the hippo,
the bear, and the reindeer. And, parallels to today's world also occur;
we might wonder if we are living with an American Hippo roped to a
Russian Elephant with clever modern European, African, or Middle
Eastern tortoises seeking to become the ultimate victors.

 Teaching with the metaphor, however, is not limited to the use of
animal images and stories from nature; nor does the method draw only
on the literary form of the fable or parable. Rather, metaphors emerge
all around us; they are used as examples in daily conversation and as
illustrations for most major new points of view. Metaphors are, in fact,
constantly used to prompt insight;* they are essential in aiding the

---

*The term insight is used consistently throughout this book to mean an intuitive
appreciation or understanding, a new realization. Parables and fables have traditionally

development of intellectual understanding, because *they depict the basic pattern of a concept through common referents*. Because metaphors inherently model the concept being discussed, they appear in all literary forms—in political debate, stage plays, intellectual treatises, legal briefs, homilies, folk songs, and poetry. Metaphors are, in fact, word pictures of the thoughts we wish to express; they portray working images of the words and concepts we use in daily interaction with one another. Consider this advice on political co-optation:

> *In baiting a mouse-trap with cheese, always leave room*
> *for the mouse.*
>
> Hector Hugh Munro, "Saki" (1870–1916)
> from *The Infernal Parliament*

We could talk at length on political co-optation, or the need to internalize and identify with the strategies or thoughts that control the politicians' actions. Munro's mousetrap "with room for the mouse" succinctly sums up the concept—leaving intellectual space for us to expand. The metaphor does, in fact, co-opt us. We find mousetraps everywhere; in politics, in schooling, in family decision making; indeed, in any situation where there is a hidden agenda or ulterior motive, the persuader needs to remember the purpose of the trap is not to display cheese but to catch mice.

The truth is that wisdom is often best expressed in the natural pictures that words can paint. Consider these examples on the nature of love:

> *There is a land of the living and a land of the dead, and the*
> *bridge is love.*
>
> Thornton Wilder
> *The Bridge of San Luis Rey*
>
> *Money will buy a fine dog, but only love will make him*
> *wag his tail.*
>
> Ulster (Northern Ireland) *Post*
>
> *Man has here two and a half minutes—one to smile, one to sigh,*
> *and a half to love; for in the midst of this minute, he dies.*
>
> Jean Paul Richter
>
> *Love: A season's pass on the shuttle between heaven and hell.*
>
> Don Dickerman

---

expanded the scope of a given concept being taught. The process of relating the lesson to life eventually produces a moment of new understanding, a moment of insight, a moment of real life application.

*Love rules without a sword, love binds without a cord.*

Anonymous

*Love is the doorway through which the human soul passes from selfishness to service and from solitude to kinship with all mankind.*

Anonymous

Each metaphor speaks of the human condition we all experience—the passage through joy and sorrow—the transforming power of the human emotion called "love." We could speak different languages, have roots in totally different cultures, and yet, the truth of these examples would identify a universal quality we all recognize. Love is acceptance, a decision to be vulnerable, a decision to be linked with others; it makes us fragile and incredibly strong. Love is a basic paradox of the human condition.

The metaphor thus creates an image which sparks insight, insight that causes us to perceive the world differently. The parable, one of the most widely recognized forms of the metaphor, is an excellent example of this natural teaching process. Consider the following two examples of "truth" defined in the midst of political persecution. First, listen to the wisdom of Jesus of Nazareth when questioned by a lawyer, "Who is my neighbor?" then compare his message with Nasrudin's response to "What is inner truth?" Both confront the issue of being truthful in the arena of political moral judgment.

From the *Book of Luke:*

*A man was on his way from Jerusalem down to Jericho when he fell in with robbers, who stripped him, beat him, and went off leaving him half dead. It so happened that a priest was going down by the same road; but when he saw him, he went past on the other side. So too, a Levite came to the place, and when he saw him went past on the other side. But a Samaritan who was making the journey came upon him, and when he saw him was moved to pity. He went up and bandaged his wounds, bathing them with oil and wine. Then he lifted him on to his own beast, brought him to an inn, and looked after him there. Next day he produced two silver pieces and gave them to the innkeeper, and said, 'Look after him; and if you spend any more, I will repay you on my way back.'*

*Which of these three do you think was neighbor to the man who fell into the hands of the robber? The lawyer answered, 'The one who showed him kindness.' Jesus said, 'Go and do as he did.'*

And from the Sufi stories of Idries Shah:

*"Laws, as such, do not make people better," said Nasrudin to the king; "they must practice certain things, in order to become attuned to 'inner truth.' This form of truth resembles apparent truth only slightly."*

*The king decided that he could, and would, make people observe the truth. He could make them practice truthfulness. His city was entered by a bridge. On this he built a gallows. The following day, when the gates were opened at dawn, the Captain of the Guard was stationed with a squad of troops to examine all who entered.*

*An announcement was made: "Everyone will be questioned. If he tells the truth, he will be allowed to enter. If he lies, he will be hanged." Nasrudin stepped forward. "Where are you going?" "I am on my way," said Nasrudin slowly, "to be hanged." "We don't believe you!" "Very well, if I have told a lie, hang me!" "But, if we hang you for lying, we will have made what you said come true!" "That's right! Now you know what truth is—YOUR TRUTH!"*

While both stories are metaphoric in nature and didactic in purpose, one teaches that truth is seeing that all people are part of you; the other teaches that all truth is relative to the eye (perspective) of the beholder. In the story of the good Samaritan, we are challenged by the truth of universal love—"Go and do as he did!" Such an answer shocked the listeners who heard Jesus suggest such an idea; in that day, no one believed anything good of someone from Samaria. The Sufi story, while less direct, also forces the listener to pause and reflect upon the essence of the message—is it true that truth is relative to perspective and therefore always illusive? Paradoxical stories, such as these, teach the complexity of perspective—morality is the product of the one who seeks it. Both the Sufi story and Jesus's parable confound and challenge the listener's mind to affirm a basic sense of social justice.

However, just as the master teacher varies the purpose of using the parable, the fable, and the story, we, too, must vary the use of metaphoric teaching. Metaphors can teach content or process, concept or sequence. Inherent in the use of all metaphors (whether found in parables, allegories, analogies, fables, or folk tales), is an insight moment for the learner—an illuminating "I get it!" or "aha!" moment that occurs when the concept is "seen" with all its implications. This insight moment creates a vivid picture in the mind of the learner; it is a moment of creative juxtaposition, a moment of putting the unlikely together to create a unique synergy. The metaphor (in any form) taps into our personal system for insights and provides enjoyable, energetic moments of revelation. When such learning occurs, we have, in fact, tapped the domain of the other brain—the right side of the cerebrum.

## THE METAPHORIC METHOD—RECENT CONTRIBUTIONS

Two paths of inquiry—the study of metaphoric linguistics and the research on brain specialization and information processing—have converged in the development of metaphoric teaching strategies. These paths converged primarily in the work of two writers/researchers/teachers: W.J.J. Gordon and Bob Samples. These creative and intuitive authors broke the ground and created the foundation for the metaphoric teaching models developed in this book. Their insightful contributions (products of both research and creative spontaneity) have defined metaphoric teaching as an accepted generic instructional strategy, a strategy that is now highly effective with all instructional levels from kindergarten to junior high to graduate schools and with all populations from handicapped to gifted to corporate officers.

When Gordon's *The Metaphorical Way of Learning and Knowing* first appeared in 1966, it represented the result of twenty-three years of observation and research in the area of creative problem solving. Gordon's approach consisted of two primary methods: the first method is called "Making the Strange Familiar," that is, using what we already know (for example, the basic functioning of the amoeba) to understand something we don't know (the history of the Massachusetts Bay Colony); the second method is called "Making the Familiar Strange," suggesting to the artist that instead of picturing a tree as a solid form in space, the tree could be seen as a "hole" within a solid block of air.

Gordon's Synectic Education Systems taught us to use the metaphor to stimulate creative conceptual leaps in the thinker. The results of his work (especially his work in industrial problem solving) challenged educators to recognize the impact the metaphor could have in classrooms; from science to social studies, from language classes to vocational training, from math to P.E., the metaphor can be an effective, efficient teaching tool.

Essentially, Gordon's approach consists of three metaphoric categories: the direct analogy, the personal analogy, and the compressed conflict analogy. Use of these analogy categories prompts creative connections in the learner's mind:

1. *Direct Analogy* (developing a comparison of unlike items)
   What living things in nature are shaped like a zero?

   Compare a plow with something. (A plow is as powerful as the bow of a ship—why?)
2. *Personal Analogy* (personally becoming something you are not)
   Imagine that you are a spider who is trying to spin a web on a rainy, stormy day. As the spider, what does the storm do to you—and how do you feel about it?

   Imagine that you are a boomerang of an Australian native bushman . . . He throws you at the kangeroo. How do you feel as you fly towards the kangaroo?

3. Compressed Conflict Analogy (using words and phrases that conflict sharply when in juxtaposition with one another)
   *Delicate armor* describes a bank safe. Explain.
   An example of *repulsive attraction* could be . . .

Gordon sought to prompt new creative connections with these analogies; he designed his model, "synectics," to help corporate "think tanks" innovate and change the set perceptual patterns that limit new ideas and new perspectives. We have found these three forms of the metaphor highly effective in aiding the mastery of both subject matter and concept.

Let us consider, for example, direct analogies that link earth science (volcanic action) and the American revolution. (Direct analogies compare two subjects, the familiar and unfamiliar, with one another.) The teacher could begin by asking students to compare the magma of a volcano with the blood of the human body; then the comparison could be followed with:

What do you know that is like a volcano?
Is this something with a hard exterior and a potentially explosive interior?
What do you know in the world of living things that is similar to the volcano?

Such questions prompt creative, exciting images for the student; one may expect such unpredictable answers as:

I think sneezing is like a volcano.
I think the brain is like a volcano, because the cranium is hard, but thoughts are volatile!
I think the octopus is like a volcano, because it "explodes" with a black fluid when it is disturbed.

Following these direct analogies, the teacher could introduce personal analogies (analogies that force the learner to become personally involved with the metaphor being used):

Imagine you are an American colonist. In what ways would you be like a volcano?
Imagine you are a shepherd using an archaic sheep counting system that requires carrying around hundreds of pebbles. How would your feelings be like those of the colonists dealing with the British?

Personal analogies cause even more insightful responses from students. Typical comments would include:

I would be ready to explode; one small upset might make me boiling mad! I would think that I was not valued as a human being!

Finally, the third category of analogies—compressed conflict analogies—would capitalize on the energy and insight generated by the first two. (Compressed conflict analogies place conflicting images and concepts in juxtaposition with one another.) The teacher could continue the lesson by posing such improbable connections as:

Does a volcano have a right to erupt?
If the British were fighting with lawn mowers, what were the American colonists using?

A flurry of creative perspectives will follow. Students enjoy forcing the right brain to ponder the unconventional analogy. The process results in personal integration of the concept and subject matter at hand; for example:

It's a complex issue. The volcano can't help erupting when it is stimulated to the explosive level by forces beyond its control, but it's sad for all those who are hurt.
I think the American colonists were like David with Goliath—I think the Americans had sling shots. I guess, that's what people mean when they say the British lost the war, because they followed conventional war tactics. They just tried to mow people down; they didn't count on bullets coming from behind the trees and stone walls.

The obvious benefits of Gordon's metaphoric categories emerge when we apply them in instructional settings. The categories often produce a flood of insights and creative thoughts. In a time when we are pressed for additional instructional time to teach the basics and often feel pressured to show concrete results in standardized tests,* the metaphor offers a powerful alternative for effective assimilation of concept and information. Startling results can be accomplished by the judicious, ongoing use of metaphoric teaching strategies. The automatic enthusiasm, increased efficiency of concept mastery, and quick energy produced by using the metaphor can bring excitement and life to the classrooms of the 1980s.

The Gordon method of synectics, however, has limits in terms of daily use in the classroom. By necessity, it links a structured teaching approach with an inherently creative process. This is often difficult to accomplish without extensive training in the use of synectic categories.

---

*The results of the authors' research with "Back to the Basics" instruction is outlined later in this chapter.

Nevertheless those teachers who have mastered the skill have had considerable success in using Gordon's method as a highly creative, conceptual tool—a tool that does not require memorization and continual recall as "proofs" of learning. For these people, synectics has been a definitive step forward—an exciting approach that balances content and creative thinking in the classroom.

In summarizing Gordon's contribution, we might look at the work of Jacob Bronowski. In his book, *Science and Human Values* (1956), Bronowski describes a "synectic" process although he does not call it that; the process he describes is the imaginative leap from the familiar (the Greek image of the atom) to the strange (the highly limited nineteenth-century knowledge of chemistry) which produced a new synthesis—the discovery of today's "modern atom." Certainly, "making the familiar strange and the strange familiar" marked *The Metaphorical Way* as a trail-blazing expedition in creative problem solving.

It was not only the work of W. J. J. Gordon, however, that originally sparked our interest in the potential of metaphoric teaching, but also the writings of Bob Samples, and in particular his book, *The Metaphoric Mind* (1976). In this book, an intriguing blend of left-hemisphere theory and right-hemisphere extension of the theory, Samples speculates on the rise of the rational mind. He suggests that the metaphoric mind (right brain) predates the rational mind (left brain); in Samples' words:

No one knows where it happened. Maybe it was in Sumeria . . . perhaps the Indus Valley or in some culture not yet discovered . . . but the wandering ways of the metaphoric mind performed a frightening act of submission. They accepted the dominance of the rational mind.

Nevertheless, according to Samples, "The rational mind is all too aware that all knowledge is metaphoric." Consequently, as Samples conceptualizes it, "The rational mind is threatened by the parent"—the metaphoric mind. It is as though the left brain continually seeks to maintain a position of dominance and control.

Samples believes that children, unfettered by cognitive intellectual chains, are in a better position than most adults to benefit from metaphoric instruction. Children accept the method readily; they respond naturally to images and welcome the spontaneity of insight. They are considerably less cynical and more open. Questions with no "right" or "wrong" answers delight and thrill the young mind! Conversely, adult learners often need highly structured introductions to the metaphoric lesson; their left brains must be reassured of the existence of the right brain's alternate information-processing and of the logic of "listening" to the right brain through the aid of images.

Samples' *Metaphoric Mind* introduced four modes of metaphoric thought. These modes were extremely helpful to the authors; they provided the theoretical underpinning for the subsequent model this book describes. These four modes (Symbolic/Metaphoric, Synergistic/Comparative/Metaphoric, Integrative/Metaphoric, and Inventive/Metaphoric) significantly influenced the initial design of our metaphoric lessons;* we describe them in detail here because they were so critical in the early conceptualization of our four-level teaching method. Samples' modes framed the instructional house we later built —a house where creativity and concept live in partnership with content and sequence.

## The Symbolic/Metaphoric Mode

This mode exists "Whenever a symbol, either abstract or visual, is substituted for some object, process, or condition."

For example: the word "butterfly" or the picture of a butterfly is used to represent the actual animal in nature.

The most common abstract symbols are letters of the alphabet, numerals, and technical symbols. Visual symbols include logos, road signs, trademarks, and images of all sorts. Pictographic language, such as the Japanese "Kanji," is also included in visual symbolization.

Although both types of symbols have a visual aspect, the more abstract symbols of phonetic language systems appeal primarily to the thought-processing of the left hemisphere; visual symbols (including pictographic language alphabets) appeal to the image-processing of the right hemisphere. In fact, in Japan, one finds that people who suffer left brain damage lose the ability to read and write in Katakana (the abstract, phonetic alphabet of daily commerce) and people with right brain damage lose their ability to read and write in Kanji (the visual, pictographic language of poetry and ancient literature).

The symbolic/metaphoric mode is the mode most often used in the classroom; it is this mode we use when we learn to read, to count, to understand that there is meaning ascribed to the many images we have in our world. Visual symbols, symbols to stand for the actual,

---

*Samples further defines these concepts and extends their application in his *Whole-school Book* (1977). Samples' approach is not sequential; each mode has independent classroom potential. In the Sanders model we have actively included sequence in the metaphoric lesson; as inheritors of a left-brain schooling process, we find metaphoric sequencing allows each hemisphere to equally reinforce and support each other. As such, it has an integrative effect in teaching concept with content, process with product, and it allows easy access to the experiential learning model we describe in Chapter 5.

real objects, experiences, and qualities we encounter in life, are the primary building blocks of school curriculum. Teaching students to add and subtract, to read the thoughts of others, to recognize the pictures of other cultures, to appreciate images that teach us about the world around us, to categorize the world in terms of language and defined concepts—these are all examples of the symbolic/metaphoric mode.

Every time the student realizes that a symbol or picture is being used to take the place of a real object, a real experience, or a real sensation, the student is functioning in the symbolic/metaphoric mode. This mode predates the use of written language; it dates back to prehistoric man and the images he painted on cave walls and sculpture. That a word or picture can substitute for the real thing is one of the earliest discoveries we make as children—it is a discovery we never stop exploring.

## The Synergistic/Comparative Metaphoric Mode

Synergistic, in this case, refers to the quality of achieving an effect that is greater than the sum of the separate parts of the given system.

An example of this might be comparing the different elements of the circulatory system to the various representations of the legend of road map in order to understand both the road map and the circulatory system better.

Synergy also occurs when we use parables to explain subject matter concepts. Consider this situation where the teacher is explaining the economic opportunism of farmers in the 1960s with the following parable from Berechiah, the "Jewish Aesop" of the eleventh century:

*A small fish caught in a net said to a fisherman, "I am too little to be a good catch, please spare me. Whether you roast me or broil me, I will not fill your stomach. Let me go, and I will grow for another two years. Then you catch me again, and I will be seven times as fat. Then, when you boil me, it will make you glad."*

*But the fisherman answered, "Better a little fish now in my hands than a great leviathan which my neighbor will catch a year from now."*

The overall impact of the above parable, used to explain the perspective of entrepreneurial agriculture, is certainly greater than the message of the story or the discussion of farming in 1960. The fable suggests in compact, image-rich fashion that it is considerably better to harvest the profits of today than count upon the possible profits of tomorrow. Again, this eight-hundred-year-old fable parallels the modern aphorism, "A bird in the hand is worth two in the bush."

Integral to the use of the synergistic/comparative metaphoric mode is combining more than one thought, more than one image, more than one experience—the overall impact produces a "synthesis of energy" —a moment of synergy. We use this mode every time we teach by the use of a story, a fable, a parable, an example from the student's own experience or life. It is the mode of comparison, the mode that allows us to understand the unfamiliar with the use of familiar objects, experiences, and sensations—it applies the characteristics of what is known to extend the understanding of what is not known. Through the use of this mode, we can gain an appreciation of the "big picture"—the overall implications of what we are learning, studying, and experiencing.

From the first time students learn what it is to call "wolf, wolf," to the comparative studies of American and world literature, we are employing the synergistic/comparative metaphoric mode. The story is understood for itself; and the story also comments allegorically on the nature of the subject we are studying. This ability to recognize both the literal and the figurative as simultaneous statements of the concept at hand is exciting to the mind; the lesson becomes "real," and the classroom comes alive.

## The Integrative/Metaphoric Mode

This mode involves getting both the physical and psychic attributes of the learner in sensual contact with the metaphoric image being used. "It is a total re-entry," according to Samples, "into the mainstream of nature."

This level is exemplified in the guided fantasy experiences, where the learner "sees" in his/her mind the time movie of the earth's history or "becomes" the caterpillar and discovers the dynamic restructuring of the cocoon.

If the teacher demonstrates the process of the water cycle (or if the students experience the "rainbow guided fantasy"), if students experience the strike cycle of the praying mantis by using their bodies in role-play (or become this little animal in a guided fantasy), we are allowing this integrative mode to become part of the instructional process. On the other hand, students writing a report on the water cycle or the feeding habits of the praying mantis would not be in the integrative/metaphoric mode, but rather their thoughts would be in the abstract/symbolic mode. Integral to the integrative/metaphoric mode is providing an experience for the students to personally feel, reflect upon, and sense actual contact with the image.

This integrative/metaphoric mode is present every time students dramatize the lesson they are learning, role-play the situation they are attempting to understand, participate in simulated experiences that create "realistic conditions." It requires that the student (himself or herself) become the subject under consideration; its dividends include the development of empathy, the recognition of situational limits and opportunities, and the awakening of creative perspective.

This book uses the guided fantasy journey as a basic teaching strategy for reaching the integrative/metaphoric mode. With the use of the student's own imagination, we can stimulate the experiences of every metaphoric image we introduce. The resource is immediate; it requires only the quiet concentration of the students and the internal imagery of their minds.

## The Inventive/Metaphoric Mode

This mode creates a new level of personal awareness and creative perception. It is the mode of the natural mind, and it is, in and of itself, synergistic and original.

Samples quotes Jonas Salk on this mode:

The artist draws upon that part of the mind that functions beneath consciousness . . . while the scientist, by and large, but not exclusively, uses that part of the mind that functions in consciousness. The part of the mind that functions beneath consciousness also operates during consciousness. . . . It is necessary to learn how to draw more upon it and employ it for solving the problems of life, of survival, and of evolution. Wisdom arises from both parts of the mind.

The inventive/metaphoric mode is private; it is the mode responsible for Lister's insight on the application of carbolic acid to the problem of hospital sterilization; it is the mode responsible for the German biologist Rudolf Virchow's proposal of the biological law of the cell. It is the mode of the creative that exists in all of us—it prompts creativity to contribute to the logic and reason of the left brain. The mode itself establishes a need to creatively respond to the metaphor.

It is this inventive/metaphoric mode that allows us to make creative leaps in our understanding of the concept; to help students experience this mode, we must teach them to value insight—their own personal moments of "I get it!" or "aha!" Classrooms—where risk taking is valued (not judged as foolish), where conceptual blocks are exposed (not maintained), where wonder and curiosity are integral to learning (not accidental by-products)—are "safe" places for students to experience and pursue inventive/metaphoric activities.

This inventive/metaphoric mode allows the student to break conventional boundaries and systems, to risk improbable connections, to spot image "clues" to the problems with which he or she is wrestling.

It is the mode of the creative thinker, the maverick, the nonconforming marcher who hears the different drum. We can help students experience this exciting mode of thought by teaching them to look for the unusual perspective, to "prove true" the compressed/conflict analogies, to explore the implications of improbable (yet highly creative) insight metaphors; concept and metaphoric image can be linked, and their unlikely merger will produce amazing results: new combinations, new viewpoints, and sometimes entirely new thoughts.

With these four categories of metaphoric modes, Samples enhances the synectics of Gordon and brings metaphoric teaching a significant step closer to daily classroom application. As modern masters of the metaphor, both Gordon and Samples suggest more than a simple technique for learning better and faster; rather, they introduce an almost revolutionary educational premise: namely, that the metaphoric mind (our right brain's ability for imagery) can positively and continually impact the rational mind (our left brain's ability for logic and order), and that this impact is synergistic.

What Gordon and Samples teach us (and what researchers into hemispheric processing confirm) is that creativity, concept attainment, and the metaphor are mutually facilitating, that, while concept attainment is unquestionably obtainable without creativity and the metaphor, the distance between conceptual ignorance and conceptual understanding is quickly and efficiently traversed in the vehicle we call the metaphoric method. Exactly how to do this is the subject of the next chapter.

## BIBLIOGRAPHY

Bronowski, Jacob. *Science and Human Values.* New York: J. Messner, 1956.
Gordon, W.J.J. *The Metaphorical Way of Learning and Knowing.* Cambridge, Mass.: Porpoise Books, 1966.
Hadas, Moses. *Fables of a Jewish Aesop* (Translated from the Fox Fables of Berechiah Ha-Nakdan). New York: Columbia University Press, 1967.
Paivio, Allen. *Imagery and Verbal Processes.* New York: Holt, Rinehart and Winston, 1971.
Samples, Bob, Cheryl Charles, and Dick Barnhart. *The Wholeschool Book.* Reading, Mass.: Addison-Wesley, 1977.
Samples, Bob. *The Metaphoric Mind.* Reading, Mass.: Addison-Wesley, 1976.
Shah, Idries. *The Exploits of the Incomparable Mulla Nasrudin.* New York: E.P. Dutton, 1972.

# CHAPTER 4

# Creativity, Concept Attainment, and Metaphoric Teaching

## A LOOK FORWARD

The bicycle is a basically simple machine; its wheels, frame, chain, sprockets, brakes, handle bars, and seat are designed to function as a whole, to produce a vehicle that carries people faster and with less effort than walking. We understand the bicycle when we see it, however, not as a series of separate, mechanical parts (none of which alone can transport us), but as a totality of interacting parts. Teaching, learning, managing behavior, stimulating interest, and exciting minds, while by no means as simple a process, operate on much the same principle as the bicycle. The activities require interrelatedness in order to function best.

Yet, although we, as educators, easily acknowledge the wheel as less functional, less enjoyable, and less productive when it is separate from the frame, sprockets, chain, handle bars, and seat, we often accept the mandate of the current "back to basics" movement to separate, rather than integrate, learning activities in the classroom. Thus, in schools, we have math time (chains), reading time (wheels), writing time (sprockets); we have chemistry class (handlebars), and American history (seats), but we seldom have an ideal opportunity to assemble the separate parts (subjects) into a functional whole (education).

Metaphoric lessons encourage such assemblages in the regular classroom. Metaphoric lessons, in fact, naturally provide a linking format for integrating language, earth science, and social studies (The "Time Movie" Lesson) or life science, history, and language (The "Change/Butterfly" Lesson) and implemented metaphoric lessons, therefore, are best when designed as part of the normal teaching schedule; to see metaphoric teaching only as a "fun activity" or as "the creativity lesson" for the week is to shortchange the inherent potential of the method.

Indeed, one of the major strengths of the metaphoric method is its ability to affect a number of subjects and processes simultaneously. In a time when we are faced with the frustration of needing to teach multilevel information—basic grammar (the use of the alphabet in utilizing the Dewey Decimal System), sophisticated concepts (the economics of slavery in the antebellum South), and variant thought processes (creative interpretation of power politics)—we suggest a solution: meeting these instructional demands through the use of metaphoric teaching. For with the metaphor, we gain the ability to sensibly interrelate the basics, to interestingly connect personal experience and concept development, and to regularly encourage creativity as a normal part of classroom interaction.*

This chapter then, begins with a brief look at creativity, moves to a "real life" presentation of a metaphoric lesson that integrates the teaching of basics, concepts, and creativity, and explores and delineates a streamlined strategy for teaching concept development. Finally, using the information derived from recent left/right brain research, the chapter considers the question of creativity in a much larger context, particularly as it applies to "making bicycles" in the classroom. Behind all of this, like a great undiscovered oil reserve, lies the power of the metaphoric image.

> *Working with creativity resembles working with electricity.*
> *In neither case do we understand very fully what "it" is, but*
> *may gradually learn how to partially uncover "its" potential and*
> *set the stage so "it" turns on a little, and otherwise learn*
> *to work with "it."*
>
> Calvin Taylor and Robert L. Ellison

Developing the metaphoric teaching model described in this book confirmed our belief in the essential truth of the Taylor and Ellison description of working with creativity. We have examined and probed the right brain's "modus operandi" in order to find a way to consciously and effectively utilize it within the regular classroom. Indeed, to "set-up" the right brain, to uncover its potential and to encourage the release of this potential in the classroom has presented countless challenges. In order to continually define and refine the method, we have

---

*In the elementary classroom, the problem often seems overwhelming: we must daily balance the need to concentrate on the basics (reading skills, composition skills, and math skills) with encouraging scientific inquiry (Why is the rhino becoming extinct?), helping students develop personal judgment (Why do we value individual freedom?), and teaching the interrelatedness of what we learn (a story about the rhino, the governmental system of an African dictatorship, the role of human superstition, and the economics of free universal education).

We want our students to discover that killing rhinos for superstitious reasons can be related to the budgeting of money for free schooling when the country is governed by dictatorship. Each day can be a challenge to find these connections—to allow students to discover that separate instructional lessons can coalesce for an understanding of life as a whole.

presented numerous metaphoric lessons in elementary and secondary classrooms. Many of these lessons have been demonstrated with audiences of ten to fifteen classroom teachers in attendance. These presentations have had enormous success; we have, in fact, learned much about how to work with teaching strategies that are image-directed (metaphoric) rather than recall-directed; through these demonstration lessons, more importantly, we have observed the synergistic impact of metaphoric teaching on the total learning process.*

In late March 1980 we presented The "Change/Butterfly" Lesson to a class of twenty-seven fifth- and sixth-grade students. After the lesson we held a question and answer period for the twelve teachers who had been observers. One of the teachers asked a question that seemed to summarize a central concern of many classroom teachers:

I have to concentrate on language, math, and reading skills; my kids are tested for growth in these areas only. In addition, I have to switch my class often, and I lose my class for at least forty-five minutes a day for P.E., art, or music. When do I teach creativity? Isn't that what the art teacher is supposed to do?

This is a very real question in these times, a question that reflects both the increased pressures teachers are feeling to produce measurable results on standardized tests, and the common assumption that anything that does not directly contribute to these measurable results is educationally and intellectually expendable. Further complicating the teacher's dilemma is the widely held supposition that standardized achievement tests do not measure "creativity" in any of its forms; rather, there is a common belief that these tests measure only basic knowledge and the ability to read, comprehend, or recall factual information. Upon closer examination, however, we find that standardized tests often do measure growth in the ability to think conceptually, and although we would not suggest that using creativity to improve test scores is the only justification for teaching creativity, nevertheless, creative thinking can lead to critical thinking and conceptual facility —and when it does, the results are astonishing. Consider an actual case history: (Teacher: Ms. Simonton, age twenty-eight, seven years teaching experience, fourth-grade class, fairly typical suburban school.)

Ms. Simonton asked us to visit her class and demonstrate The "Change/Butterfly" Lesson (see page 57); she also invited both her

---

*The impact of "right-brain-targeted" strategies is, of course, not limited to the right brain. It is important to remember that the brain, though functionally separated, is integrally linked. This caution is necessitated by the propensity of some individuals to put too much emphasis on the separateness of the duality of function as opposed to the synergy of hemispheric interplay. It's the active exchange of information between the hemispheres that maximizes the insights and conceptual development of the individual.

principal and district curriculum coordinator to observe. Before designing the actual lesson, we asked what the children were already learning about change. We have discovered that metaphoric lessons are even
more effective when presented in an integrated format with subject
matter; as we have mentioned, the metaphoric method is designed to
integrate subjects, not to be used alone as an interesting amusement
for the right brain's enjoyment.

The students were struggling with paragraph revision—learning to
proofread, to rewrite their thoughts, to restructure the order and arrangement of their sentences. We were intrigued with the possibility
of improving writing skills through the use of metaphors. What if we
could link rewriting a paragraph with a metaphoric concept? Could we
change a routine, "boring," "have to" exercise into something challeng-
ing, creative, and highly motivational?

On Tuesday morning, between the reading period and the recess
break, we began the lesson: "Today, we are going to learn something
new about rewriting paragraphs—about the ways we can change them
to allow them to become our best work." (The students quietly groaned.
Their teacher had told them that today would be a special day, an
exciting day with a new lady to teach them—they were ready for
"hippocampal stimulation!") "But, we are going to learn about paragraphs in a different way than you have ever experienced. We are going
to have a lesson where there are no right answers and no wrong answers." (At this point, one of the students actually said, "No kidding?")

"To learn about *changing,* we are going to learn about a little animal
who teaches us all about what it means to change." Thus began the
lesson on the butterfly. Images came first: greeting cards, pictures, and
household articles with butterflies on them flooded the front of the
room. Of special interest to the students was the New York Metropolitan Museum of Art's huge folding book on butterflies. The children
were fascinated by the hundreds of butterfly images.

After the students had absorbed the images, we posed the question,
"How are you like a butterfly?" They were reminded not to say anything out loud, just to think of the answer in their own head; when
everyone had an answer, we began. As the answers came from all
around the room (each student "in turn" or the process would have
been chaos), we were surprised to hear how many responded that they
were like the butterfly because, "I like to fly." Many of today's suburban children are experienced travellers; responses from urban students
might differ considerably. Other students were more introspective;
they were like the butterfly because they loved the fields and flowers
or they saw themselves as soft and gentle.

The third element of the metaphoric lesson, the guided fantasy, was
the highlight of the session for the students. They relaxed, listened, and

silently participated (except for one who apparently mentally "sat it out," his eyes occasionally opening and darting quickly around the room, who looked slightly embarrassed—perhaps because he did not have the attention of the class). After the guided fantasy, we debriefed the experience. The students were truly excited; they began to realize how special, how unique, each individual student's own experience had been; the silence (under the pressure of extra excitement) of all the students while any one student shared the details of his/her guided fantasy gave additional support to the personal, unique nature of each student's experience.

The fourth level, the creative insight level, allowed us to return to the original concept to be taught—paragraph revision. On the blackboard, hidden from view by a map, we had written a paragraph taken from a fourth grader's notebook. After the debriefing, we uncovered it:

I dreemed I was walking down a dark streat. When i saw a very brite light comming toward me from the sky. I started to run i run faster and faster but the light keep comming. I turned to look it was a flying saucer. The light reeched out to me and took me on to the flying saucer. Just then my Mother waked me up.

While the students silently read the paragraph, we said: "What you see on the board is a 'caterpillar' paragraph. What we need to do is put this paragraph into a cocoon so it can become a butterfly. Does anyone want to help?"

The motivational level of the students soared. Everyone wanted to help; there was no embarrassment for "wrong" suggestions, some ideas worked and some didn't. The students found all the errors (even some we hadn't expected—e.g., small "m" in mother instead of capitalized Mother), and the corrected paragraph was written next to the original:

I *dreamed* I was walking down a dark *street when I* saw a very *bright* light *coming* toward me from the sky. I started to run. *I ran* faster and faster, but the light *kept coming.* I turned to look. It was a flying saucer. The light *reached* out and took me *into* the flying saucer. Just then, my *mother woke* me up.

We followed this activity with these comments: "Every time any one of us writes anything, we produce only caterpillars the first time around. Dr. Sanders, your teacher, your parents, even great writers, everyone must take time for the cocoon if we are going to have true butterflies when we finish. We can let writing be crawling like a caterpillar or a moment of flying like the butterfly. It just depends upon whether we are willing to change what we create—to reword our thoughts, to give them the benefit of the process that takes our written thoughts from caterpillars to butterflies."

The lesson ended, and the children returned to their classroom. When we turned to the principal and district curriculum coordinator for feedback, their comments were enthusiastic. They explained that the lesson was essentially basic "TABS" (Texas Assessment of Basic Skills) curriculum, and that many teachers were looking for a method to creatively teach the basics. Then they added, "Did you know that those children were grouped 'Low to Middle'?" (No, we didn't; they had seemed like "average" kids to us). "Well, if anyone had seen those children during the last hour, they would have sworn you were working with a group of gifted/talented kids."

This expansion of potential, this special opportunity to go beyond normal classroom performance levels is, of course, one of the outstanding side effects of the metaphoric method; generally, this chance to expand beyond the ordinary happens seldom in today's demanding classroom; in effect, the two brains had "turned on" to allow these students to experience a moment of creative giftedness. For these students, however, the impact of the lesson did not end when they left the room.

The following day, one of the students brought into the classroom a rubber stamp of a butterfly and asked, "Mrs. S., when we really write 'butterfly' papers, can we have a butterfly stamp on the top of them?" And, later in the day, when the teacher was giving a spelling quiz with the words in sentences (e.g., "Who has the *geography* book?"), she noticed that, as usual, no question marks were being placed at the end of the sentence. She was about to comment on this when, instead, she decided to refer back to the previous day's lesson: intuitively, she said, "What I see around this room are a lot of 'caterpillar' sentences." Later she commented that she had never seen pencils add question marks any faster—including one of her slow learners exclaiming, "I get it!" This lesson was followed during the next few months by Ms. Simonton's teaching of many other metaphoric lessons in this book. Although the verdict is not yet in (years will be needed for long-range assessment), the children have definitely improved their "TABS" skills and their parents and administration are delighted. Indeed, this case suggests that efficient teaching of the academic basics might be noticeably enhanced through the focused attention of the "image brain."

We cite this sample case study because it is typical of the results we have been finding when metaphoric teaching is brought into the classroom. Students do learn more, both more effectively and more efficiently, when they understand conceptually why they are learning. The classroom becomes a place of excitement and basic skills are mastered much faster when both "brains" are creatively and consciously focused on the same topic.

Additionally, with the use of metaphoric strategies, the instructional choice does not have to be mutually exclusive: that is, do we teach kids to read or do we teach them to be imaginative? Do we teach content or do we teach insight? Do we teach separate content areas or do we link subject matter through creative thinking? These choices no longer haunt us, because teaching creativity is not an "either, or" proposition. Creativity and cognitive development, content and insight, thoughts and intuitions, are not mutually exclusive: in fact, they are complementary. Creativity can be, in fact, the sun, the lights, and the colors of our intellectual rainbow—the energy that enhances and highlights the potential of our perception—the sum of our thoughts, feelings and actions. Creativity links images with function, logic with concept. It hooks both of the special thought processes of the left/right brains—it complements the abilities of both hemispheres. Creativity is contrast, but it is also comparison; creativity is intuitive, but it is also metaphoric.

## VARIATIONS ON THE THEME–CONCEPT ATTAINMENT

One of the major problems in teaching concepts, in moving students toward concept attainment (the ability not only to "know" but to be able to use and to understand the concept), lies in helping students grasp the "big picture" as to why they are learning a given concept and its basic subject matter. All too often the student memorizes the specific information we give him or her and misses *why* it is being learned. This problem can stem from approaching concept attributes too literally, too logically (too "left-brained"). In order to gain an understanding of the concept, the student needs to view the subject matter holistically—as fitting into an overall pattern. To respond to this need (the need for an overall perception of the importance of the lesson), we can use metaphors in the early stages of introducing a new concept.

Metaphoric thinking can continually, and in many different forms, creatively unlock the conceptual potential of the right brain. Strategies for tapping into this ability to "get the picture of what's being taught" are not limited to the metaphoric method as we have so far described it in this book. Although the essential elements included in the following concept attainment model have been derived from the basic metaphoric model, they can be further explored in terms of concept attributes and concept mastery. Indeed, it is not a far jump from a strategy that teaches concept mastery to a strategy that teaches concept through experience; both are needed in the classroom, and both, we submit, draw upon the essential nature of concept itself—both focus upon the student's ability to perceive the concept and its implications rather than simply to memorize the concept's definition and its text-defined context.

As an example, let's return to the concept of "change." As we noted, change is an all-pervasive concept both in our schools and in our lives. Change appears in the elementary school curriculum in practically all subject areas. In science, for example, many textbook or kit programs stress the fact that the universe is in constant change; by high school, the science curriculum has expanded to include the concept of change in matter or change in regard to the laws of thermodynamics. The concept of change, however, is not limited to science curriculum; rather, it is a cross-curricular concept that we, as teachers, deal with directly or indirectly in many subject matter areas on a daily basis. Consider the following teaching moments when a lesson on change, as a concept, would help students grasp the overall process they are studying.

| | |
|---|---|
| In a reading group | Changing to a new book; changing focus from reading skills and phonetic skills to comprehension and speed-reading skills. |
| In a math class | Changing from the concept of adding to the concept of multiplying as repeated addition; changing from arithmetical to algebraic computation. |
| In a history class | Understanding historical change from monarchy to democracy; perceiving the struggle in changing from an agricultural society to a technological society. |
| In a social studies class | Changing the basic values of students from unquestioning acceptance of peer group values to conscious, personal decision making. |
| In a geology class | Perceiving the impact of physical changes on earth; noting the changes in the erosion pattern of a given land mass. |
| In a spelling class | Changing stress and phonetic patterns to include longer words. |
| In a typing class | Changing the basic conscious striking of typewriter keys to a highly spontaneous psychomotor response. |
| In a foreign language | Changing one language's verbal associations with visual stimuli to another language's associations; changing cultural norms to accept a different cultural value system and its vocabulary. |

In an English class                Changing students' attitudes toward
                                   quality reading materials; changing class
                                   appreciation levels toward theme, struc-
                                   ture, characterization, and plot develop-
                                   ment.

The list could go on and on. All around us, teaching requires helping
students understand the nature of change.

Marriages change, people change, politics change; both as students
and as adults, we are constantly dealing with the paradox of change—
change is one permanent constant aspect of the universe. Change is, in
fact, a basic human dilemma, a crossroads, a decision-making moment;
it is a dilemma that recent popular works of nonfiction *(Passages)*,
fiction *(Covenant)* and even movies *(The Four Seasons* and *Ordinary
People)* have explored in depth in the attempt to help people examine
and accept this basic "fact of life."

Because of its importance in life, change has been a subject for
comment throughout the ages. As early as 513 B.C., we find Heraclitus
reminding his listeners that with change, "All is flux, nothing is stationary." In the late sixteenth century, Richard Hooker extended this
definition with the following understanding of change's impact on the
individual: "Change is not made without inconvenience, even from
worse to better." Still later, in Washington Irving's *Tales of a Traveller,*
we find a nineteenth-century metaphor that explores the psychology of
change: "There is a certain relief in change, even though it be from bad
to worse; as I have found in traveling in a stage-coach, that it is often
a comfort to shift one's position and be bruised in a new place." And,
probably the best-known description for change in our lives comes from
a much-quoted Shakespearean metaphor many of us memorized in
high school; in *As You Like It,* Shakespeare vividly portrays the changing roles we play throughout our lives:

> *All the world's a stage,*
> *And all the men and women merely players;*
> *They have their exits and their entrances,*
> *And one man in his time plays many parts,*
> *His acts being seven ages. At first, the infant,*
> *Mewling and puking in the nurse's arms.*
> *Then the whining schoolboy, with his satchel,*
> *And shining morning face, creeping like a snail*
> *Unwillingly to school. And then the lover,*
> *Sighing like a furnace, with a woeful ballad*
> *Made to his mistress' eyebrow. Then a soldier,*
> *Full of strange oaths and bearded like the pard,*
> *Jealous in honor, sudden and quick in quarrel,*
> *Seeking the bubble reputation*

*Even in the cannon's mouth. And then the justice,*
*In fair round belly with good capon lined,*
*With eyes severe and beard of formal cut,*
*Full of wise saws and modern instances;*
*And so he plays his part. The sixth age shifts*
*Into the lean and slippered pantaloon,*
*With spectacles on nose and pouch on side;*
*His youthful hose, well saved, a world too wide*
*For his shrunk shank, and his big manly voice,*
*Turning again toward childish treble, pipes*
*And whistles in his sound. Last scene of all,*
*That tends this strange eventful history,*
*Is second childishness and mere oblivion,*
*Sans teeth, sans eyes, sans taste, sans everything.*

**(II, vii)**

In the school curriculum we must often deal with *change* as subject matter specific when, in reality, change is a global concept, impinging on almost everything we do. The change we learn about in geology can serve as a metaphor for the change we study in psychology*—but, too often, it doesn't. Why is a pervasive concept such as *change* so often poorly understood by students and adults, whether it is being related to mathematics, science, or social studies?

We suggest that the lack of understanding is a result of the individual's conscious definition of change. The concept *as such* (Ding an sich) is often defined only in terms of the accepted "left-brain" definition. To truly define the concept, we must look at the overall definition of change, a definition derived from information in *both* brains. In order to understand this, we need to look at two separate definitions; first, a conventional definition for change:

*Change:*   Definition 1 (adapted from Webster's):
1) to make radically different or to make different in some particular; 2) to replace with another; 3) to make a shift from one to another; 4) to undergo loss or modification; 5) to put fresh clothes or covering on.

In other words, to change is to make something different, to vary the form, to substitute, shift, or undergo variation. This definition is

---

*We can describe the growth of psychological perspective, for example, as the "sands of time"; the sudden emergence of overwhelming feelings as an "eruption" or an "earthquake of feelings"—emotions that have shifted too quickly and are now out of control!

We can view therapy as a process of "uncovering the layers of trauma and defense mechanisms"—to gain a perspective on what "has been deposited and has hardened into place"; people can even find it helpful to view their lives as having had an "ice age when glaciers covered their dreams and feelings" and a time that has still left "people dinosaurs" in their minds to haunt their present lives.

logical, consistent, and reasonable in terms of the instances where using the word change will be appropriate.

However, there is second operational definition occurring simultaneously with this literal (left-brain definition. It is a figurative (figure or image) definition that emerges in pictures in the user's or listener's mind—pictures derived from the cultural moments in which the word was learned and most often used. We first discovered this "right brain" definitional level (although not referred to as such) in *Metaphors We Live By* (Lakoff and Johnson, 1980). In an exciting examination of linguistic interpretations, Lakoff and Johnson suggest that the literal definition (the normal way we define concepts in the classroom—"Let's look it up in the dictionary") summarizes only the explicit properties of the concept—i.e., what has been intellectually accepted as true and consistent. (This kind of definition we call "left brain.")

Lakoff and Johnson further suggest that the conventional definition is only part of any given concept:

Metaphor is for most people a device of the poetic imagination and the rhetorical flourish—a matter of extraordinary rather than ordinary language. Moreover, metaphor is typically viewed as characteristic of language alone, a matter of words rather than thought or action. For this reason, most people think they can get along perfectly well without the metaphor. We have found, on the contrary, that metaphor is pervasive in everyday life, not just in language but in thought and action. Our ordinary conceptual system, in terms of which we both think and act, is fundamentally metaphorical in nature.

These linguistic researchers claim that behind each conventional definition of a concept is an "interactional" definition, a definition developed as a result of the social context in which the concept is used, a definition that is as important for the concept being expressed as is the dictionary definition. Built upon the cultural value system of those who first teach the concept (usually parents and peers), the interactional definition is identified by discovering the underlying social metaphors that provide the individual's personal images of how the concept works.

Lakoff and Johnson use the concept of argument as their primary example; in their model, the accepted dictionary definition of argument is:

*Argument:* Proof, theme, subject matter, a reason offered for or against something, a debate, controversy, or discussion a process of reasoning.

But does this definition really help us fully understand the concept of argument? They suggest not. The best way to understand what argument is like is in examining the word argument in its interactional context, the context in which we use it. For example, are we talking about argument in terms of a debate, a law class, or a contract dispute? In context, the word argument is further defined by the "the interactional metaphors" that accompany it. Argument, for example, could mean "war." Consider these typical examples:

Your claims are *indefensible.* He *attacked* every weak point in my argument. His criticisms were right on *target.* I *demolished* his argument. I've never *won* an argument against him. You disagree? Okay, *shoot.* If you use that *strategy,* he'll *wipe you out.* He *shot down* all my arguments.

But argument can also be seen in terms of other metaphors. If we are teaching history, social studies, science (or even debate or law from a different viewpoint), we might find the cultural metaphor of "building" more helpful. This alternate definition provides an image of argument as a reasonable process of assembling information, of facts building upon themselves, of theory substantiating theory:

Is that the *foundation* of your argument? It might *need more support.* Your initial *premise is shaky.* We need more facts or the argument will *fall apart.* We need *to construct a strong platform* for it. Here are some additional facts *to shore up* the theory and provide a *buttress with solid support. Without this foundation, your argument may collapse for lack of a framework* to support additional facts and data.

With this additional imagery (argument as war or as building), we expand the dictionary definition of argument. "Proof, theme, subject matter, a reason offered for or against something, a debate, controversy, or discussion, a process of reasoning" does not offer holistic understanding—or, the "big picture" of how the concept affects us personally. Showing students that some people see arguing as a battle will prepare them for the emotional conflict that often accompanies an argument. Expanding their view of argument (to also define argument as a process of building) will help students gain an appreciation for the painstaking process of creating strong, reasonable arguments that prevent explosive emotional conflict.

How do these two definitions, the conventional and the interactional, relate to concept development (and specifically the concept of change) in the classroom? Let's look again at the metaphoric images (the right-brain pictures) our culture attaches to the process of change and then explore how we can use metaphoric teaching to provide alternative images for this "right-brain" definition—images that students can experientially develop with an interactional context that will enrich their understanding of what is meant by changing.

We begin with another look at Webster's definition of change:

Change: . . . to make radically different, to make different in some particular, to replace with another, to make a shift from one to another, to undergo loss or modification, to put fresh clothes or clothing on.

This definition is essentially rational, analytical, "left-brain" in orientation. It is simple, straightforward, valueless. But, it is not what change commonly means in our daily lives. In everyday living, the concept of change is influenced by the metaphors of each individual's personal experiences:

*Change*   Definition 2 (derived from cultural comments we hear all around us):
*"Change* your attitude, young lady (young man)!"
*"Change* the channel, I don't want to watch that."
*"Change* your clothes, they'll get dirty."
*"Change* your bed, you need to learn to take care of yourself!"
"If I could only *change* the color of this room."
"If he *changes* one more thing, I'll go up in smoke!"
"Do I ever need a *change* in my life!"
This definition expresses our prevailing images of change—1) fix it, 2) improve what is currently happening, 3) get something better, 4) change is emotional or physical work, 5) change involves a quality move, usually from bad to good.

When we examine the context in which we commonly use the word, *change* expands in meaning; it becomes more than the left brain, rational, and linear definition of "replacing or making different"; change means "Improve it!" Suddenly, all the everyday experiences we have had with the word "change" begin to color the tidy, literal dictionary definition. In fact, the metaphors that accompany the process of changing (the cultural images that the right brain has perceived) influence what we feel about changing and even our understanding of what is being communicated with this word.

When we as adults tell young people, "I want you to change your attitude," we are not saying, "I want you to try a different attitude or an attitude shift." We are, in fact, telling them, "Improve (fix) your attitude to come up to the standards I want." The child is very aware that we are saying "Your attitude had better improve." He or she knows that the comment is not neutral, and that the change will definitely involve emotional (perhaps, even physical) effort.* The problem

---

*While writing this section of the book, our nephew, Aaron, came to visit us in Houston. Aaron is nine, and it seemed an ideal moment to check perceptions with a soon-to-be fourth grader. I asked him what it means to "Change your attitude." He responded with, "I had that problem last year." I asked further, "What was the prob-

is that we have not realized that these images exist independent of our conscious awareness and that they can actively influence the perceived meaning of every word we use. When confronted with these cultural, hidden messages, we tend to insist that we meant the literal definition: "I merely suggested that he change his present attitude and try adopting a new way of looking at things."

How pervasive is the FIX IT! IMPROVE IT! metaphoric definition of change? Look at these examples: "Change the tire," means you have either a flat tire or a worn tire. "Change the bed," means it needs fresh linen. "Times are changing," means either a shift toward improvement or a slip backward. We rarely use change merely to mean "make something different." Although we know that the word "change" (strictly speaking) means to "replace," we all tacitly agree that the "replacing" should be the "bettering of the situation." The underlying metaphor of change (namely not to replace but to improve) can, however, be perceived as a demand or as criticism by the students who hear the word in the classroom. For example:

> This year you will really *change* the way you think about science.
>
> You're in high school now, and you'll find significant *changes* occurring in the way you view homework assignments.
>
> As you *change* your skill level this year, you'll see a new way to view you, your friends, and your world.

What we really want is to have our students view changing as normal growth, as expansion of what already exists, as seeking one's potential or fulfillment. As with the seed that becomes the flower, the idea that becomes democracy, the invention that allows people, separated by hundreds of miles, to talk to each other—we want students to value the original seed, idea, and invention, as well as the later products that evolve from the original thought. The beginning is not always inferior; change is becoming, but becoming does not mean devaluing the initial accomplishment of producing the seed, creating the idea, or inventing the new product.

---

lem?" He explained, "My teacher didn't like me telling her when it was time for recess, that we had already studied that part of the book, or that we were done with our workbooks."

"What did you do about it?" I asked, Aaron answered slowly, "My dad teaches me a lot, too, Auntie. My dad said he thought I would learn a lot if I found out how to win the 'citizen of the month' award from my teacher. I did, too! Two months later, I won the 'citizen of the month' award!"

Not only did Aaron confirm our findings—"Change your attitude." meant "Don't give me so much trouble!"—but he gave a good example of the wisdom that can come from parents who understand what the teacher is trying to communicate. Aaron learned a valuable lesson in politics; the teacher "changed her attitude" toward him.

To create a sense of change as an opportunity (not criticism of the status quo), we must offer alternative images of what change can be to modify the current images our students hold. The metaphoric lesson does this well; as the student learns that changing can mean the process of *becoming* (like the transformation of the butterfly), the student also learns to value the caterpillar phase. The butterfly becomes a symbol of what the caterpillar can become, not a criticism of life in its initial growth stages. The attitude that "There's something wrong with you, or you wouldn't need to change" is challenged by a new attitude —"Changing means following your destiny, seeking your potential; it doesn't mean there's something wrong with what you are." This new attitude frees the student and extends an invitation to expand and grow. It suggests that the present level of performance is worthy of respect and pride; then it encourages a continuing process of growth.

All concepts have both literal and metaphoric definitions. Awareness of these image definitions can greatly aid classroom understanding of any concept. Let's take another concept, another word we use daily in classrooms everywhere—"math." When we look up "mathematics" in Webster's dictionary, we find the literal definition of the word to be:

*Math*   Definition 1 (adapted from Webster's): 1) the science of numbers and their operations, interrelations, combinations, generalizations, and abstractions, and of space configurations and their structure; 2) a branch of operation in, or use of mathematics (the *mathematics* of physical chemistry).

This definition of mathematics speaks to a select audience—to people who define math as the logical, sequential, scientific process of manipulating numbers and space configurations. While we know this to be an accurate definition of the science of mathematics, it has little meaning to fourth graders who are wrestling with fractions, decimals, and two digit multiplication. Fourth graders define "math" with the cultural images that their parents and peers have provided:

*Math*   Definition 2 (derived from cultural comments we hear all around us):

"Okay, it's time to get your *math* book out and do your homework."

"He has had some trouble with English, but boy is he ever good at *math.*"

*"Math* means you have to learn to be precise."

"I hated *math,* too, when I was in school!"

"Your dad has always been a whiz at *math*—I bet you'll do well, too."

"What I want to know is did you do your *math* homework before you started to watch this T.V. show."

Thus, we have the prevailing images of math—1) math is serious study and means work; 2) math ability means you really are intelligent; 3) math is so hard that it's all right to hate doing it; 4) people who do well in math are going to "make it" in life.

To the young student, math is not a science of numbers but a subject with rigid rules, something you are either good at or not; math homework must be done even if other homework is not done; math tests how smart you are. These "IQ" images of math terrorize students who have trouble initially conceptualizing what math is all about. In fact, these beginning negative moments of fear can follow the student throughout his or her educational experience. In contrast, math as a puzzle, as a tool for making your life easier, as a way to solve problems, or as a language of numbers instead of words, is often overlooked. The metaphoric lesson is a quick, enjoyable way to provide such alternative images of math for each student in your class.*

## Concepts—Definitions with Waistlines

What do "image definitions" (right-brain cultural perceptions) mean to the classroom teacher? First, we must recognize that our students rarely share our own personal "image definitions" for the words we use (we all have different cultural experiences; as teachers, we have experiences that are a "generation apart" from those of our students). Second, we must assume that these image definitions differ from individual to individual within the classroom (such "concept pictures" depend upon all the home and classroom experiences the student has had with the word at hand). Third, and most important, we need to identify a positive image of classroom concepts that we want students to adopt into their own lives; such positive images can then be taught quickly and effectively through the use of the metaphoric method. We can, in fact, tap the metaphoric brain (the right brain) and teach these concepts easily and consensually. In a very short time, students can arrive at agreed upon definitions for most instructional concepts;** and, in the process, the essence and characteristics of the concept (the image and metaphors behind the word) can be identified and classified.

For example, let's assume that you want to teach the concept of "tolerance" or "to tolerate" to a seventh grade class:

---

*Please see Part II of this book for guidelines in developing metaphoric lessons for your class. (Several examples and techniques are outlined.)

**Yes, while it is possible to get students to agree on a common definition of what it means to be "courteous," "have self-discipline," "the right attitude," or "be self-starters," it is also possible to develop agreement on concepts such as, "democracy," "aesthetic appreciation," "socialization," "theme versus plot," "political awareness," and a host of other concepts you would like them all to share.

*Step 1.* Have the students go to the blackboard and write down sentences that are typical of the way they have heard people use the words "tolerate" or "tolerance" in everyday life.

Encourage the students to write the sentence the way they have heard it.

I can't *tolerate* all the noise in this house!

I wish you would *tolerate* your little sister and include her in your games.

The doctor says I can't *tolerate* penicillin.

Steel has a *tolerance* that makes it better for making swords—they don't break.

Our minister tells us we should *tolerate* everybody.

I won't *tolerate* you acting this way!

These plants will not *tolerate* this cold weather.

My mother can't *tolerate* the way I keep my room.

*Step 2.* Now, ask the class to see if they can find a word (or set of words) that can substitute for "tolerance" or "tolerate" in the sentences they have written.

*"Don't like it!"*

*"Be nice."*

*"Can't take it!"*

*Step 3.* Next, ask the students which values go with the word "tolerate" or "tolerance."

*"Ought to do it."*

*"Right thing to do."*

*"It's an ultimatum."*

*"Good people do it."*

*"It's the moral thing to do."*

*Step 4.* Then, ask the students how they feel if they are being "tolerant." This involves going back to the initial sentences and checking how they feel about being "tolerant."

*"Strong—able to take it."*

*"Doing the right thing—what you're supposed to do."*

*"Powerful—I can handle anything."*

*"Accepted for what I am—not criticized."*

*Step 5.* Finally, ask the students how they feel if they are not being "tolerant."

*"I'm in trouble."*

*"Someone is angry with me."*

*"I feel guilty."*

*"I can't take it."*
*"I don't feel very good about it."*
This exercise has now generated a working definition of what tolerance means to the students in your class. Tolerance can mean "moral obligation," "a sense of being strong enough to take obstacles," and "a sense of being accepted." With this increased awareness, you can now introduce the definitions of tolerate and tolerance adapted from Webster's:

*Tolerate:* (1) to endure or resist the action of (as a drug) without grave or lasting injury;
*Tolerance:* (1) to have a sympathy or indulgence for the beliefs or practices that differ from one's own;
(2) the act of allowing something.

You will find that students will be excited not only because they came so close to the dictionary definition, but because they also discovered additional information about the word "tolerate." They found that being tolerant is considered "morally good" in our country, that being tolerant is "learning how to accept differences," and that being tolerant "makes you feel powerful."

This process, therefore, accomplishes two things: first, it defines the pictures that the right brain perceived with the word "tolerance" (the church, Mom, a sense of power or strength); and second, it provides the literal definition that Webster's gives us (endurance, sympathy, empathy, the ability to allow things to be as they are).

To increase this awareness of tolerance as the "acceptance of things as they are," you could follow this introduction with a metaphoric lesson. In searching for metaphors of positive images of tolerance, we thought of a garden—a garden with all kinds of plants and flowers, a place where time schedules for growth are encouraged and cultivated. This "seasonal" garden always has some kind of produce ready for harvesting, some kind of flower ready for picking. In many ways, it is a symbol of a special quality—the quality of accepting differences in all types of people and in the things they set out to accomplish.

To teach the concept of tolerance, you might develop your own metaphoric lesson (the garden is a good metaphor for tolerance) or you might want to implement some of the following activities that encourage students to put the concept of tolerance into context with the subject matter they are studying:
Elementary students could:

Create a neighborhood TOLERANCE MAP—a map of all the differing cultural centers and churches in the neighborhood.

Develop a class TOLERANCE TREE—a tree of the class where each student is a leaf with his or her special beliefs or values.

Write a chronicle of "E.T." returning to the earth ten years after his visit and documenting how his lesson of tolerance affected the children he met.

Trace, historically, the role of TOLERANCE in creating the power, diversity, and strength of the United States.

Conduct an ethnological study (like *Foxfire*) of the backgrounds of leading businessmen and women in the city (town) who have contributed as civic leaders to shaping the United Way (the scouting activities, the Junior League, the Democratic/Republican parties, any significant civic group).

Create a TOLERANCE GARDEN where everyone in the class has a spot of land to grow something special.

And, Secondary Students could:

Trace the role of tolerance in the development of the English language (from Anglo-Saxon/Norman influence to the multitude of outside cultural contributions in today's English language).

Identify the effect (or lack) of tolerance in a central character in literature (Othello, Silas Marner, or Maggie in *The Thornbirds*).

Test their own sense of tolerance in learning new definitions for concepts in a foreign language (Germans say they "love" something only with strong, genuine devotion; everything else is "I have it gladly" or "I like it").

Investigate the role of tolerance in the development of a winning team (football, basketball, soccer).

Study one role of tolerance in community or local politics; identify where tolerance is encouraged and where it is not encouraged.

Experiment with levels of tolerance in the chemistry lab (which elements can be tolerated by water, which elements cannot).

The possibilities for applying the concept of tolerance to the subject matter at hand are endless; if the concept is central to what you are teaching, you will find many opportunities to design follow-up activities. We have offered these suggestions just to get you thinking creatively about the many applications you and your students can think up.

In summary, there are literal definitions (those we identify with the help of Webster's dictionary) and cultural definitions (those pictures we perceived when we first learned the concept at home or at school); these definitions affect every concept we teach. Helping students identify both definitions (the words of the left brain and the pictures of the right brain) increases their total understanding and allows them to create a "Gestalt" for the concept. In the case above, students learned that the literal definition of "tolerance" (the capacity to endure unfavorable environments, to sympathize or empathize with the beliefs and practices of those who differ from us, and to allow a deviation from the standardized norm) has attendant pictures with it (the image of the Church, personal images of acceptance, and social dividends that come with allowing and welcoming differences in perspectives, goals, tasks, and viewpoints). Both the cognitive and aesthetic dimensions of the concept are enhanced and clarified; these two levels of perceived meaning (what we know logically and what we have experienced in terms of cultural images) then become integrated and expand to a more consciously recognized definition of what we mean by being tolerant.

This multistage process will allow any given concept to expand the student's awareness, awaken a personal sense of new images, and add new meanings for commonly held beliefs; simultaneously, it will develop clearer limits and definitions to the specific content areas we seek to teach and help our students comprehend.

This process, which both expands and contracts the student's conceptual awareness, also prepares each student for the realization that information (concepts and factual information) can be learned, not just memorized—that learning can occur through creative, image-related activities. This process of looking at literal and cultural perceptions also teaches the student to value his or her own experiential and metaphoric sources of knowledge. Examining literal definitions of concepts in terms of personal experiences with these same concepts places "life" knowledge on an equal plane with "book" knowledge.

In metaphoric teaching, the brain of image experience is the key to the brain of analytical information; in a cyclical fashion, each ultimately influences the other. This is the essence of the method, the method originally based upon a learning model that incorporates experience and information into a concept-oriented learning strategy. This model, the experiential learning model, is the subject of the next chapter.

## BIBLIOGRAPHY

Lakoff, George, and Johnson, Mark. *Metaphors We Live By*. Chicago: University of Chicago Press, 1980.

Salk, Jonas. *The Survival of the Wisest*. New York: Harper and Row, 1973.

Taylor, C., and Ellison, R. "Moving Toward Working Models in Creativity: Utah Creativity Experiences and Insights." In Irving Taylor and J. W. Getzels, *Perspective in Creativity*. Chicago: Aldine, 1975.

# CHAPTER 5

# The Experiential Learning Model

## A LOOK FORWARD

It is a long trail from Aristotle's counsel that "the greatest thing by far is to be metaphorical . . . that to metaphorize well is a sign of genius because (this ability) implies intuitive perception of the similarity inherent in the dissimilar." (Poetics, 1459a 3–8),* to today's classroom where students are learning to compare complex concepts to systems of nature, metaphors of experience, and models of creative imagery. But as has been noted in previous chapters, this metaphoric path has been traveled often by history's greatest teachers, statesmen, and historical leaders. Jesus of Nazareth, William Pitt, Otto von Bismarck and countless others intuitively grasped the power of relating their messages to human experience through the use of a familiar image; their metaphors are still powerful instructional tools for wisdom and insight. How quickly we grasp Jesus's fitting of "a camel through the eye of a needle," Pitt's "parks are the lungs of England," and Bismarck's "War can only be carried out through . . . blood and iron." Over and over, political, religious, and educational leaders have captured our minds with metaphors; metaphors that explain and expand philosophical treaties, spiritual revelations, didactic prose, political world views.

Few of the eulogies which were delivered immediately after the assassination of Dr. Martin Luther King, Jr., failed to mention his "I Have Been to the Mountain" speech. The speech was a metaphoric summary of a committed man's lifelong struggle; in the speech, King spoke eloquently and emotionally of not fearing death because he had experienced the ecstasy of his own life's worth—a moment of total self fulfillment captured in the metaphoric phrase, "I have been to the mountain." With simple clarity and overpowering force, the metaphor expresses King's faith in the purposefulness of the climb. In fact, the secret of the metaphor lies in the expanding impact of its crystalline image; the metaphoric image extends our perceptions, our understand-

---

*This famous quote from Aristotle is often rendered, "But the greatest thing by far is to be master of the metaphor" rather than "But the greatest thing by far is to be metaphorical." The Greek: to "metaphorikon einai" literally means "to be metaphorical," to see life experience as a metaphor rather than merely to use a metaphor to convince readers.

ings, and our explanations—it creates a picture of the message we seek to communicate.

Strangely, our search for a basic strategy to develop an instructional model for right-brain imagery began with only a vague appreciation of the power of the metaphor; our search actually began with an effort to create a teaching model that would increase concept facility with middle school students who were being taught by first-semester student teachers. Only when we had already designed a working model for these metaphoric lessons did we realize that the metaphor is continually used in the writings and teachings of history's great leaders. Our research, therefore, began not with conscious awareness of the almost serendipitous power of the metaphor, but rather with the adaptation of a recent theoretical model—the experiential learning model.

First articulated in the work of Kurt Lewin in the late 1940s, the experiential learning model resurfaced in studies by Kolb in the mid-1970s. Our acceptance of its basic tenets dramatically changed the ways in which we taught our students both in the college classroom and in the public school.* Kolb's model provides a conceptual link for relating recent discoveries in educational theory with the ancient, proven, teaching methods. For example, both the old methods and new models share the view that learning is cyclic in nature; both the ancient teacher and modern experiential researcher share the assumption that learning is an integrated process, integrated not only in terms of subject matter, but also in terms of thoughts, behaviors, and feelings. This chapter, then, focuses on the experiential learning model and its specific relationship to metaphoric teaching.

## THE EXPERIENTIAL LEARNING MODEL

We once visited a classroom in Eugene, Oregon, where the teacher had assured us she was doing an "experiential learning" lesson—and, indeed, to a point, she was. She had booked the district's school bus each Wednesday morning for six consecutive weeks, had reached an agreement with other teachers in her building regarding student schedules, and was taking her eighth-grade social studies class on a series of career education visits to various retail outlets in the area for the purpose of exploring career opportunities available to her students when they graduate.

---

*Kolb's basic tenet is: "Immediate concrete experience is the basis for observation and reflection. These observations are assimilated into a theory from which new implications for action can be deduced. These implications or hypotheses then serve as guides interacting to create new experiences." (Kolb, 1975, p. 1)

After each field trip the class would return to the school, and during the next class session, they would discuss the career opportunities observed during the trip. That was it. There were no other experiential activities in the career education curriculum. To this teacher, as to many others, experiential learning meant just that—having an experience, usually a field trip or a "hands-on" laboratory lesson.

There had been a lot of logistical planning and effort in this lesson; it was obvious that the teacher knew the value of actual experience and the total integration it can provide the learner. However, with a few additional tools, this unit and additional experiential lessons could have been greatly enhanced. What our teacher did not know is that experiential learning does not have to be confined to actual "doing." Experiential learning can be brought into the classroom through the minds and imagination of the learners. Students do not have to leave the building to gain a sense of actual contact; the mind can provide the experience almost as realistically as the actual setting. The mind is a storehouse, even in the youngest learner, of incredible information and experience.

Two factors could immediately enrich this lesson on career education: first, a conceptual understanding of experiential learning, knowing what's involved in helping the learner gain maximum understanding of the experience at hand; second, supplemental classroom metaphoric exercises to increase personal awareness of values and preferences toward specific careers.

How could an understanding of the experiential learning model and metaphoric lesson planning aid our teacher's instruction? Let's look at Kolb's model and how it applies to metaphoric teaching. It suggests definite implications for classroom teachers. It differs from many current instructional models in a number of significant ways:

1. Students are not merely given subject matter information (although understanding of subject matter is important to the model).
2. The basis of the learning is concrete experience.
3. Time for reflection and integration is built into the lesson.
4. Generalizations are derived from real experience; experience is not seen as a future moment when the present generalizations might be applicable.

Kolb's work was not done with classroom teachers as a primary focus; rather, his interest lay in theories of group process. But he was very close to a model that would meet the needs of classroom teachers. We adapted the model with the following results.

The attractiveness of this revised model is its simplicity and general adaptability to most classroom settings; for our purposes, the meta-

**Kolb's Experiential Learning Model (1975)**

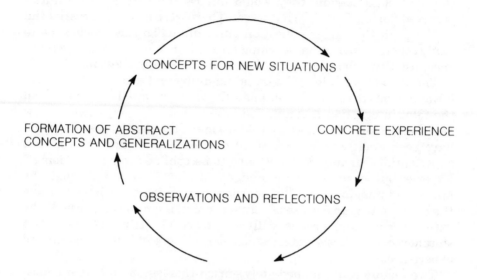

phoric method fits well within its broad tenets. The following examination of each of the four components of this model (focus, experience, assessment, integration) is intended to help you better understand how experiential learning merges well with metaphoric teaching to adapt to the needs of your classroom. The cycle of these four components repeats itself synergistically as students are encouraged to experience and become aware of the concepts they are learning.

## The First Phase: The Focus

The *focus moment* precedes the lesson and functions as a conceptual advance organizer (Ausbel, 1963);* the advance organizer, presented before the actual lesson begins, introduces, in "capsulized form," the overall concept, idea, or thought to be covered during the lesson. In our example of the career education unit, the advance organizer would provide a perspective from which to view the experience of the field

---

*The advance organizer "sets the stage" for the lesson to be taught; in a mini-lesson form, the advance organizer explains the import, scope, and overall concept that underlies the lesson at hand. It helps the learner know what is coming next, how the instruction fits into the subject matter as a whole, and why the lesson about to be experienced is important to the understanding of the concept as a whole.

We have found that the use of a metaphoric image as an advance organizer is effective, motivating, and highly efficient. Students are quickly focused upon the concept they are learning and how this concept works.

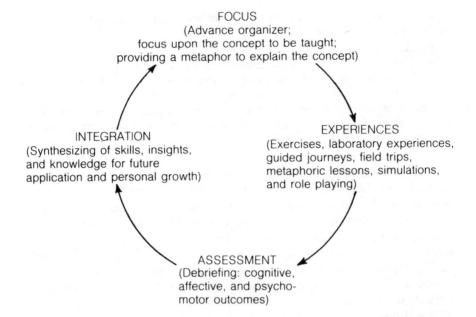

FOCUS
(Advance organizer;
focus upon the concept to be taught;
providing a metaphor to explain the concept)

INTEGRATION
(Synthesizing of skills, insights,
and knowledge for future
application and personal growth)

EXPERIENCES
(Exercises, laboratory experiences,
guided journeys, field trips,
metaphoric lessons, simulations,
and role playing)

ASSESSMENT
(Debriefing: cognitive,
affective, and psycho-
motor outcomes)

trip. Consider the following perspectives and their accompanying focus metaphors:

"Today, we will be looking at examples of management careers in retail business settings."

This means we will be visiting several stores and looking for the ways people manage each other in each store setting. In a way, it's a lot like visiting a protected wilderness, where the "animal" species we are observing is MAN. As we visit each store, see if you can spot the leader of the pack and what that person is doing.

What differences in leadership style can be seen on this field trip? Are some store managers a lot like lions? Others like bull elephants? And, others like lookout gazelles? Identify the management styles you see operating in this "human wilderness" we are visiting today.

or

"Today, we will be watching for the ways the jobs we are observing are interdependent upon one another."

If we were looking at animals in the African veldt, how would each animal's position depend upon the other animals all around him? Do some animals need certain other animals to survive?

Think of the ways the jobs we see on this field trip are very similar. How do these jobs depend upon one another for survival in the "business veldt"? How is the interdependence of the business world similar and dissimilar to the interdependence of the African veldt?

or

"Today, we will be looking for how many different jobs are actually connected to the daily functions of a bank."

Think for a moment what it would be like if we were to visit a rain forest today. How many different large animals could we find in one acre of forest? In a way, we will be doing something similar in our visit to the bank today.

Let's try to identify all the roles and positions that we can find in this "human rain forest." We will need to look closely for all the jobs, both visible and not so visible. How many different jobs are there in this acre of human beings—this acre in a "people forest" called a bank?

Advance organizers are important to concept formation; they provide an "anchor" where information and ideas received during the instructional period can be attached. Using advance organizers seems to cause the brain to "agree" to program the new information and ideas under a specific memory topic; information, skills, and insights are then mentally "filed" with the same basic retrieval system—namely, under the focus concept of the lesson. Subsequently, new knowledge is added to what the learner already knows about the subject being discussed, and the lesson further refines and clarifies the concept in terms of the subject matter at hand.

In a way, advance organizers work in similar fashion to the threads on a stove bolt; they are the critical elements in fastening new knowledge to what is already known. They are the beginning of integrating the information with the concept; each thread on the bolt represents something the learner already knows from previous experience or study. Advance organizers in this eighth-grade social studies class would remind the students of things they know about interdependent systems: previously learned information from other classes, from television and from their families.

Choosing appropriate advance organizers requires careful thought as to what you want to teach. The following suggestions are helpful in identifying the focus for any lesson; we have used the "career education" lesson as an example.

1. *Identify the basic concept to be presented.*
   Each lesson has several basic ideas or thoughts that could be explored. Choose one of these and use it to help the students gain an overall focus for the lesson. Any of the following topics could be the basic concept of the "career education" lesson:
   A. Students will learn to identify basic personnel procedures.
   B. Students will compare quantity of tasks assigned each worker with quality of task performance.
   C. Students will determine their own feelings and attitudes towards the jobs they are observing.

D. Students will compare the salaries and relative job benefits in the various retail outlets they visit.

There are countless possible foci for any given lesson; it is important to the learning process that you single out the most appropriate focus, the one that summarizes what you want your students to learn. Once you have identified the focus, the next step is to provide a metaphoric advance organizer as well.

2. *Start at the concept level and provide metaphoric examples.*

A metaphoric example will help the students see "the big picture." It helps them identify the *pattern* of the activity they are about to have.

A. *Personnel Procedures*

Think of the management strategies that a head lion uses for keeping the whole pride at work. Then, think of the very different management strategies used by a head chimpanzee who is keeping the whole chimpanzee colony at work.

How many different personnel procedures are used in each group we find in our human wilderness? Do these management strategies vary from department to department? Why?

B. *Quantity of Task versus Quality of Performance*

If we were to look over the different roles inside the "lion pride" or the "chimpanzee colony," who would do the same jobs most of the time? Who would have the most important tasks? Who has a task where the quality is more vital to the whole group than the amount of times the task is done?

C. *Personal Feelings and Attitudes*

Is there a difference in our world between being like a lion and being like a lioness? How do you feel about these differences? How would you personally feel if you were beginning on the bottom of the career ladder? If you were in a middle management level? If you were the head of the company? Would your style be like . . . a lion? A gazelle? An eagle? or ___?

D. *Relative Salaries and Job Benefits*

What's the difference in the wilderness between leading a lion pride and leading a chimpanzee colony? What benefits go to the lion? What benefits go to the chimpanzee? Is there a price that the lion pays? Is there a different price that the chimpanzee pays?

In each role, there are built-in job benefits and built-in liabilities. For instance, everyone fears the lion. And it's easier to capture the chimpanzee—or is it? In today's field trip, look for the leadership roles in each store; how many different kinds of groups do you see? How do the leaders differ? What are the job benefits and prices each different kind of leader enjoys and pays?

3. *Compare the concept with information or experiences that the students already have.*

   This process helps students connect what is being experienced with past knowledge and experience.

   A. *Personnel Procedures* may be similar to classroom rules or the "laws of the jungle."

   B. *Quantity versus Quality Issues* can be seen in terms of homework assignments or the differing activities carried out by members of the chimpanzee colony.

   C. *Personal Feelings and Attitudes* can be compared to the first dance the student ever attended or to the possible attitudes of being a lion, a boa constrictor or a zebra—coping with life in the jungle.

   D. *Job Benefits* will relate directly to student career goals. What are the benefits of going to college? Of vocational training? Armed Services? Your own family business? Job benefits can also be linked to the differences in being the "head" animal versus one of the group being led. What's the difference between being the dominant male lion or a member of the pride? Of being the queen bee or a worker bee? The "head" zebra or a member of the herd?

   These comparisons yield valuable perspectives on the long term versus short term issues of job performance and job selection.

4. *After using the advance organizer as a focus, expand the basic focus with more specific suggestions.*

   Begin by introducing the general concept, and then follow with specific perceptual cues that your students can look for:

   A. *Personnel procedures*—"Try to notice how people communicate with one another and whether or not this communication changes when they talk to their boss."

   B. *Quantity versus quality*—"How many times does the same behavior get repeated versus a single behavior enacted once a day but directly affecting the overall functions of everyone in the department?"

   C. *Personal feelings*—"Today, we'll be exploring our own feelings towards selling; as you watch people doing their jobs, try to imagine how you would be feeling if you were doing that job."

   D. *Job benefits*—"If you had the job and its pay, could you go home at night without work to do? Would you spend your weekends at the office? What freedom comes with a salaried position? Which freedom would you prefer?"

   Encourage your students to look for unexpected insights. The way employees punch their time cards, joke or don't joke on the job, spend "break time"—all these behaviors can reveal important subtle information.

Whether you are teaching the necessity of personnel procedures, the delegation of job assignments, the awareness of personal attitudes, or the hidden benefits of job definitions, you'll find these anecdotal observations invaluable.

In summary, using a focus moment—a time to introduce the advance organizer for the lesson—can provide huge dividends in terms of the learning process. It helps each student perceive the conceptual purpose of the instructional activity (in this case, the field trip). This perception of purpose, then, prompts a conscious awareness of subsequent experience, insights and information-gathering; new knowledge can be mentally "filed" as clarifying the concept to be mastered. Using advance organizers, then, helps the information "make sense" to the learner; perception is focused, not arbitrary and disorganized. Once the pattern is established by the metaphoric focus you provide, new information enhances the pattern; the logic of the lesson becomes more apparent; the student knows WHY he or she is learning the lesson.

## The Second Phase: The Experience

At first thought, providing classroom experience is not earthshakingly new. Much of what happens in schools involves doing: whether students are reading books, writing papers, or taking tests, they are rarely inactive. Yet, all of us have had the nagging feeling that something was missing; for example, we know that, by themselves, repeated time tests in multiplication facts do not (innately) increase student motivation to do more tests. We would like to suggest that what is often missing in conventional instruction is the utilization of the affective feelings, insights and images of the individual student—that is, the involvement of the learner in a total learning process, where two brain hemispheres are considered and integrated. This process focuses both the logical, analytical brain and the image, conceptual brain.

Using feelings and images (metaphors) to enhance conceptual understanding is not merely teaching students to express their feelings and attitudes; rather, this method will create a working pattern in each student's mind as to how the concept and subject matter are related. "Doing" becomes more than repeating classroom activities long ago labelled by the student as "boring." Doing can become an actual encounter with what's being learned, whether it is a real life experience or a simulated experience within the individual student's mind.

In the experiential learning model, mastery of the concept depends primarily upon the design of the *experience* that follows the initial *focus*. In the eighth-grade social studies class, visiting the retail outlet stores provided ideal experiences to explore potential career directions.

However, there were other experiences available: the students could have journeyed in their minds to stores they knew and later compared these experiences with the real thing; they could have revisited the field trip stores in their minds to discover additional feelings and details they had forgotten; they could have role played the communication they saw between employer and employee, between customer and clerk, between their teacher and themselves. They could have used natural metaphors to understand the environment of the store: was the store like a bee hive? Like a rabbit warren? Like a hurricane? Or like a hot, dull summer afternoon?

Perhaps we can better explain this experiential component and its potential with the following case history which happened to us a few years ago.

Late one Thursday afternoon while working with a group of fourth-grade teachers designing new curriculum, we found ourselves stymied in responding to teachers who wanted desperately to give their students a sense of the incredible variety of life under the surface of the ocean. Obviously, we couldn't take the students scuba diving; films were a possibility, but basically passive; illustrated books did not even come close to the sense of awe the teachers sought. Then one teacher mentioned an idea he had seen in a popular magazine for elementary teachers.

We took two large sheets (25-feet long, 20-feet wide) of clear plastic and used duct tape to attach them to one another. Next, we cut a small hole in the side of the plastic and put a large house fan into the opening. Turning the fan on full power, we inflated the "bubble" into a large semi-transparent plastic bag. Then, we cut a three-foot slit in the bag and put duct tape on either side of the slit. We brought in two film projectors with undersea footage and sound, an overhead projector with transparencies of underwater scenes, and two automatic slide projectors with slide cartridges of sea life. The bubble accommodated seven students at a time. Anxiously, we turned on the machines and temporarily sealed the entrance. The results were incredible! Schools of fish seemed to dance on one side of the plastic while sea anenomes flowed gently across the other; sharks, barracuda, and manta rays appeared to swim menacingly only a few feet away. It was all there, the beauty, the mystery, the danger of being underwater.

At the time, we thought that this experience was unobtainable in any other way, short of renting a submersible or swimming with heavy scuba gear. We did not yet know that metaphoric teaching could approximate similar conditions. (We should add, as well, that the bubble later surrendered to the enthusiasm of an excited young learner who got overly involved watching antelope and elephants scurry across the African grasslands; it was never reconstructed.)

With a guided fantasy experience, a very similar awareness could have been created. Because Jacques Cousteau and James Bond, "Wild Kingdom." and Walt Disney, PBS specials and *Raiders of the Lost Ark* have already provided a vast image bank of working metaphors for our students to draw upon, they can enjoy an encounter with the ocean's depths without ever leaving their desks. The guided fantasy simply brings the images into focus; it allows the students to build and expand on the information and pictures already available in their minds.

It is important to note that we are not claiming that students can experience phenomena and environments for which they have no information, for example, asking them to imagine life on Mars (it would greatly resemble life on Earth or a science fiction movie they have seen). What we are claiming is that given visual clues and brief past experiences (from books, movies, or television), students can conjure up an encounter in the mind that allows them to feel and envision the totality of the ocean, the African veldt, or the busy urban marketplace; that their minds are ready image resources for a directed, enriching mental journey which you, the teacher, can prompt, focus, stimulate, and shape.

The experience phase of the model thus includes a metaphoric or real activity in which thoughts (sea anenomes may look like swaying flowers but are really live animals), feelings (it is scary underwater), and skills (my sense of balance changes while I am floating underwater) are integrated within the learning activity. The student's brain is fully stimulated; learning potential is exponentially increased.

Think of the instructional possibilities inherent in the experience phase of this learning model. Reading about the ancient city of Zimbabwe is, by nature, passive, but staging a dramatization of the event or taking a guided image journey to Zimbabwe's city center becomes an active learning process; thoughts, actions, and feelings can be combined, a total experience can be created. Most teachers find that seatwork with math problems increases student ability to add fractions, but it seldom captures student enthusiasm or attention. They also find that providing a learning center where actual fraction pieces are assembled and manipulated involves the student totally and often motivates even the slowest learner.*

This does not mean we should neglect the proven and useful methods of classroom instruction that we have found effective; we do not suggest discarding techniques long used and proven valuable—techniques such as the presentation of math problems in workbooks, the use of vocabulary recall examinations, the assignment of information topics for

---

*This motivation is daily evidenced in "electronic" games and the enthusiasm they generate.

essay writing. What we are advocating, however, is that these methods be supplemented, augmented, enriched by the regular use of experiential exercises—particularly the metaphoric lesson. Our rationale lies in the basic truth that the student who journeys as a virus to the nerve cells of the human body, that the class who nonverbally experiences empathy in a "shoe" walk (p. 213), and those parents who envision a day in the life of their child at school during a guided fantasy, all share something in common—a deeper, more lasting understanding of the concept and information being learned.

The activities of Phase II in the Experiential Learning Model, then, are essential to discovering how the focus concept works, how it feels, how it can be experienced. Experience is at the heart of metaphoric teaching; it provides the data bank for conceptual learning. Active attention to this phase of the lesson will bring new insights for you as a teacher, will increase creativity in your classroom, and will renew your enjoyment of the curriculum being presented.

Although integrated experience is the heart of metaphoric teaching, it does not by itself make for effective instruction. Whether we take a guided mental journey or stage a dramatization of a famous event, we are experiencing a total learning moment when all three domains (the cognitive, the affective, and the psychomotor) work together. This learning, however, will not surface consciously and coalesce into awareness unless the next two phases of the experiential learning model are also implemented.

## The Third Phase: The Assessment

The question "What did we learn?" is an important element in capturing what has been experientially presented in Phase II. *Assessment* itself takes many forms: writing a paper, role playing what has just happened, taking a quiz, or *debriefing** through questions and discussion. Although "debriefing" has become a 1980s buzzword in education, its importance should not be discounted. Too often, "Let's debrief what we did today" is answered with "I liked it" or "I thought it went really well." And, too often, these responses become the sum total of the debriefing. Stopping at this basic level is selling the skill of debriefing short. Debriefing is a valuable skill that can enhance not only metaphoric teaching and experiential learning, but all teaching. As an instructional tool, it is as essential to the learning process as the advance organizer. Debriefing does not mean finding out whether the day went well; it means helping each student discover *what* he or she has felt,

---

*"Debriefing" refers to a questioning process that allows the teacher to assess the overall impact of the lesson—cognitively, affectively, and behaviorally.

thought, and experienced during the instructional activity. Debriefing extends learning in much the same way that watching the slides of your favorite vacation is always an expanding moment. Each time you see those slides, you discover something new (cognitive), gain a different perspective (affective), or think how you might better have taken that picture (psychomotor).

The key to debriefing (assessing the overall impact of the experience) is to pose questions that probe all three of these domains of the student's learning—cognition (new knowledge and information), affect (new feelings and values) and psychomotor development (new skills, behaviors, and actions). Timing of this assessment is a critical element; debriefing should occur immediately after the experiential activity.* To aid you in developing your own questions for such activities, we have included the following guidelines which we use regularly in our teacher in-service workshops:

1. *Use small group feedback first.*
   We usually begin any debriefing of the experience in groups of two or three. This allows participants to share their perceptions without fear of being somehow "wrong." This usually occurs either in a structured dyad or in group discussion.
   We've found that after people are comfortable with sharing their thoughts in a small group setting, they can share these insights with the total group far more easily.
   To prompt whole group sharing, we use either a clear transparency, butcher paper, or the blackboard to record their responses. The more people see their actual words recorded visibly in front of the group, the more they will continue to share. The process is similar to brainstorming; the facilitator must be careful not to edit the wording of the group members.
2. *Provide your own personal examples as a model for the discussion.*
   Self-disclosure should be used as an example of the instructions you want the class to follow.
   For example, if I ask you to consider your feelings as a seashell lying on the bottom of the ocean and to identify one insight these feelings give you, then I might add:

   "What comes to my mind is the sense of beauty all around me. I'm safe because there's no danger of my falling; the world I'm living in is incredibly beautiful—filled with so many living creatures and plants . . .

---

*Yes, frustrating as it may be, it is actually better to provide less of an experience (in length and scope) in order to allow adequate time for the debriefing questions to be considered.

"When I think more about this, I realize that a feeling of safety is important to me in my daily world—and that I am always attracted to what is aesthetically pleasing to me."

or

"Thinking of the ocean and the fate of the seashell makes me realize how many outside forces there are—the fish, the ocean currents, the scuba divers, the shifts in the ocean's floor. I wonder if I have any role at all: am I just a pawn in the total experience?"

"When I think about these feelings, I realize that a lot of my life involves observing, not doing. It seems like I keep waiting for things to happen—I rarely make the changes myself!"

When a personal example is given, the group can expand on the question; everyone has a bird's eye view of what's expected—vivid examples and responses often come forth.*
After giving such an example, always be sure to pose the question again.

"So, what I would like each of you to think about are the feelings you had as a sea shell on the bottom of the ocean floor. What insights can you gain from these feelings? . . . Now, would you share these thoughts with your partners (small group)?"

3. *Avoid questions that have all "yes" or "no" answers; use open-ended questions that do not have "right" or "wrong" responses.*
"Yes" or "no" answers stop the flow of ideas and the conscious reflection upon the instructional activity the students have experienced. Try to avoid questions like, "Do you have any thoughts or feelings about what we just experienced?" Answers to this question often include glazed looks and unthinking responses reflected in nodding or shaking of the head.

Do ask questions such as, "What were your thoughts or feelings about the exercise we just had? Why do you think you thought (felt) that way?" These questions prompt explanations and self disclosure, the conscious consideration of the experience that has just happened.

4. *Create a hypothetical context for your questions; it lessens the sense of personal threat and "wrong" perspectives.*
Some of the best debriefing questions involve totally hooking the curiosity and imagination of the right brain:

---

*A word of caution, however—never spend a long time on your own example. Its merit lies in the model it provides, not in the excitement you have for your own thoughts. Too overwhelming an example can cause students to discount their own thoughts.

"What does it feel like to be a virus inside the blue/red canal?"

"If you were a buyer for a large department store, what problems would be most difficult?"

"If you were to explain to your parents tonight what today's lesson was all about, what would you feel is the most important part to mention?"

"Thinking about the 'human bee hive' you saw today in the department store, who would you say was the queen bee? The worker bees? The drones? Which role would you like to have? Why?"

Expansion questions, that is, questions that call for imagination as well as logic in order to respond (Gallagher, 1963) are helpful in assisting students to debrief their thoughts, feelings, and newly developed skills. An expansion question such as "What might the schools do to save endangered species?" might encourage students to reveal otherwise "hidden" insights and information.

5. *Remember the "why" of the exercise as well as the "how."*
Debriefing is a time to return to the focus (the advance organizer) and the overall concept being taught. Take this time to determine if your students understand *why* they did the exercise and *how* it relates to their lives and what they've previously learned.

"As you remember, the focus of this lesson is learning *what happens when people CHANGE*. What have you now learned about the process of changing?"

"As we mentioned earlier, the focus of this lesson is *seeing the ocean as a huge underwater 'forest' of animals*. What have you now learned about the ocean that causes you to see the ocean differently?"

"We began this unit thinking about *the differences between quality of tasks accomplished and quantity of tasks assigned*. What is the difference, then, between the daily work of the store manager and the daily work of the salesclerk?"

Refocusing upon the concept underlying the lesson allows the student an opportunity to link the new thoughts and feelings with subject matter information that has been previously assimilated. It brings the learning full circle; it allows the experience to widen the learning "file" the student has created in his/her mind for this topic.

6. *Do make every effort to hear what your students are telling you; make certain that you acknowledge their comments and recognize their insights.*
We find that paraphrasing or repeating back to people as accurately as you can the insights they have shared is a powerful motiva-

tor. This does not mean that each comment should be repeated, but ideas that need clarifying or that you need to shorten for recording on the board are prime candidates for restatement.

In addition, try to "save" the "off-the-wall" comments; students (people in general, for that matter) do not like to be embarrassed by "wrong" answers; if the comment is a little "unusual," we do our utmost to find a context in which the comment is helpful and expands or prompts an insight in all of us; if a student were to say something like:

"Well, I just think the ocean can't be an underwater forest, because it has fish not animals!"

You could respond to this comment with something like:

"That's a good point, there is a difference between fish and animals, and the ocean is very different from a forest in many ways. But, what if we were to call the ocean a 'water forest,' which fish would be like a mountain lion? Which like deer?"

Certain elements are consistent products of a well-planned debriefing of experiential lessons; every debriefing should include the following points:

1. *Concepts* should be clarified and expanded.
2. *Experiences* should be viewed objectively in terms of what the students learned, felt, and gained in skills.
3. *Essential Information* should be reviewed and refocused.
4. *Attitudes and Values* should be respected, probed, and protected from peer judgment or cross-examination.

As the debriefing concludes, encourage summary statements for students regarding the overall experience; provide your own model of honest self-reflection; point out the benefits of open feedback from the class; and—take time to tie the parts together. The payoffs for you, the teacher, are immediate; you will be able to assess what your students have actually learned.

Remember, debriefing is a time to check and see if instructional goals are being met and if important points have been clearly identified; it is not a time to "correct" with grading as the objective. Making debriefing a quiz defeats its overall purpose. Rather, encourage questions from both learner and teacher, a time for all to respond to and probe the new knowledge. With such purpose, debriefing becomes a shared moment that increases mutual understanding and causes insights to be generated.

Remember that central to the process of debriefing is the expanding of self-awareness; it is a process of prompting insight and extending each student's conscious thoughts about the activity he or she has just experienced. Every comment is an opportunity for more conceptual understanding. Every observation is a challenge for increased perspective. As the whole class actively listens to one another, the Phase II Experience and the Phase I Focus of the lesson merge and become more than the sum of their parts.

You will know the debriefing is succeeding when the smiles, raised hands, and general enthusiasm for insights actually capture the mood of the class. For as students learn to use insight as an assessment tool (to become consciously aware of personal knowledge as a valid outcome of experience), a wonderful moment of conscious learning and introspection occurs; shared, these moments have a synergy that touches everyone, and, as was discussed in Chapter 1, these moments of insight serve as preludes to the moment of illumination—a moment critical to creative thinking.

## The Fourth Phase: The Integration

At first impression, the *moment of personal integration*—the actual choice to internalize what has been learned and apply it to other topics and life experiences—seems like a moment totally beyond our control. To a degree, it is true that the moment is personal and one of free choice for the student: "I may have to tell you what you want to hear, but, in the end, I don't have to believe it, use it, or apply it to my life."* However, as we learn more and more about the brain and how it works, we are discovering that experiences can have a powerful impact on individual subconscious goal-setting and conceptualization. Debriefed experiences increase this impact; the "tapes" can be stored for conscious access.

Thus, while it is true that we do not have the power to force a student to value his or her own insights with family and friends, we can facilitate personal "ownership" of new knowledge by preparing additional lessons to incorporate the basic concept and expand the implications of its metaphor. The Change/Butterfly lesson can be enriched by another unit—a unit on "growth" or the metaphoric "Reaping of the Harvest." The Perspective/Time Movie lesson can be reinforced with units on "Nature's Clocks," "Cultural Historical Markers," or other "movies" of moments in history. Each experiential lesson has the potential to be more than itself; each lesson can become a link in an ever-expanding

---

*All of us remember courses where we threw away all vestiges of the course in the attempt to erase a painful memory from our minds.

network of conceptual bridges that extend the understanding of our students.

Debriefing is naturally followed by *integration;* parts of the lesson will naturally "stick." You'll hear students saying, "I get it!" And after such moments, they will want to apply "it." In the integration phase, we actively recognize the student's need to pose new problems, ideas, and contexts for the concept and experiences they have had; we encourage their pleasure in using the new knowledge, the new attitudes, and the new skills. The design of appropriate homework can reinforce this learning; we need to see homework and class projects as opportunities to allow personal incubation to occur, to stretch the present learning moment, to apply the concept to new materials, new topics, new ideas, and new experiences.

Personal integration occurs, however, whether you plan for it or not. Students will informally discuss the lesson while they walk down the hall; parents will tell you how much their child enjoyed the "ocean" lesson or the "butterfly" lesson; student will offer to help you prepare additional metaphoric lessons. You will find that, as your students develop a sense of shared learning, they'll begin to bring in images needed for metaphoric lessons; they'll monitor class role-playing; they'll want to write class plays; they'll find community resource people. Experiential learning means involvement; coupled with metaphoric organizers, experiential learning enhances every instructional unit, excites the learner, and allows the individual to truly internalize the concept and subject matter being presented.

*Encourage the valuing of these experiences by following up on student suggestions.* Try to plan your unit flexibly so that you can take advantage of student enthusiasm and willingness to be involved with their own learning. When students approach the next similar subject topic, they will have a heightened understanding of the concept they are exploring; there will be an excitement for the personal experiences and insights they can rightfully anticipate.

A survey of retail outlets can prompt inquiry into labor unions; an ocean experience can stimulate interest in the desert; the metamorphosis of the butterfly can create curiosity toward the molting of the lobster; the "time movie" can spark a visit to ancient Rome, a walk with Napoleon on the island of Elba, or a ride in H.G. Wells' time machine. The connections are all around you and your students—as you teach them to share those personal connections, you all grow. The classroom can automatically renew itself with each new topic, and each new inquiry can be an exciting hunt for knowledge.

A visit to the business "rabbit warren" (the retail department store) can, in turn, suggest another visit—a visit to a corporate "fox den" (a management headquarters) or an in-depth look at the business "game wardens" (the union representatives). Using the Change/Butterfly lesson to introduce an instructional unit on the Reconstruction of the South can be followed with a unit on the petrochemical "flowers" that now provide a home for the butterfly (Houston, Dallas, and Atlanta). Comparing the ocean to a "watery jungle" can help students study the roles of the hunter and the hunted (or examine the plight of the fast-becoming-extinct whale).

Metaphoric possibilities are endless; each focus metaphor will suggest additional metaphors and students will continually discover more and more workable metaphors for the concepts they are learning. Often the subject matter will lend itself easily; the key lies in allowing students to explore the metaphoric image at hand, to "play" with its available insights, to welcome the challenge of improbable connections, and to value the personal energy that comes with true understanding.

Whether we use metaphors to explain the focus of an experiential learning lesson or use the metaphoric lesson to facilitate concept mastery, metaphors consistently produce results that are many times more powerful than one would anticipate. The metaphoric focus with its image-rich experience automatically encourages self-assessment and personal integration; designed as a total process, these four components challenge and excite the part of the learner's mind most untapped by classroom instruction—the brain's right hemisphere.

Focus, experience, assess, and integrate—this cyclical process reinforces conceptual understanding, generates intuitive ability to apply what is learned, and spawns a growing sense of personal enjoyment, freedom, and power. At the center of this process is an ongoing synergy of IMAGES, images that allow the student to experience the implications of the lesson, to internalize how the concept works in real life, and to organize in advance for the information the lesson will provide.

These images can be the products of a real life experience (a field trip, a role-play, a simulation game, or a laboratory exercise), or these images can be the spontaneous products of the metaphor. It is with the metaphor that an internal experience is prompted, an internal experience that expands cyclically outward and elicits the experiential learning already stored within the student's own mind.

This internal awareness—carefully focused, consciously experienced, personally assessed, and individually integrated—is the core process of the experiential learning model; thus this model enhances the metaphoric method conceptually, for it provides a working road map for each metaphoric lesson we design and teach our students. With this map in hand, we can enjoy our journey, stop to explore the special moments of insights, and know we will reach the instructional goals we have set before us.

## BIBLIOGRAPHY

Ausbel, D. *The Psychology of Meaningful Learning.* New York: Grune and Stratton, 1963.

Gallagher, James, and Aschner, M. "A Preliminary Report on Analyses of Classroom Interaction." *The Merrill Palmer Quarterly of Behavior and Development* 9, No. 3 (1963): 183–194.

Kolb, David A., and Fry, Ronald. "Toward an Applied Theory of Experiential Learning." In Cary Cooper (ed.), *Theories of Group Processes.* New York: Wilegard Sons, 1975.

# The Metaphor as a Measuring Tool

James A. Joseph, one of the U.S. representatives attached to the United Nations, tells of a village along the banks of a great West African river. For centuries, the people of this village had sailed their boats on the river, fished its waters, and traded for miles and miles up and down the river. The villagers built their boats, developed their tools, reared and educated their children for the life of a river culture; then, one day, as Joseph tells it,

They discovered that a few miles upstream, men were constructing a huge dam that would soon dry up the river. Suddenly, the villagers' design for the future, the educational strategies upon which their survival had been based, were dangerously out of date! Tomorrow would no longer be a repeat of "yesterday."

Indeed, this village is a reflection of the contemporary American situation; "up river" in our government, economy, and communication systems, there are tremendous changes taking place—changes in our resources, changes in our economic needs, changes in our vocational options. More and more flexibility is needed to respond to these changes, and this flexibility (which so many find frightening) is a natural product of "right brain," creative, metaphoric thinking.

Fortunately, just at the time when such flexibility is critical to our culture's survival, we are discovering the very source that can free our locked-in notions of the past. We are discovering that this key is the metaphor, a ready image we can use to access the conceptual creativity of our students. We *can teach* students to use new knowledge in everyday settings; we *can give* our young people tools to cope with the "dam" when the river is about to disappear. And, this new awareness (that information learned in school does apply to life) can significantly motivate and increase their desire to learn, can channel their energy to solve the difficult problems of our age, and can renew their enthusiasm toward the future.

For those of us who have always maintained that "understanding what the lesson is all about" is an important instructional goal, there now is a tool to "measure" that understanding. Regardless of the new concept you are teaching (interdependence of cell activity, tolerance for cultural diversity, courtesy for those around us, co-optation in military

147

strategies, checks and balances in democratic monarchy, osmosis in plants, or square roots in math), students can show you they understand the concept by giving real life metaphors for how the concepts work:

Interdependence can be like the interaction of a bicycle's parts—creating power and energy for movement.

Tolerance can be likened to the acceptance of many different plants in the garden, each having its own season and contribution to the overall well-being of both the garden and the gardener.

Courtesy can be seen as morning dew that encourages each flower to open its petals and enjoy the sunlight.

Co-optation can be viewed as the strategies behind a well-designed mouse trap—baiting the trap is integral to entrapping the mouse.

Democratic monarchy can be like the liberty found inside a bee hive —freedom within defined roles and clear expectations.

Osmosis can be explained as a process that resembles a sponge.

Square roots can be compared to center beams in a four-sided house.

Every concept we teach has potential pictures for the right brain to see and to understand; these holistic images are ready sources for expanding the student's ability to master the given concept, apply it appropriately, and challenge its underlying assumptions. In the end, they produce flexibility of thought, curiosity towards the given, and natural excitement for learning.

Personal growth and self awareness are also expanded with the use of the metaphor. Consider this focus metaphor:

A hammock is swinging lazily in the breeze while your friend finishes the yardwork. Are you the hammock or are you the breeze? Which role do you play in your friend's life?

As the hammock, the student may feel quiet and worn from continually supporting the friend; as the breeze, the student may feel strong and invaluable in fanning the friend; or the "hammock" may realize that he or she is sad, because the friend is working and not playing; the "breeze" may feel ignored or undervalued. The benefit lies in the discovery of unknown attitudes and feelings; comparing actions, knowledge, and feelings to the metaphoric image allows students to gain a tool for communicating with their own right brains. The images are active; they are alive with perception; they are both flexible and creative.

Metaphoric images are never stationary; they hold the potential to expand into scenarios, to allow new views of relationships, to transcend their original parameters. And, metaphors can be motivators as well; we can decide to change what the hammock is doing—to change the breeze and give it a new role.

The metaphor combines image with logic; it extends the potential of the world around us; in the metaphor, we glimpse our own passivity or involvement. We can view our own actions and those of others around us, and we can choose to change the picture we see. We can decide to become a hammock where our friend can relax and find strong support; we can decide to be a strong, refreshing breeze for those around us; or we can look for friends who will be our "hammocks" and provide us with "cool breezes." These images help us restructure our self image; they become symbols by which the right brain can "speak" to us and influence our perceptions of ourselves and those around us.

Synergy (the synthesis of several sources of energy) exists when all the parts of a system work together to create an effect greater than the sum total of each independent element working alone. Metaphors induce this synergy; they extend the implications of any thought, feeling, or hunch. They encourage creative thinking and increase the number of possible insights in any learning situation; in essence, metaphors seduce the creative brain.

The metaphoric teaching method, therefore, actively uses imagery to help students identify the relationship between concept and subject matter; with the metaphor, students learn to explore the implications of a concept, to gain perspective on conceptual boundaries, and to develop advance organizers to guide in-depth study of the subject matter. The metaphor reveals the framework of the concept, its limits and its personal impact. Through metaphoric questioning such as: "In this situation, if you were the mouse being entrapped by the cheese, how would you feel?" students perceive personal attitudes, values, and perceptions simultaneously. They learn co-optation as a concept, but they also learn how co-optation must feel and the inherent, dormant rage that may later emerge. Such metaphors allow students to see relationships from perspectives other than their own; in fact, the metaphoric method actually induces self evaluation, introspection, and conceptual understanding.

Teaching techniques that actively employ the use of the metaphor are many; they include:

*The guided fantasy:* the mental journey that allows the student's mind to explore and experience activities the physical environment cannot provide.

*The metaphoric "warm-up":* the use of metaphoric advance organizers to "explain" with focus images what the lesson's concept is all about.

*The metaphoric "warm-down":* the closure moment in which the lesson is "summed up" with an active metaphoric image.

*Metaphoric interpersonal exercises:* short, small group exercises to check the comprehension and understanding of the concept being taught.

*Open-ended personal metaphor questions:* debriefing with metaphors to aid concept mastery, identification of personal feelings and attitudes, and prompting of creative perspective.

*The expanded metaphoric lesson:* the new teaching strategy you have already seen modeled in the "Change/Butterfly" lesson and the "Time Movie" lesson.

The expanded metaphoric lesson introduces a complete teaching strategy—a strategy that can introduce a whole instructional unit, prompt an entirely new perspective on a concept already familiar to the student, or model new behaviors for classroom problem solving, scientific inquiry, or even interpersonal interaction. In actuality, the metaphor enhances any instructional strategy; from discussion to recitation, from role-playing to lecture, the possibilities for metaphoric teaching are all around us; we are, in fact, limited only by our own inability to see the images inherent in the lessons we teach.

The first part of this book, then, has explored the implications of using metaphors. We introduced a new teaching strategy (the expanded metaphoric lesson), we probed the right brain's role in defining concepts and words (the meaning of change), we introduced a six-step lesson for exploring a given concept's cultural definition (the lesson on tolerance), and we presented findings in the field of brain research and creativity that urge us, as educators, to immediately begin using metaphors in classroom instruction. We explored the metaphor's role in providing a creative experience with the subject matter being studied; we identified the metaphor's power to build upon the brain's own natural source of imagery—the right brain hemisphere. We discovered that the metaphor does, in fact, provide a bridge, a bridge that links the information of two hemispheres and creates a passageway for conscious exchange of reason and perception.

In Part II of this book, we present complete, generic metaphoric lessons that can be adapted for use at many grade levels; we also provide short "warm-ups" (advance organizers for many familiar instructional concepts) and "warm-down's" (closure metaphors for motivating students to continue their new knowledge and conceptual understanding). Behind all of this is the ever-expanding, creative elasticity of the right brain.

We have too long viewed "left-brain" skills, such as analysis, logical thought, sequential reasoning, and verbal expression, as the trunk of the tree we call education; it is time to re-assess this view. It is time to recognize that "right-brain" skills of synthesis, perception, imaging, and insight are equally valid for the growth of the tree and are the support of its branches that bear the fruits of creativity, concept attainment, and innovation.

As you read and examine Part II of this book, and as you prepare lessons that stress the value of insight, intuition, and concept attainment, you are joining a special group of people—people who have marked the trails of knowledge for centuries, who have left a wealth of information about the world in which we live. And, you are developing new intellectual tools: image tools your left brain will quickly learn to value and utilize. These are the creative tools that can respond flexibly to a fast-paced, changing society, to the split seconds of our human existence on this globe we call "earth." These new tools will, in the long run, be invaluable in assisting the "left-brain" tools we now rely upon: the tools that cope with the river in traditional ways. In order to respond to the newly dammed river as an opportunity, we must tap into the right brain's vision—we must see the future as images that can become, not facts that must be.

## BIBLIOGRAPHY

Joseph, James A. "Education for Citizenship vs. Training for Employment: The Misplaced Debate." Presented to IEL Policy Fellows, Washington, D.C. April 21, 1983.

# Creativity, the Metaphor, and the Integrated Brain: Classroom Application

Teachers are busy people! In elementary school, teachers are often responsible for teaching five, six, or even seven separate subjects daily; and in secondary school, five or six "preps" daily are not unusual. In addition, teachers are constantly confronted with meeting the individual needs of students; in fact, every class (every subject area) has students who need individualized attention, including the frequent design of individualized instruction. As teachers, we must continually prepare to meet these needs, and this almost insistent preparation time often detracts from our time (and ability) to be creative—in essence detracts from the time we need to explore new, innovative teaching strategies.

Indeed, as we respond to the instructional needs of "special" students (the gifted, the creative, the slow learners, the hyperactive, the troubled—the list goes on and on), preparation time seems to expand exponentially; eventually the need for order and system dominates. Creative hunches take time to explore, and time is a costly and precious resource in a demanding schedule.

Time is a constant concern of teachers. We try to save planning time by grouping students or we try to give attention to the overwhelming needs of our classes by teaching to the central needs of the entire class. But often this is impossible. In preparing for a fourth-grade math lesson, for example, we may (having assessed the needs of the students) find ourselves designing a basic fraction lesson for one student group, introducing two-digit multiplication to another, and reviewing the principle of "borrowing" in three-digit numerals with still a third group. Each group, then, needs at least a twenty-minute lesson, "seat work" for another thirty minutes, and "follow-up" work for the next day. All this can easily happen—just for the math lesson. Experientially, we are well aware, try as they might, teachers are busy people!

Metaphoric lessons, for all their dividends in terms of conceptual learning, creative enjoyment, and high motivational impact, do take time to prepare. For this reason, the lessons that follow in this second part of the book have been designed to be immediately useful in your class. Depending upon the grade level and sophistication of your students, you may wish to modify or expand the insight questions that follow each lesson, but the overall lesson can stand "as is" for the grade level indicated.* (Suggested instructional topics—particularly enhanced by the metaphoric lesson at hand—are included in each section as well.) The lessons themselves are our way of giving you, the busy teacher, a head start on the use of metaphoric lessons in your classroom. We have found (through both our own experiences and the reports of many in-service teachers) that the lessons are, indeed, "ready to go," that they really will save your preparation time. And, what's more—they can be used over and over.**

To assist you in developing your own metaphoric resources library, Part II has two major components: (1) a careful review of the instructional design process essential to the creation of a metaphoric lesson, and (2) developed examples of metaphoric lessons. The format and content of Part II rest on two assumptions: first, some of you will want to begin designing your own lessons immediately; second, some of you will want to try out a number of lessons before you commit yourself to the process of a full-scale design of your own original lessons. Part II, then, includes material designed to help you, whichever path you choose to begin the metaphoric teaching process.

---

*In fact, each lesson has been "field-tested," and the grade level appropriateness has been assessed, experientially explored, and defined. Except with gifted children, lessons designated for older students should be kept for higher grades (as indicated); many of the primary lessons, however, can be for everyone with just a little adjustment in insight questions and insight problems.

**Once a metaphoric lesson is developed, we have found it convenient to put the lesson, its text, props, and visual aids into a file box—marked "Change/Butterfly" lesson or "Perspective/Time Movie" lesson; using this process, we have built a small library of "instant" metaphoric lessons. In just a couple of years, you can easily develop such a library. One way to minimize your time commitment to developing these lessons is to utilize student help. If you teach your students what a metaphoric lesson is all about, they will often locate props, design appropriate guided fantasies (depending on their age), and even suggest questions that can link the metaphor with the subject matter they are studying.

# CHAPTER 6

# The Long Form:
# The Metaphoric Lesson
# as an
# Instructional Unit

## A LOOK FORWARD

It's Friday afternoon . . . Monday begins the new instructional unit in ecology. You mention to the class that next week, "We'll be looking at food chains and how nutrition relates to these chains."

Some students tell you, "We had that last year—it's all about animals eating other animals . . ." Others say, "Can't we do something that's fun?" Still others begin to tell you about "the food wheels we made last year."

You yourself begin to wonder—how sophisticated is their understanding of ecological linkages? Of nutritional protein reduction? Of their own role in the food chain? And, you ask yourself, isn't there a way to perk up this unit? A way to create a new perspective on their own food habits?

This process repeats itself over and over in classrooms; you, the teacher, know there is much to be learned in any instructional unit, many concepts to review in greater depth, many differing possible instructional goals depending upon the level of ability, past experience, and current motivation of each student. Your job is to diagnose, then design instruction; where the concept is already semi-internalized, you must reteach to overcome the confusion and lack of information that may be stumbling blocks to student progress.

How do you get started? Knowing you have a specific instructional unit with an overall concept you want to emphasize, how do you personally tackle the task of designing a special metaphoric lesson to introduce this unit? To guide you, Part II includes two basic metaphoric development forms: the long form (for the introduction of an instructional unit) and the short form (a condensed lesson plan).

Like the tax forms we fill out each year between February and April, these two forms represent different kinds of "trade offs." The short form is quicker and less time-consuming—but its "learning refund" is considerably less. Similar to the way that we can itemize deductions on the IRS long form, we can thoroughly explore a concept with the complete metaphoric lesson design. While the short form (with its compressed format and minimized planning time) meets an immediate need for quick design (and, as such, is very helpful), the long form meets a more comprehensive need—the need for instructional units that can be used each year as part of your own professional library. In truth, many teachers begin by developing the condensed lesson plan for the moment—then find themselves expanding this plan into a complete metaphoric lesson for the future. Like the IRS form, the more time you invest, the greater the return. Chapter 6, then, includes a thorough introduction and review of the process of writing the complete metaphoric lesson. Chapter 7 will explore the "short form."

## THE LONG FORM—OR PLANNING A COMPLETE METAPHORIC LESSON

Suppose you are the teacher with the food chain unit to teach; and suppose you have already realized that the unit is going to present a number of problems: What do the students already know? What are their learning styles? What is your overall instructional goal? What concepts are important? What instructional objectives are critical, and, is there a way to make the unit come alive   to avoid teaching "more of the same"?

Let's further assume that you have determined that the content of the unit really should build upon the content of last year's unit (that content was both comprehensive and essential); now, however, you realize that even though you have the content, you still have a design problem because you really want to capture the curiosity of your students. The following guidelines are intended to provide a journey through the creative instructional process itself; they are designed to help you plan that curiosity-inducing lesson. Each of the basic steps below is critical in designing a complete metaphoric lesson. Combined, these twelve steps influence both the overall success of the lesson and its delivery.

1. Background of Your Students
2. Overall Instructional Goal (or Purpose)
3. Measurable Instructional Objectives
4. Pre-Assessment Procedures
5. Basic Focus of the Lesson (the Central Concept)
6. Level I—The Metaphoric Image (or Symbol)
7. Level II—The Personal Comparison Question
8. Level III—The Interactive/Imagery Experience
9. Level IV—Creative Insight Questions
10. Postassessment Procedures
11. Materials and Equipment
12. Modifications for the Future (Personal Insights)

The next few pages will "walk you through" this process; the problem of designing a metaphoric lesson for the food chain unit will be used as an example. This lesson, then, will not only exemplify the method but will also explore the benefits of the long form design.

## 1. Background of the Students

Considering the background experiences of your students may take a few minutes or a few hours depending on a number of factors. On the surface, it seems obvious; we all know the students we are teaching— but do we? Discovering background information can mean rethinking some of the basic assumptions we have made about our students. Have we, for example, accepted the second grade teacher's evaluation of our new third graders? Have we assumed that all the students have televisions? Have we presumed that the same values and ethnic experiences are shared by all students? Have we examined the ways that the present students resemble or differ from last year's students? These are all important questions in determining the overall background of students in your class.

Suppose, for example, that you are teaching high school English. You know that your third period English "I" class requires much more structure than the "IAs" you have in fifth period; you also have an accelerated Romance literature class (first period) that is way ahead of both of them. All three classes have freshmen; all three classes cover some of the same general content and concepts, but the sophistication levels of each class are very different.

With a metaphoric lesson, you can introduce a basic concept to all three classes with the same lesson—only the Level IV "INSIGHT" questions will vary. As discussed earlier, "insight" questions are designed to link concept, content, and understanding. The level of understanding will likely be different, but the "image" experience can be shared by all three classes. Student perspective influences the insights they can gain; gifted students, for example, usually perceive "tolerance" very differently from their peers. For the gifted child, "tolerance" often means being able to accept people without judging their inadequacies—being open to the uniqueness of each individual in his or her world.

In the elementary school, background information is also critical for concept mastery. In addition to student records and past teacher evaluations, there are curriculum concerns as well. In most districts, there are five- and six-year curriculum continuity plans ("special" or "articulated" curricula)—curricula designed to provide cohesion and sequence for the elementary instruction as a whole; curricula, however, that can inadvertently overlook the problems of teaching the highly mobile students we frequently have in our classrooms.

Consider, for example, the school-wide implementation of a "spiral curriculum" model. If you are teaching a sixth-grade class where the concept "the universe is in constant change" has been built from a simple to a complex concept following the spiral curriculum model, those students who have been in the school for five years and who have followed the spiral will be very comfortable with the sixth level of conceptual expansion and understanding. However, transient "new students" may not share this same background; they may find the concept both difficult to understand and unfamiliar. Their level of understanding is also part of planning the metaphoric lesson.

Finally, total class "personalities" change from year to year; the ability level of a given class is influenced by many variables: the individual students in the class, their economic backgrounds, individual mobility and family structures, the length of time they have known one another, the quality of past teachers. One year everything works; there are few discipline problems, considerable acceleration, and a high level of success and cooperation; the next year, the same academic level of students may be very different. One or two troubled youngsters, two new students, or a missed level of skill-building can greatly affect the overall performance ability of the class. In these situations, you may decide to use the metaphoric lessons to catch students up conceptually; metaphoric lessons can provide "time-outs" where there are no "right" or "wrong" answers—rather, a moment of experiencing the "big picture."

So, who are the students you are about to teach? What's the overall background of the class about to have the "food chain" unit? Are there "hidden factors" you should know? Let's assume for purposes of our discussion that the following description fits this class:

1. *Grade Level:* This is a fifth-grade class in a suburban setting where parental involvement in schools is high.
2. *Class Cohesiveness:* Many of these students have been together since kindergarten; there are three new students, two students currently facing divorce in their families, and at least half the class is in single-parent homes; one student lives with grandparents.
3. *Ability Level:* This is an "average" class—some students are having remedial skill problems, but the majority are typical fifth graders, three are very talented.
4. *Concept Background:* The three new students know very little about "food chains." The concept is unfamiliar to them, and the overall class comfort level with the concept has unsettled them.
5. *Metaphoric Lesson Experience:* You have already used a metaphoric lesson in this class; they are willing to help locate props.
6. *Classroom:* You have a self-contained classroom; resource teachers include music, P.E., and art teachers who meet with the class weekly.
7. *Class Characteristics:* You have "mapped out" some of the overall

class demographics; you know, for example, that the students come form two basic ethnic backgrounds—Anglo and Hispanic. You decide to look at four major factors: district experience, ability level, family background, and familiarity with "food chain" concept.

**Table 1:   Background of Class***

| District Experience | Ability Level | Family Background | Familiarity with "food chain" concept |
|---|---|---|---|
| 22 have been in class together since kindergarten | 17 have skills within normal range | 9 are from single parent homes; 2 are presently facing divorce; 6 are in two-parent homes | All 22 have had past units with "food chain" as the concept to be learned; the three who have academic difficulty are still uncertain as to what the overall concept is all about |
| | 3 have difficulty with most academic subjects (do well in art, music, P.E.) | 1 is from a single-parent home; 2 are from two-parent homes (one home seems very troubled) | |
| | 2 are very gifted academically | 1 comes from a single-parent home; other from two-parent home | Both of these students are sure they know the unit already |
| one student was "new" last year | normal ability | Army career family; father is an officer | This student agrees with the other two—they already know the material |
| two students are "new" this year | one is very talented (academically and in art, music, P.E.), other has normal ability | Talented student's father was transferred and mother is unhappy; other student is living with grandparents | Both students are unfamiliar with the unit, concept and basic assumptions of a "food chain" |

*Of course, this kind of in-depth assessment of student background cannot be done for every metaphoric lesson. Doing the first three columns (District Experience, Ability Level, and Family Background) about the third week of school is a good idea, then whenever you are about to teach a new concept, the fourth column (Familiarity with Concept) can be completed.

Several interesting deductions can be made from this kind of table. They will influence your overall design of the lesson. For example:

1. The dissenting students are asking the creative challenge; one is probably seeking peer acceptance (the child with Army background).
2. Several students are having conceptual difficulties and could benefit from a clearer image of what they are learning.
3. At least 25% of the class are currently under considerable stress; the lesson's side effects of relaxing participants can be helpful for these young people.
4. The students have had considerable experience with the overall content material, but they lack conceptual understanding of its significance.

While analyzing background factors is not a cure-all, by any means, it can be a valuable aid in assessing the emotional climate, motivational level, and previous experiences that will influence class response to the lesson at hand.

## 2. Instructional Goal

After viewing the general background of your students in preparation for this lesson, take a "time-out" for yourself—a time to think about and mentally define the overall concept you want students to learn in this instructional unit. Why are you teaching this unit? What overall principle or perception is important for them to gain?

You could, for example, decide to make your instructional goal any one of the following:

*Concept 1*　Cohesion is a necessary factor of a natural ecosystem (protecting natural "food chains").

*Concept 2*　Animal homes are independent "food chain" systems.

*Concept 3*　Interrupted food chains may cause extinction.

You will find that each instructional unit has many possible concepts to focus upon, many potentially valid instructional goals. In fact, in many ways, the instructional goal is like a city to which we would like to travel—the goal is the final destination of our instructional journey. Reaching this instructional goal (the actual mastery of the concept and its related content material) involves careful planning of instructional objectives, learning activities, and assessment measures. This planning process is much like creating a travel plan, deciding upon a mode of transportation, and gathering the prerequisite information for your itinerary.

Deciding upon the instructional goal, then, is Step 2 in both the design of the instructional unit and the design of the metaphoric lesson. In fact, this decision serves two essential purposes:

(1) It helps you, the teacher, define the overall concept you want students to understand.
(2) It helps you, the teacher, develop a clearer idea of what you want students to master in terms of specific information.

With every instructional unit, there are many possibilities for concepts and related content material. Choosing the instructional goal will mean narrowing down these possibilities.

For example, in this unit, do you want your students to:

*Goal 1* value "food chains" as necessary links for survival? (Related to Concept 1)

*Goal 2* see their own homes as human "food chains" that provide for their survival? (Related to Concept 2)

*Goal 3* recognize the plight of endangered species who have experienced interrupted food chains? The panda with its bamboo food shortage is such an example. (Related to Concept 3)

No doubt you are thinking of still more possibilities. For the purpose of developing this lesson plan together, however, let's choose "Goal 1" as our instructional goal—valuing "food chains" as necessary links in the natural order of our present world's survival.

## 3. Instructional Objectives

Instructional objectives, also known as "measurable learner outcomes," define how we will reach our final destination (the instructional goal) and how we will recognize this destination (the indicators of having mastered this goal) once we get there.* If we see the goal as the city to which we are journeying, then the instructional objectives might be likened to:

1. *The Transportation System*  How (specifically) will we travel to this city (goal)?
2. *The Time Schedule*  What will happen when?
3. *Estimated Time and Place of Arrival*  How will we know we actually get there?
4. *Checkpoints to Keep on the Right Travel Plan*  What indicates that we are headed in the right direction? How can we be sure? What can be actually observed?

Each instructional objective relates specifically to measurable behaviors, attitudes and content material; thus instructional objectives have four primary components:

---

*The instructional goal is the overall learning destination for both the left and right brains; the instructional objectives are specified means for reaching this destination and are designed to involve the left/right brains actively in the learning process.

# THE INSTRUCTIONAL GOAL:

## UNDERSTANDING THE FOOD CHAIN

FOOD CHAIN

# THE OBJECTIVES

## TRANSPORTATION ▪ TIME SCHEDULE ▪ Estimated Time of Arrival ▪ CHECKPOINTS

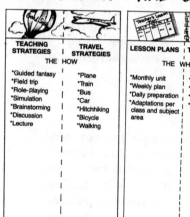

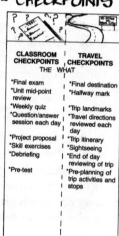

| TEACHING STRATEGIES | TRAVEL STRATEGIES | LESSON PLANS | TRAVEL PLANS | INSTRUCTIONAL MILESTONES | ARRIVAL POINTS | CLASSROOM CHECKPOINTS | TRAVEL CHECKPOINTS |
|---|---|---|---|---|---|---|---|
| THE HOW | | THE WHEN | | THE WHERE | | THE WHAT | |
| *Guided fantasy | *Plane | *Monthly unit | *Trip itinerary | *Mastery of the food chain unit 6/20 | *Arrival in destination city 6/20 | *Final exam | *Final destination |
| *Field trip | *Train | *Weekly plan | *Weekly key cities | *Review of food chain unit 6/19 | *Next to last city 6/19 | *Unit mid-point review | *Halfway mark |
| *Role-playing | *Bus | *Daily preparation | *Daily travel plan | | | *Weekly quiz | *Trip landmarks |
| *Simulation | *Car | *Adaptations per class and subject area | *Next stop | *Completion of class projects 6/17 | *Last visit with relatives 6/17 | *Question/answer session each day | *Travel directions reviewed each day |
| *Brainstorming | *Hitchhiking | | | *Class field trip 6/13 | *Famous Landmark 6/13 | | *Trip itinerary |
| *Discussion | *Bicycle | | | | | *Project proposal | *Sightseeing |
| *Lecture | *Walking | | | *Student proposals class projects 6/7 | *Pacing trip after week of travel 6/7 | *Skill exercises | *End of day reviewing of trip |
| | | | | *Class syllabus 6/1 | *Travel plan 6/1 | *Debriefing | *Pre-planning of trip activities and stops |
| | | | | *Pre-test for food chain knowledge and experience 5/25 | *Pre-planning of possible stops and visits along route 5/25 | *Pre-test | |

# THE CONCEPT TO BE LEARNED:     THE FOOD CHAIN

162

1. *Objectives can be measured:* We can know, for example, whether or not students can outline a food chain, identify the energy path within it, and state their choice of a personal food chain they see and value in their home environment.
2. *Objectives identify a level of performance that we consider acceptable for mastery:* We want the full outline, or, we have four elements in the energy path, or, we are looking for at least four living animals or plants in the neighborhood food chain.
3. *Objectives define the time schedule for the completion of the objective:* When do we want them to outline the food chain—in the first two days? When do we want them to identify the energy path of a specific food chain—at the end of the unit, in their projects, on the unit exam? And when do we want them to choose a personal food chain to study, observe, and learn to value—during the unit, in the last week of the project or as part of a field trip?
4. *Objectives identify the teacher's expectations for performance in one or more of three learning domains:* cognitive (informative skills), affective (emotional, creative, and valuing skills), and psychomotor (motor coordinator skills).

In the case of this instructional unit on food chains, you define the following overall instructional objectives as appropriate to the overall goal of *Awareness of Cohesion within a Natural Ecosystem:*

1. That by the end of the first week of instruction, students will be able to identify the energy path of three land-based food chains. (Cognitive—information gathering)
2. That by the end of the second week of instruction, students will choose a food chain in their own environment that they will observe and trace, and define ways they believe it is essential to the survival of those within the chain. (Affective—valuing experience)
3. That by the end of the instructional unit, students will construct a three dimensional model of a land-based or marine-based food chain that is crucial as a natural linking system for the animals within it. (Psychomotor—skill-building)

Including all three learning domains (cognitive, affective, and psychomotor) significantly enriches the overall focus, direction, and impact of the lesson. People have many needs: They need to expand their knowledge and information (cognitive), they need to examine their values and attitudes (affective), and they need to continually gain new actual skills for coping with and changing their environment (psychomotor). Addressing needs holistically allows the total mind to develop. Metaphoric lessons, for this reason, are designed to allow affective experiences and psychomotor skill-building to be in partnership with cognitive information-gathering and assimilation.

Let's consider some additional examples of instructional objectives within these categories; the following objectives actively focus both the left and right brain processes upon the learning process:*

| | |
|---|---|
| Cognitive Outcomes: (facts, knowledge, subject-oriented information) | Upon the completion of the metaphoric lesson, students will identify five trophic levels within a food chain. |
| | Upon the completion of the instructional unit, students will define the role of detritus feeders within a given food chain. |
| Affective Outcomes: (values, attitudes, awareness of personal feelings) | Upon the completion of the metaphoric lesson, students will express their feelings about survival within a given food chain and the survival of the food chain itself. |
| | Upon the completion of the instructional unit, students will examine their own personal attitudes towards "kill or be killed," "natural selection," and "survival of the fittest." |
| Psychomotor Outcomes: (actual motor skills, new motor coordination, and the ability to perform new behaviors) | Upon the completion of the metaphoric lesson, students will visualize the journey of protein through a specific food chain. |
| | Upon the completion of the instructional unit, students will physically locate and see a living food chain within their own neighborhood; this food chain will then be depicted in a three dimensional model the student will build. |

These instructional objectives are designed in terms of two time schedules: the specific learning outcomes influenced by the metaphoric lesson and the specific learning outcomes to be achieved by the end of the overall instructional unit.

The metaphoric lesson is a conceptual introduction for the unit; it is not the entire unit itself. It can help students understand the "big picture" of what is about to be learned, but the unit itself will have many learning activities—the metaphoric lesson is but one of these learning activities.

Instructional objectives, however (whether you are designing the metaphoric lesson or an entire new instructional unit), are important building blocks for the instructional design process. They help guide specific behaviors, spell out the conditions for performance, and provide a measuring tool for determining success and mastery.

---

*While it is not true that all cognitive outcomes are left brain and all affective outcomes are right brain, it is true that many of the cognitive learning objectives involve sequential, fact-oriented kinds of information, and that many of the affective objectives prompt curiosity, a sense of where things fit in personally, and aesthetic appreciation of innate beauty or perfection in the pattern. Psychomotor objectives involve many skill levels including the basic motor coordination of the cerebellum.

## 4. Pre-assessment Procedures

Pre-assessment of the class's knowledge levels, affective attitudes, and psychomotor skills can occur either formally or informally; pre-assessment itself is the moment when you actually check your own personal estimate of student background ability and determine as accurately as you can the sophistication level of student information, understanding, and ability.

Formally, pre-assessment involves three kinds of testing: *a general inventory* (what do the students know about natural survival?), *a topic survey* (what do the students know about eco-systems?), and *a diagnostic analysis* (how familiar are the students with terms such as "food chain," "energy path," and "detritus feeders"?) The last assessment can save you and your students hours of repeating information they already know.

Informally, we pre-assess by questioning students, by posing problems for them to solve, or by introducing a learning simulation where knowledge of the basic information is critical to the experience. *In either case (formal or informal) the purpose of pre-assessment is the same: to discover the cognitive, affective, and psychomotor skills the students already possess.* It is a moment to check the appropriateness of the instructional goal, the timeliness of the concepts you are teaching, and the specific instructional objectives you are intending to accomplish.

In essence, pre-assessment means determining whether the information, attitudes, and skills you want students to have at the end of the unit need to be taught. Is it possible that they already know the material? That they have already developed the attitudes? That they already have the skills? If so, you can design your unit around more sophisticated concepts, more sophisticated information, and more sophisticated skill application. If not, you know you are on target and those who are complaining have "personal agendas" they are satisfying—these personal needs will also be better anticipated and met.

Pre-assessment means involving both "left-brain" thinking and "right-brain" thinking—checking what the student knows logically and factually and checking the overall image ("big picture") the student has. You'll need to pretest the facts, manner of reasoning, and overall knowledge the students have concerning the unit at hand: can they define the basic topics, terms, and processes? And you'll need to assess their level of conceptual understanding: Do they "know" how the concept actually works? Can they apply the concept to other situations?

Information levels can be pre-assessed conventionally, using quizzes, questions, definitions, discussions. But conceptual understanding should be pre-assessed differently, usually with problem solving, instructional games, simulations, role playing, and/or the use of "concept metaphors." For the purposes of this unit on food chains, let's assume that you have already pretested your students and discovered that the majority of the students have a working knowledge of 25% of the terms, topics, and definitions included in the unit; this means you will be able to assume a higher level of general knowledge when you begin the unit. However, you are puzzled as to whether or not they really "understand" the words, processes, or concepts these seem to define. What do they know experientially about:

the *strength* of an interlocking food chain?

or . . . the *interdependence* of each link in the food chain?

or . . . the *vulnerability* of all the links when a foreign element is introduced?

or . . . the *awareness that humans can terminate links in a food chain and threaten the survival of the entire food chain's life forms?*

To assess this understanding, we must find ways to have students show us they can apply the knowledge they recite. This means solving a problem in which the concept is central to the solution; role-playing their understanding, or devising metaphors that demonstrate that they understand how the concept works.

For example, if you want to assess the students' understanding of interdependence, you might begin with questions about the way a bicycle works, the way the parts of an automobile work, or the way each member of the family supports the roles of one another. Then, you could ask the students to think of examples in nature where interdependence is critical to survival of the animals involved:

where young animals need their mothers.

where one animal provides the warning signal for others (like the beaver in the pond or the monkey in the forest).

where one animal is the food supply of another (like the mackerel and the tuna, the zebra and the lion).

Their answers will reveal very quickly the level of their understanding, and this information will help you modify, enrich, or speed up the time schedule you have developed for teaching your instructional unit. It will also help you design an appropriate metaphoric lesson. You may discover, for example, that the first two concepts (strength and interdependence) are well integrated into the students' understanding of food chain; however, you may also discover that vulnerability and the influence of outside intervention are not well understood and need to be the overall focus of the unit.

*How does pre-assessing the conceptual understanding work?* Let's look at some additional examples of concepts you may want to teach. Suppose you are teaching a foreign language and want to introduce the concept of dialect. You could begin with examples of different terms used for the same item: "common pins" in New England are "straight pins" everywhere else; "I'm fixin' to do it" in the South means "I'm getting ready to do it" in the North; "you, guys!" in the West is often rendered "y'all" in the South. Next, instead of explaining the concept, ask the class to explain what is happening. Why do these terms differ? If we're all speaking English, why do these differences occur? The class will "solve the problem" and explain to you what dialects are all about. This, in turn, will lead you into a German lesson on the differences between Berliner German and Bavarian German, Quebec French and Parisian French, Mexican Spanish and Castilian Spanish.

Or, suppose you are about to teach a unit on Westward Expansion in the early 1850s. You could ask the class what happens when new people move into their neighborhoods (this can be extremely revealing in terms of neighborhood norms, customs, and established patterns). What happens when new people enter the class? Have any of them ever moved? What happened to them when they moved? Their answers will lay the groundwork for your unit:

"We had a new condominium building go up near us; it meant widening our street." "We were really afraid of our new neighbors; we didn't know any Vietnamese." "When I moved here, I was really sad to leave all my friends behind—I didn't know if I'd find new friends!"

What happens with a move? New resources are needed; new customs and ideas are introduced; fears of not being accepted and leaving behind what is known arise. The Westward Expansion had all of these elements: How the settlers coped with these demands can be the conceptual basis of your unit.

In summary, the pre-assessment of *subject matter* means checking to determine whether the information you want students to have at the end of the unit is already present at the beginning, while the pre-assessment of *conceptual understanding* means posing the concept (to be learned) within a familiar framework in order to determine whether a "working understanding" of the concept already exists. Each lesson has an infinite number of concepts we can focus upon. In the food chain lesson, we can find many other related concepts: "compassion" for the role animals play within the food chain; "respect" for natural systems and their order; "protection" for dwindling natural resources; "sensitivity" to immediate neighborhood changes. The essential problem is to clearly identify the specific overriding concept that best enriches student understanding of the instructional unit.

Pre-assessment, then, clarifies both the instructional objectives and the concept focus of your unit. As information increases in terms of what your students do and do not know, you will find yourself rethinking and modifying the overall content emphasis of the unit. Flexibility in restructuring what you have planned can make the difference between an adequate instructional design and a highly efficient (and effective) instructional design.

## 5. The Image Focus of the Metaphoric Lesson

Having decided upon the primary concept you will emphasize (the value of food chains as necessary links in the natural order of our present world's survival), the next step is to identify a workable metaphor for illustrating this concept. Answering these four basic questions will assist you in selecting the appropriate metaphor:

1. *What are the basic characteristics of the concept you are teaching?*
   A "break" in the system will endanger the viability of the entire system.
   Each element in the system is dependent upon the links before it—and ultimately upon the links that proceed from it.
   The overall smoothness of the system can be taken for granted.
   Small parts can become strong while working together for mutual benefit.
2. *What objects, animals or systems available in the everyday world can symbolize these characteristics?*
   The spokes in a bicycle wheel
   The parts of an automobile
   The role of the honey bee in pollinating flowers
   The actual linking function of chains
3. *Which of these symbols is most assessible in terms of props, materials, and concrete examples?*
   Any one of the above bicycle wheels, automobiles, honey bees, or chains (in a variety of forms) can be found in our everyday world. Each will "work" as the metaphor; the "chain" has been chosen as an example here because there are many kinds of "chains" available —and because the word "chain" is used in the concept of a "food chain."
4. *What materials do you have readily available to use with the image you have selected?*
   Gold chain, Christmas tree chains, bicycle chain, tire chains, graph of a "food chain" within the human body, pictures of Great Wall of China, a graph of the Pony Express stations, a map of a supermarket

chain, a picture of a "human chain" putting out a fire with buckets, a picture of people reaching their hands around the earth, a color slide of people chained together in mountain climbing, and a cartoon in which a crazy chain reaction wakes up the central character.

If question 4 produces too few examples, "regroup" to question 2. The metaphor will work; it is important that your choice be one that you personally feel like "playing with"—one that you find enjoyable and worth investigation. This design process actively recognizes the need to keep the right brain focused on creative alternatives and the "play" aspect of creative problem solving.

Symbols abound for every classroom concept you would like to teach. For example, in teaching the concept of prejudice, you could look at the treatment of expensive trees versus everyday trees in a garden shop (there are needs that all trees have, but the owner is often more concerned with trees that offer the greatest financial rewards). Is prejudice based upon financial concerns? The discussion that would naturally follow the introduction of this metaphor could prove very revealing to both you, the teacher, and your students.

Suppose you are teaching a unit on ethnocentrism; you might find the history of an island to be a helpful metaphor. Ethnocentrism is an island effect, and it often means considering the ways the people being studied were isolated and apart from the mainstream of things. As you open your mind to potential metaphors for each concept you are teaching, you'll find that the images will seem to literally "flash" through your mind: Democracy can be taught with the metaphor of a natural dam in a river (the beaver may create the system, but it takes all the animals and plant life working together to create a healthy, ongoing environment). The concept of time management can be the story of the tortoise and the hare (do you rush into things and then procrastinate, or do you plod along and always finish?). Opportunism and entrepreneurial capitalism can be likened to the habits of the shrew (an animal that dies in four hours if it doesn't eat; thus, the shrew is always on the lookout for new food sources and willing to consider types of food other animals ignore). Interpersonal skills can become active images as well: Listening can mean becoming a human mirror (learning to accurately take in the information being shared in order to more accurately "reflect" the message back). Perception-checking can be compared to a recording system (has the message been received correctly with the right tone, emphasis, and without background interference?). The ability to describe another person's feelings can be seen as keeping a careful eye on the seismograph (to be on the lookout for sudden shifts, earthquakes, and volcanic action—so similar to the effects of explosive emotions). Confronting and resolving conflict may mean learning to defuse potential bombs and redirecting that energy for productivity (nuclear energy for electricity instead of for warfare). For every concept you would like to teach, there are countless potential images to explore: images that will lend immediate, creative perspective on how the concept itself actually works.

## 6. The Metaphoric Focus (Level I)

Once you have chosen a concept (valuing the interdependence of the food chain) and have identified an image symbol (metaphor) to represent this concept (the physical "chains" we see all around us), the development of the metaphoric lesson begins to rely on "image thinking" as well as logical thinking. In creating Level I of the Metaphoric Lesson, it is essential to collect all the materials and symbols you can find that are examples of the metaphor you are using.* In the case of food chains, you would seek out and collect as many concrete examples of "chains" as you can.

Collecting your examples can be a highly energizing experience as you allow your mind to consider all the different objects and pictures you have on hand that suggest "chains." This is a time to encourage right-brain imagery to "play with" existing resources in order to create new connections for seeing the metaphor (for example, the Pony Express map can be seen as a chain of mail stations); in fact, the ability to "see chains everywhere" increases as you actually put these images in front of you and allow yourself to "see" the chains. More and more possibilities will be sparked as the right brain begins to perceive these images and expand creatively.**

Focusing on the image level often becomes self-reinforcing; the more images you see, the more that are suggested. Take the concept of specialization, for example. You may be thinking in terms of specialized products, services, or even biological niches. A highly effective metaphoric image is the blank check. As you begin to gather up physical examples of checks, you will find all kinds of specialized checks: personal checks, cashier's checks, traveller's checks, money order checks, payroll checks, credit card "checks," and transfer checks. Checks come in many colors, sizes, types and uses. Taking the "blank check" as a metaphor for specialization, you can explore the evolution of the check in commercial trading:

---

*We do this first before we write the whole lesson. This process of "seeing" our images, touching and manipulating them, and totally experiencing the metaphor, allows a richer awareness for the right brain's input to the design process.

**A short report on how one teacher "learned" to identify a workable metaphor for her lesson follows later in this chapter. This initial introduction for developing the metaphor lesson provides the bridge for right-brain involvement in understanding what the concept is all about.

1. Students can begin with barter and symbols for barter.
2. They can then explore the use of scarce symbols of wealth (gold, pearls, and even livestock).
3. Next, they can trace the minting of coins, the printing of paper money, the use of bank drafts, personal checks, and payroll checks.
4. Finally, they can look at newer forms of checks—credit cards and the magnetic strips of computerized tape that determine our records by today's mechanical tellers.

In a short time, perhaps only hours, students can discover that the bank check has introduced a whole world of specialization—a world that becomes an intriguing guided fantasy as a microcosm of the process of specializing.

In our food chain lesson, this step means collecting and examining all the physical examples of "chains" you have: the gold chain, the Christmas tree paper chain, the bicycle chain, tire chains, the graph of a "human chain" that stretches around the world, the pictures of the Great Wall of China, the Pony Express stations, people climbing a mountain (chained together by rope); it means searching for unique "chains"—a map of a "supermarket chain," a "human chain" of people putting out a fire with buckets, a picture of children holding hands around the world, a cartoon of a crazy "chain reaction" set-up for waking up the central character, and a graphic food chain illustration.

### 7. Personal Comparison (Level 2)

Once you have examined these metaphoric images—the objects, pictures, illustrations, slides, and objects—it is time to design the personal comparison phase of the metaphoric lesson. This process allows both the right and left brains to focus on the conceptual task, and it encourages the students to personally value the experience they are having. To develop this awareness, we must "structure" a moment when (right-brain) nonverbal perception can be negotiated into (left-brain) verbal reasoning. For the purposes of these lessons, this means developing comparison questions.

There are several ways to design a comparison question. Central of all these ways is the process of comparing the image to the insight it suggests:

Choose a "chain" in the group we've just seen that reminds you of yourself and the way you live your life.
If you were to compare yourself to one of the chains we have just seen, which one would you choose?

How are you like the bicycle chain?
Think of a way you and the gold chain are just the same.

It is important to pose the question in a way that the student must answer more than "yes" or "no." For example, "Can you think of a way that you and the gold chain are alike?" can be answered easily by "no." If the option is given to the rational brain to control the response, it will. Also, try to avoid situations where the analysis becomes critical to the answer: "How is the bicycle chain like your life?" can cause the student to think there is a "right answer" and thereby limit the spontaneity and imagery of the process; the left brain will control and generate "good," "logical" answers whenever there is a possibility of "correct" responses.

The personal comparison phase is like the prologue to the epic, the prelude to the symphony; it "warms up" the participants and sets the stage for the next level, the interactive/imagery experience. The personal comparison moment literally causes intuitive/insight moments within the students; they will be amazed at the new perspectives they will gain about their lives:

"I see myself as the master link of a bicycle chain, because I'm always helping my mom understand my older brother and my older brother to understand my mom. If something happened to me, they would never connect!"
"I'm like the ½-inch case hardened chain I lock my bike with, once I latch on to somebody, I just don't let go."
"I feel like the first domino in the chain, I know if I get depressed, I take a lot of others with me."
"I related to the Pony Express chain, because I am always on the go and I always am doing things for other people."

Because these insights will be personal and potentially revealing, do not ask students to explain them. Simply accept the comments and continue with the lesson; if someone says something that could be misunderstood, refocus the class's attention on yourself with something equally personal. This will move the spotlight to you, the person most capable of handling the attention. Generally speaking, students reveal their feelings in direct ratio to your ability to handle them; if you are personally reluctant to delve deeply into emotional insights, they will be, too. And this is all right. The comparison time is not psychoanalysis; it is classroom instruction. Its purpose is personal insight, not therapy.

We have used directed dyads very successfully at this level of questioning; in directed dyads (pairs) students share with only one other person. After the sharing period, examples that students wish to share with the entire group can then be elicited. The openness of the group, the sophistication of the overall communication, and the concept/ image you are using, will essentially determine whether directed dyads or large group sharing will yield the greatest learning. Younger students enjoy the group sharing; older students often prefer the privacy and potential for insight of directed dyads.

### 8. The Interactive/Imagery Phase

In most lessons found in this book, the interactive/imagery phase is an abstract, right-brain exercise, the guided fantasy. In this case, the focus is on valuing the interdependence of the food chain, and because that sense of interdependence can be experienced physically as well as intellectually, this lesson will feature another type of interactive experience, the pantomime.

The assignment, then, is to put your students in groups of four and have them select one of the chains to represent. They are then to design and present a pantomime of one of the types of chains. This task is more difficult than it might first appear. For example, how could they represent a gold chain (a series of interlocking links) as opposed to a bicycle chain (also a series of interlocking links)? How could they pantomime a steel chain as opposed to a paper chain, a people chain as opposed to a "chain of events"? No two groups should have the same type of chain to pantomime; they should also be free to select types of chains that you did not include in the pictures or other images shown in phase 2 of the lesson. Some other chains they might come up with are: island chains, chain letters, chain gangs, computer program "loops," chain reactions, chain saws, chain pumps, or chain stitches. In each pantomime, the students will be demonstrating both to themselves and to the audience the critical nature of each link, that is, the way in which each link depends on both the one that precedes it and the one that follows it.

### 9. Creative Insight Questions

Once the students have completed the pantomime presentation of the various "chains," the next step is to connect the insights derived from this interactive experience with the concept of the lesson (the value of food chains as necessary links for survival). In linking the new understanding of the vital nature of each link in the chain with the students' old knowledge regarding food chains, you can prompt new insights, awarenesses, and understandings.

The questions can be discussed in dyads, in small groups, or as a whole class. Choose from the following:

1. Vegetation is the master link of food chains. Why?
2. Natural selection is Nature's case hardening. Why?
3. Unusual climactic phenomena are Nature's bolt cutters. Why?
4. Time is stronger than any link. Why?
5. If algae are the alpha of the food chain, what is the omega?
6. Extinction of a species sets off a "chain reaction" in food chains. Why?
7. Canine teeth are the carnivores' master link. Why?
8. Silk is to lace as oxygen is to food chains. Why?

Remember, the purpose of these questions is to link concept and interaction in order to produce increased concept mastery. Seek the response that reflects depth and insight, make certain it is shared with the entire class.

## 10. Postassessment

The postassessment measures need to refer back to the instructional objectives designed in step 3 and, like the pre-assessment measures, the postassessment can be either formal (pencil and paper) or informal (a general round of questions). This lesson has three basic objectives, one each in the cognitive, affective, and psychomotor domains. Thus, your questions should assess the students' attainment of these objectives:

1. Identify the energy paths of three land-based food chains.
2. Which food chain did you choose to observe? Define the ways in which each link in the food chain depends on the other. How does this relate to the ecological values conflict of government-sponsored resource management; U.S. free-enterprise resource management?
3. Construct a three-dimensional model of a land- or marine-based food chain.

Assessing the students' level of growth from pre-assessment to post-assessment provides evidence of the impact of the metaphoric exercise and establishes a firm base from which to evaluate the impact of the lesson.

## 11. Materials and Equipment

To complete this lesson you will need:

*Props:* Chains of different shapes, sizes, and uses ranging from paper chains to bicycle chains to anchor chains to gold chains. Pictures of human chains and the Great Wall and of mountain climbers chained together. Perhaps illustrations of chain reactions or chains of events.

*Audio-visual:* Overhead projector, screen, transparencies featuring chains.

*Instructional Materials:* A pretest and a posttest, some specific written ideas on the interactive pantomime, insight questions.

## 12. Personal Insights and Revisions

The pantomime was difficult for some students; the next time I teach this lesson, I'm going to give more background on how to do a pantomime and then give them some practice before they do the chains.

The insight questions really worked well; don't change them.

I need some new props next time; every time I find a chain or a picture of a chain I am going to put it in this box. For example, I didn't use the image of a "chain smoker." Is breaking a link, that is, skipping a regularly scheduled time for a cigarette, one way to break the chain smoking habit?

Overall, I was very pleased with this lesson.

*Now that we have introduced the basic design sequence for developing a metaphoric lesson, and looked at the process that might proceed writing your first lessons, let's review these steps with the use of a familiar concept and a lesson we introduced earlier in the book. Let's return to the "Change/Butterfly" lesson—but let's return with a difference. This time we will look at the design of the lesson, particularly in terms of your role as the learner, and the role(s) your students might play. Each step of the basic "long form" design format will be reviewed; in addition, we will fill out this form as if you were our intended student and the lesson were beginning now.*

# METAPHORIC TEACHING LESSON PLAN
# The Change/Butterfly Lesson Revisited
*The Long Form: A Participant's Guide*

*1. Background of the Class.*   Describe your students, the instructional unit you are teaching, the grade level, and any special factors important for understanding the classroom environment.

For this lesson, the "students" are the readers of this book; most of you are teachers with one to twenty years of teaching experience. Many of you are currently enrolled in a graduate course in a college of education. Some of you are undergraduates, training specialists, and teacher educators; all of you are curious and determined to find out more about the creative brain. As teachers, you have teaching experiences that vary from kindergarten to college classrooms, but all of you, whether teachers, trainers, or students of the brain, share a common interest—an interest in increasing your own personal skill in planning, designing, presenting, and evaluating teaching strategies that involve the right brain's knowledge, imagery, and creativity.

As a background, you have already read information related to right/left brain research findings, metaphoric teaching (modern and past), concept attainment, and creativity as a process. We will assume, therefore, that our "class" has (at the very least) a reader's experience with metaphoric teaching and insight moments.

*2. Instructional Goals.*   Describe the overall purpose of teaching the lesson. Include the concept you want your students to learn and the context for this concept within the instructional unit you are teaching.

There are two instructional goals for this lesson: (1) The students (you, the reader) will be able to design metaphoric lessons; and (2) the students will be able to identify the role "risk" plays in any decision to change a set pattern of behavior and values.

Two basic concepts will also be taught: first, patterning in designing a metaphoric lesson (the twelve-step sequence is like the sequence of going from caterpillar to cocoon to butterfly), and second, changing as an experience that you cannot completely predict (the caterpillar does not know what the butterfly will look like, how fast it will fly, or what its life style will be).

177

*3. Instructional Objectives.* Specify the learner outcomes you will measure; relate these outcomes to the concept you are teaching. Include objectives for cognitive, affective, and psychomotor learning.

After you, the reader (the student for this lesson), have read this section ("The Change/Butterfly Lesson Revisited"), you will be able to:

Cognitive Outcomes (New Information): Identify the four metaphoric levels of the Metaphoric Teaching Model: Focus, Comparison, Interactive/Imagery, and Insight Moment.

Describe the basic characteristics of a guided fantasy: personal visualization, imagery, and a personal moment of being (or interacting with) the metaphoric image.

Use the Metaphoric Lesson Design Format to create a new metaphoric lesson.

Affective Outcomes (New attitudes): Give personal examples of how the butterfly's experience is similar to experiences we have had in life.

Share personal insights as to how the use of a metaphoric lesson will aid other students in understanding how the overall concept works.

Have personal confidence that you could design a metaphoric lesson to use in your classroom.

Psychomotor Outcomes (New motor skills): Write and lead a guided fantasy of your own choosing.

Visualize the experience of the caterpillar as it journeys across a meadow, up a tree, into its own cocoon, and then flies with its own new wings—back across the same meadow.

Use debriefing questions to help students discover the variety, diversity, and commonality of their own experiences with the image.

The metaphoric lesson provides three things simultaneously: new information, new attitudes, and new motor skills. It will increase the effectiveness of the lesson if you take time to ask yourself—*cognitive:* What is this new information? *Affective:* What are these new attitudes? And *psychomotor:* What new motor skills have been developed?

*4. Pre-assessment.* Design a formal or informal "pretest" to find out how much the students already know about the concept that is to be taught. Write out these questions even if you will be using them orally.

Because the readers of this book have many different teaching experiences and training backgrounds, we decided to provide a pretest questionnaire to help you personally assess your own familiarity with the change process and the overall use of metaphors in teaching. With very little modification, this questionnaire can be used with almost any group of students.

## PRETEST QUESTIONS

The following questions are to help the instructor assess the present level of knowledge in the class concerning metaphoric teaching and the factors involved in change/metamorphosis. They will not be graded; please answer as honestly as you can.

1. Have you ever used the metaphor, fable or parable to teach a concept to your students? If so, please explain.
2. What characteristics are inherent in any change situation? In other words, what factors or functions are always present when something is changing?
3. Have you ever experienced a guided fantasy? Please explain.
4. What feelings do people encounter when they are experiencing a significant change in their life?
5. Think of a lesson you like to teach. How important is the overall concept of this lesson? How do you check to see if your students have the "big picture"?

Invest the additional time to find out what your students already know. In terms of the left/right brain, the information will be invaluable. The left brain is often impatient with details it already "knows"; the right brain may not have an adequate supply of mental images. If your students have never experienced seeing a caterpillar or butterfly in a natural environment, they have considerably fewer visual images to use in the lesson. If this image supply is not as large as you predicted, provide more visual examples in class. If students already know some of the factual information you thought they did not, you can adapt the lesson to increase the sophistication of the information you will present.

*5. Basic Focus of the Lesson.* Choose a metaphor to illustrate the concept you are going to teach. If you have difficulty choosing this metaphor, answer the following questions.

A. *What are the basic characteristics of the concept you are teaching?*
   A pattern to be followed
   Outcome cannot be predicted while you are in the midst of the process

Raw materials will be used in a new order or rearranged
There is a sense of vulnerability, uncertainty, and risk

B. *What objects, animals, systems of nature, or common, everyday items could symbolize these characteristics?*
The water cycle
The egg
Larva to adult in certain amphibians (tadpole to frog)
Larva to adult in certain insects (caterpillar to butterfly)
The baking of cake
Metamorphosis in crustaceans (lobster molting)

C. *Which of these objects is most accessible in terms of props and concrete examples? And, which would be fun and enjoyable to present?*
The butterfly—metamorphosis example;

D. *List all the materials you have readily available to use with this metaphor.*
Several greeting cards with butterflies, a butterfly calendar, a poster with a butterfly emerging from the cocoon, a water color painting of a butterfly, three butterfly pillows, a butterfly candle, a butterfly sculpture, a butterfly key chain, and a butterfly batik cloth hanging.

Sometimes you will discover that the metaphor is exciting, and energizing, but too demanding in terms of gathering up all the props. The baking of a cake will illustrate the concept of changing and could be the basis of a metaphoric lesson; however, unless you are an experienced baker, managing all the ingredients could present difficulties. Primary in choosing the metaphor is choosing an image with which you personally enjoy working; your nonverbal enthusiasm will excite the people you teach. For example, we have a friend who loves frogs; she could design the concept of change around the experience of the tadpole and enjoy collecting all the props and visual examples.

*6. The Metaphoric Focus.*   Describe the order of materials and symbols that will be used to focus the class on the metaphoric image of the lesson.

Our "class" begins with a verbal introduction to *change* and metamorphosis as a concept and a visual introduction of the metaphoric image we will use to symbolize the process of change—a tiny animal that reminds us of changing whenever we see its image, the butterfly. To capture your right brain's attention, we need pictures, sculptures, objects with butterfly images. To allow this process to occur, take time right now to find specific pictures and objects of the butterfly that you have handy in your home; butterfly imagery found on stationery, posters, or greeting cards, as well as in magazines, are ideal and often readily accessible.

You'll find that the butterfly pictures immediately stimulate your right brain; your right brain will be "aware" that you are "listening" to its input. Take time to look carefully at the pictures; if you can, put them in front of you on the desk or table where you are reading. The images will remain a ready supply of visual stimuli for the right brain's continued involvement in the lesson.

Next, study the word "butterfly" and ask yourself to notice how this word conjures up the images you have just seen, and even expands them to "moving images." Now look at the butterfly images in this book and those all around you; try to put these images in order of most realistic to most abstract. Your left and right brains will be actively exchanging information to do this; it is the right brain that says (in effect), "it's similar in shape," and the left brain that says (in actuality), "it lacks the correct details." You will feel creatively stimulated as you sort them out. Examples we have often used include:

First, photographs of real butterflies

Second, greeting cards with real butterflies

Third, a poster of a butterfly with inspirational message

Fourth, a butterfly sculpture

Fifth, a stained glass butterfly

Sixth, a batik cloth hanging

Seventh, a mosaic pillow butterfly

People often hesitate at categorizing the unusual butterfly images, but these strange images are of critical importance. Unusual images give the learner time and space to realize that the categorization of a "butterfly" in your mind is a conscious choice—a choice based on both item and function. We follow this experience with these questions:

1. Did any of you hesitate when putting the images in order?
2. Which image caused the hesitation? Why?
3. Was there a "debate" in your mind?
4. Did you finally find yourself saying, "Ok, if you want to see it as butterfly that's all right, but it sure is an abstract picture of one."
5. What's the perceptual difference between the real representation of the butterfly (the photograph) and the more abstract images of the butterfly? What happens in your mind?

At this point, we encourage our students to realize that the metaphor for change is just like the picture of the butterfly; it is an image standing for the real experience. *In this case, the butterfly image will be used to help us understand what happens when something changes and metamorphosis (transformation) occurs.*

*7. The Personal Comparison.*   Design a comparison question that will be used for the class to identify with the object.

At this level you are asked to compare yourself with the metaphor; in doing so, you will discover unexpected, immediate, insights about yourself, your values, and your insightfulness into your own life. Take a moment, right now, to consider your answer to this question:

If you were to think of a way that you and the butterfly are alike, what would that way be?

Next, write your answer down, and spend a moment or so contemplating what that answer is offering you as insights about your life and the way you are living it.

Next, the comparison answer is shared with the class. This isn't possible to create for you, but we decided to give you our own personal answers to the question—a sharing moment for the reader and the authors:

DON: I think the butterfly teaches me that the anxiety and restructuring of the cocoon phase is more than just getting wings—it is preparing for the opportunity to view the world from a new perspective.

The butterfly, unlike the caterpillar, can look across the meadow, can see up beyond the flowers, and can look down on the panorama of its world. It can soar as well as move along the ground.

I suppose that in a way I'm a lot like the butterfly; the butterfly is a culmination of phases—phases that are fragile. Life involves moments of being both fragile and vulnerable and I have certainly experienced this feeling of fragility and vulnerability during various "cocoon" phases.

JUDY: I relate easily to the caterpillar stage of the butterfly; much of my childhood involved "crawling" through the day. I was different from other kids, set aside as "the brain." My social skills and self-esteem suffered. I constantly looked at others for acceptance and approval.

My young adult years were spent creating a large, community-based, university practicum program; when I look back on these years, they were definitely a "cocoon" period for me. I reevaluated my values, and I learned to like myself.

The happiness I now enjoy every day could never have been predicted when I was a nineteen-year-old; a frightened, vulnerable, little caterpillar. For me, the butterfly symbolizes the potential within me. I think my life has been a series of caterpillar-to-butterfly moments.

This time-out to formulate your own answer is crucial to the process of using the metaphoric lesson with your students; they will "share" if you do. It is also important not to decide on an answer and always keep that answer; answers change as our own life perspectives change —daily and even hourly. If you "keep" the same answer, you run the risk of being perceived as "canned."

As we noted above, in a classroom situation we use two basic sharing formats: total group sharing and sharing in dyads or triads. Students should be instructed not to "explain" their answers but to accept the answers given. Unless your group includes adults with considerable closeness, answers like those we gave you will not occur. Instead, class answers will be more like:

We both like to fly and see new places.

We both like beautiful colors all around us.

My adult life has been like the cocoon opening.

We are both sometimes very vulnerable, but always gentle to others.

We are both very different now from where we began as children with limited information and responsibility.

My friends are my flowers; I enjoy visiting them the way a butterfly visits a meadow.

My classroom is a cocoon for all my little caterpillars; I try to keep it a safe place both to learn and to change perspective.


If the answers are shared in the total group, you may want to take a moment to "highlight" the overall messages—to sum up the verbal pictures that have been given:


In summary, the butterfly has reminded us of the freedom we enjoy as adults who have weathered the process of growing up and changing. When we think of our own students, we are reminded of their vulnerability, of the changing that lies ahead of them and of the need to create a safe place for these changes to occur.

And, all of us shared an overall perception of the beauty and excitement that comes from allowing change to happen in our lives.


Keep your summary general; students should not feel they are "competing" for your attention. An awareness of a possible "correct answer" to the comparison question will cause the left brain to dominate; personal insights will dwindle in number and depth.

With particularly perceptive groups, you might want to pose the following additional debriefing questions:

1. Why is the sharing process so enjoyable?
2. Why are your responses often so different?
3. What did you personally learn about yourself?
4. What did you learn about others in the class? Your partner in the dyad?

Answers will usually center around the uniqueness of each person, the intimacy and closeness that was shared, the commonality of experiences within the group. In a forty-five-minute class session, Levels I and II may be all you will present on the first day; the next level and the insight moment may be "saved" for the second day. You will need to experiment with your timing and the responses of your class to learn whether the lesson should "break" at this point. If you do decide to wait until the next day, take time to "debrief" the experience and tie "changing" back to the subject matter.

As I said in the beginning of this class period, we will be looking at the process of change as it occurs(ed)
    in the South after the Civil War
    in the Industrial Revolution
    in multiplying instead of adding
    in chemical experiments
    in typing skills you will gain
    in governments that overthrew their monarchs
    in_____
This moment of change requires a period of vulnerability and great reorganization—a period much like the process of the cocoon, which we will look at tomorrow.

*8. Interactive/Imagery Experience.*   Design a participatory nonverbal exercise, roleplay, or guided fantasy experience for your students. The purpose of this is to actively involve the student with the image or object.

We have chosen a guided fantasy for this level; it is a quick, easily accessible experience that we can provide the reader. (Please see page 63.) We also could suggest the following interactive experiences for achieving the same basic purpose—the awareness of what it means to be the butterfly:

A role-play "debate" between a caterpillar and a butterfly as to whether or not the caterpillar should build a cocoon.

A nonverbal enactment of being the crawling caterpillar and becoming the free, high-flying butterfly—after the "time-out" change process of the cocoon.

A visit to a field of butterflies and a personal moment of studying one butterfly and what it does with its life. Then, a follow-up experience with caterpillars (or vice versa).

The guided fantasy is a good vehicle for providing the interactive experience and simultaneously providing a relaxation experience and "time-out" moment from the general stress of daily classroom pressures. It brings you directly into the life of the caterpillar and the everyday experiences of a little animal who must "crawl" with limited vision. Although you read this fantasy earlier in the book, take time now to reread the guided journey of the caterpillar and allow yourself to actually "experience" the images that your right brain will be willing to provide you.*

## The Dialogue

Imagine you are a caterpillar in a far away meadow . . . It is a warm, sunny day, and you are on the far edge of a beautiful, green meadow . . . Looking up at the sky, you see puffy, white clouds on a clear, blue horizon . . . Take a moment to look at yourself carefully . . . What color are you? . . . Are you a fuzzy caterpillar? . . . Are you a sleek, shiny caterpillar?

Now begin your journey across the meadow . . . You are moving slowly, but surely, across the green, soft grass . . . towards the distant edge of the meadow where the forest begins . . . Ahead of you are some flowers . . . They smell sweet and fresh in the meadow air . . . Crawl slowly toward them, toward one flower in particular . . . When you are directly under the flower, look up at it. . . . What kind of a flower is it? . . . What does it look like? . . . What colors can you see? . . . Is it special?

Now look ahead of you . . . There is a clump of trees in the distance ahead . . . Slowly, begin the long process of making your journey toward them . . . The grass is new and slightly damp from the dew . . . It feels like moss as you crawl over it . . . Soon you come to a rock . . . You know you must crawl up over it and down the other side . . . What does it look like? . . . How does it feel? . . . How big is it? . . . After you crawl past the rock, you encounter only more soft, pleasant grass until you come upon a footprint in your path . . . Move closer to it, and look at it

---

*If possible, tape record this fantasy and listen to it in a darkened room where you can't be disturbed, or have a friend read the fantasy to you in a similar setting at a slow pace. Tell your friend that if your arm is raised, it means the friend is reading too fast.

carefully . . . Who or what made this footprint? . . . Now crawl past the footprint and continue your journey.

As you near the edge of the meadow, you can see many trees . . . They are tall, green, and inviting. One of the trees is especially beautiful . . . You decide to go up to that tree . . . When you are really close, you can smell the bark of the tree and feel a difference in the ground underneath you . . . You decide to leave the meadow below and to climb the tree . . . Slowly, start up the trunk of the special tree in front of you . . . You will find the tree easy to climb, exciting to feel . . . As you climb the trunk, you feel a little breeze . . . It ripples across your body, but it doesn't stop you from the climbing. When you reach the first tree limb, crawl out on the limb and look for a special twig, a twig that will be your home . . . When you see that special twig, crawl onto it, and wait for a moment.

Soon, a strange thing is happening . . . You are beginning to spin a beautiful, silky substance around and around the twig . . . This is something you have never done before, but it feels comfortable and natural . . . You know somehow that this little tent is going to be your new home . . . It feels very soft and very safe . . . When your cocoon is all made, close the opening with more of your silky substance.

Now, time is going by . . . You feel night coming, then day, then other nights, and several days go by . . . Soon, you can feel yourself changing . . . All that is you is still there in the soft, quiet home, but all of you seems to be restructuring, to be transforming . . . It is almost like melting and reforming . . . It is strange, wonderful, and very special . . . The days continue to go by, weeks go by, and the outside world seems to cease for you. All there is is the reorganization, the changing of what is you.

Then, one day you feel the sun . . . It is coming in through the cocoon and seems to be beckoning you to come out and feel its warmth . . . You reach forward with one of your limbs, and you open a hole in the cocoon . . . Damp, and barely strong enough to crawl out, you slowly inch your way out of the cocoon and into the sunshine . . . You find the twig is still there, the sky is still blue above your head, but the weeks have changed the scene . . . It is late spring, it is warm, and it is beautiful.

You can feel the sun drying you off, and a strange new body seems to be yours . . . There are huge wing-like arms for you, and you look in wonder at them . . . What color are they? . . . What do you look like? . . . Then, slowly a little breeze comes and lifts you off the tree . . . You are flying out over the meadow, back to where the flowers were at the edge of the meadow . . . Down below is a special flower you want to visit . . . You glide down to this flower, and you smell the sweet nectar within

. . . You perch on its petal . . . Look at the meadow, the sky, and back at the trees . . . It is a glorious day . . . It is a moment of splendor . . . It is a moment to remember. Now, slowly, when you are ready to leave, and not before, return from that meadow and from your flower . . . Come back to this classroom, and when you are truly ready, open your eyes.

### Debriefing the Guided Fantasy

There are a series of questions to debrief the guided fantasy of the butterfly journey on pages 65-67 of this book. However, the experience you have just had is different from that of your students (indeed, each guided fantasy is a unique, nonreplicable experience), so we have included additional debriefing questions for you to consider:

1. Describe the meadow you saw in the fantasy.
   *Is it a "meadow" you would like to create in your classroom and share with your students?*
2. What did the flower look like when you saw it from below or from above?
   *How is the experience with differing perspectives valuable for your students? How could it help them understand change in the instructional unit you are teaching?*
3. When you came to the rock, did it seem like an insurmountable obstacle?
   *Do your students see some kinds of subject matter as being that rock? How can you better get them up and over the rock? How did we help to get you over it? (We told you you could do it; we never accepted the possibility that you couldn't.)*
4. Next, you saw a footprint.
   *What kind of a footprint did you see? Did it change? First impressions are often stereotypical; second looks are frequently richer and more enhancing. How does this insight apply to your students?*
5. What thoughts went through your mind when you were choosing the twig for building your cocoon?
   *How are these considerations similar to those of a student deciding to trust you?*
6. What did it feel like to be in the cocoon?
   *Was it a little frightening or anxiety-producing? How is this feeling similar to changing even when you know you are safe? How is the cocoon experience like the counselor/client relationship? Like the teacher/student relationship?*
7. When you knew you were reorganizing, did you know you would be leaving things behind that you enjoyed?

> *Often the unwillingness to leave behind what's familiar keeps us all from the future we could have.*

8. Remember when you emerged from the cocoon and discovered you could fly.

   *What did it feel like? How have you had this feeling before? When? Where? (Whenever we master "change," we experience the excitement of flight.)*

9. How did the meadow change when you saw it from above?

   *How do you want your students to see your classroom, the things they are learning, the potential of their own lives?*

10. How did you feel when you had to leave the meadow and come back to the text of the book?

    *Students love the imagery experience but coming back to application of it is often difficult; try to give them imagery moments every week —it will strengthen their creativity, innovations, and ability to see things from original perspectives. Gradually students will come to view the application moments as being every bit as important as the image moments.*

Considering the answers to the above questions will enrich your own understanding of what the lesson can teach your students. Using the debriefing questions with your students facilitates their conceptual experience and appreciation of the metaphoric journey. Additionally, the sharing of the concrete pictures each student generated will help your students appreciate the unique images that each person brings to the experience. The individual imagination of each student creates details different from everyone else. Students who were not sure they wanted to "go on the guided fantasy" are amazed at the enthusiasm and excitement of those who went. They will join in the next time you present a metaphoric lesson; be sure to avoid singling them out and remain accepting of their hesitancy. For some people, two or three such journeys are needed before their right brain will really "take over" consciously and provide the vivid images others have immediately.

*9. The Creative Insight Moment.*   List the questions and compressed metaphors you will use to link the concept and metaphor together. Think of improbable connections and analogies that could be creatively thought of as "true."

Building from the experiences of the other levels, these analogies often force original perspective and new understanding. Think about these statements; see if you can "prove" each statement to be true:

| Instructional<br>Goal #1<br>*Understanding the Metaphoric<br>Pattern* | Instructional<br>Goal #2<br>*Appreciating the Unpredictable<br>Nature of Changing* |
|---|---|
| 1. Level I and II (Focus and Comparison) are caterpillar stages. Level III (Interactive/Imagery) is the cocoon. Level IV (Creative Insight) is the butterfly's moment of flight. | 1. To change is to enter a cocoon. |
| | 2. Forced change opens the cocoon before its time. |
| | 3. Changing the values of childhood means creating wings for being an adult. |
| 2. Designing a metaphoric lesson is creating the "magic moment" of an opening cocoon. | 4. In life's "cocoon" periods, we first experience anxiety before we find the freedom to soar. |
| 3. Mastering a concept is having your own set of wings; you can still "crawl" if you want, but now you can also fly. | 5. Many people choose to stay caterpillars forever—rather than risk the uncertainty of the cocoon's impact and the life that follows. |
| 4. A guided fantasy is a cocoon. | 6. The home is the tree where the cocoon is attached; the classroom is the cocoon itself. |
| 5. Insight is a moment of flying. | 7. Self esteem soars after we experience the vulnerability of our caterpillar stage. The impact of a "safe" cocoon, and the potential of creating our own new self image. |
| 6. In the beginning, the concept we are teaching is only potential, like the caterpillar before it begins its journey. | |

Each insight statement is designed to prompt an awareness of how things fit together. The guided fantasy is a moment in which the student really reorganizes what he or she thinks about changing and the potential of allowing change to occur. Telling the student, "A guided fantasy is a cocoon," allows the student to envision the process without being told the teacher's insight. In fact, as you read each analogy, you discover more and more insights as to how the overall lesson could fit into your instructional unit.

The reconstruction of the South was an untimely, prematurely opened cocoon; people suffered from the exploitation of "carpetbaggers" who arrived while the "caterpillars" could no longer crawl and the "butterflies" were yet to evolve. The computer has become industry's instant cocoon—where ideas and information can be reorganized with lightning speed into countless patterns. Multiplication is, indeed, for the third grader, like gaining wings after two years of constant "crawling." The implications go on and on. Look at the subject you teach, its basic concepts, and the realizations you want students to gain. You can apply the metamorphosis process everywhere. In foreign language, it means having a way to explain the "plateaus" students encounter in assimilating new words and grammatical structure; in science, it means new respect for laboratory experiments as "cocoon" moments; in history, it means looking for the stages within specific cultures, nations, and peoples (When was the U.S. a caterpillar? In a cocoon stage? A butterfly? And does the process repeat itself?); in geography, you might see the Ice Age as a gigantic cocoon; in sociology, you might identify the family as the primary cocoon of life. The list can continue indefinitely; you will be limited only by seeking "right answers." In fact, there are no "right answers" (left-brain biases); there are only the myriad possible patterns, images, and implications. Take time to seek these out.

*10. Postassessment.* Describe the evaluative measures you will use to determine the outcome of your lesson. These measures will relate back to the instructional objectives you designed in Step 3 of this form.

The test of effective teaching is whether or not the learners really gain the projected new information, new attitudes, and new skills. To determine the impact of the lesson, we must return to the stated outcomes we predicted for you, the reader. If you were to design your own metaphoric teaching lesson now, you could demonstrate that you have learned the following:

1. That the lesson has four metaphoric levels: FOCUS, COMPARISON, INTERACTIVE/IMAGERY, and CREATIVE INSIGHT.
2. That you have mastered the design process of writing a guided fantasy.
3. That you can use the Metaphoric Design Format to create your own lesson.
4. That you can develop debriefing questions which prompt students to discover their own individuality and commonality with others.

However, we can also check your understanding of the design process and the unpredictable nature of change by using a posttest instrument. Take a moment to fill out the following posttest, and then "test" your answers against the "key" that has been provided. This self-evaluation will help you determine what parts (if any) of the overall design format need review or further study. (Remember that this type of assessment is more "left brain," that having to choose and verbalize words is considerably different from organizing images; nevertheless, it is critical to the success of the metaphoric lesson that we also focus upon left-brain knowledge, information, and skills.)

## POSTTEST QUESTIONS
### The Change/Butterfly Lesson

| Goal 1: Understanding How to Design Metaphoric Lessons | ANSWER KEY |
|---|---|
| 1. Name two reasons why the background of the student is important to the design of the lesson. | 1. Concept may be very familiar.<br>2. Metaphor may be unknown.<br>3. Students may be less capable or more capable than you thought. |
| 2. Define the difference between a goal and an instructional objective. | Goals are the ultimate learning we want students to have. Objectives are the actual, measureable skills and behaviors that they can achieve to show they have attained this learning: new attitudes, new information, and new performance skills. |
| 3. Give two benefits for using a pre-assessment before presenting your metaphoric lesson. | 1. Checks skill and concept level.<br>2. Provides an advance organizer.<br>3. Prompts personal motivation.<br>4. Takes an attitude inventory.<br>5. Shows where students started.<br>6. Can be a set induction. |
| 4. How does the concept relate to the metaphoric image? | The metaphor is chosen to show how the concept works; it is a familiar example that the student already understands. It provides a pattern that the concept fits. When the student understands this pattern, it can be applied to the subject matter easily. |
| 5. What are three important considerations in choosing the metaphor you will use? | 1. Basic characteristics are the the same.<br>2. Easily accessible props.<br>3. You personally enjoy the image. |
| 6. How does Level I (The Metaphoric Focus) involve the right brain's attention? | The right brain is stimulated by all the actual, physical objects pictures, and images. |
| 7. Name two immediate benefits to Level II's (The Personal Comparison) activity? | 1. Students stop intellectualizing.<br>2. Students share with one another.<br>3. Students experience insight.<br>4. Sharing sets an open climate. |
| 8. In Level III (The Interactive/Imagery Experience), the student becomes the metaphoric image. How can you design this experience? | 1. Use a guided fantasy experience.<br>2. Role play the metaphoric image's daily life or functions.<br>3. Nonverbally enact the metaphor's activities.<br>4. Visit with the metaphor and hold an imaginary conversation. |

| *Goal 1: Understanding How to Design Metaphoric Lessons* | *ANSWER KEY* |
|---|---|
| 9. Describe three benefits of having a guided fantasy experience? | 1. Visualization experience. 2. Relaxation moment. 3. Sense of metaphor's overall message. 4. A "time-out" from daily lessons. 5. A moment of personal soaring. |
| 10. How does the brain respond to the improbable connections that Level IV (The Creative Insight Moment) poses? | The right brain searches for a possible pattern; it will seek a way in which the statement can be "true." When such a possibility is found, the left brain develops a reasonable explanation. |
| 11. Why use a posttest? When should it be used? | The posttest helps you determine the overall understanding of the concept you are teaching. You can use it either right after the lesson or you can use it on the following day. |

| *Goal 2: Understanding the Nature of Changing* | *ANSWER KEY* |
|---|---|
| 12. Think of a time in your life when you experienced a significant change in your life style. | It could be a new child in the family, a time when you moved to another city, the first few weeks of being at college, your marriage, or, perhaps, a divorce. |
| 13. In the early stages of this change, you were like the caterpillar. How? | You had limited vision as to what the change would mean in your life; you were overwhelmed; you probably felt like you were "crawling." |
| 14. There was a time when you were reorganizing your skills, attitudes, values, and overall ability to deal with the change. It was much the same as being in the cocoon. Why? | You felt vulnerable, not in control, and maybe even impatient. It is difficult to build the new knowledge that allows you to cope with an abrupt change. It takes time. |
| 15. What adjectives describe how you felt during this time of adjusting? | You could feel vulnerable, frightened, angry to be at the mercy of things, uneasy, often anxious, pressured, even stressed—filled with an ongoing feeling of things being out of your control. There might also be an element of being excited and anticipating the unknown. |
| 16. When did you know you had developed your "wings" and could cope with the new change? | This usually involves an unpredicted moment when you felt very much at ease and able to handle the new |

**POSTTEST QUESTIONS** *(Continued)*

| Goal 2: Understanding the Nature of Changing | ANSWER KEY |
|---|---|
| | situation, its problems, and its obstacles. You could see the "big picture." |
| 17. Did your point of view change after you became more at ease with the new life style? Could you now see the situations from more than one perspective? | This ability to see the situation from both sides, the ability to see the meadow from below and from above, is a benefit we often overlook when we are in the midst of coping with the new life change. |
| 18. What advice would you give to the young caterpillars you have in the classroom? | They'll have these questions: is it worth it? Will I really gain the ability to handle this change? Why do I feel so much risk? So much vulnerability? Answer sincerely with your own personal wisdom; there is a thrill in mastering the new situation, a sense of joy in new skills, and a realization that you are in charge of your own life. |

*11. Materials and Equipment*   Make yourself a list of all props, supplies, audio–visual equipment, and instructional materials that you will need to teach this lesson.

*Props:* Butterfly cards, sculpture, stained glass figure, batik wall hanging, blue watercolor painting, poster of emerging butterfly, butterfly pillow, and Metropolitan Museum of Art Book of Butterflies.

*Audio–visual Equipment:* Overhead projector, screen, and butterfly transparencies

*Instructional Materials:* Pretest, script to the guided fantasy, debriefing sheet for insight questions, posttest, and answer key

This check list can be a lifesaver in moments when your time is really pressed.

*12. Personal Insights and Revision.*   Include insights you gained as a result of presenting the lesson. Note areas you are exploring and new ways to connect the metaphor with the concept you are teaching. Describe changes you would make in the future.

You could be thinking something like:

"I'm not sure, but it looks like fun. I won't really know how powerful it is until I have used it and seen the results with my students."

"I wonder what significant "change" experience I would like to teach using the lesson as an introduction."

"I think I would like to write a metaphoric lesson about _____ using _____ as my image. I wonder if I can do it?"

"I never thought I would have so many insights about myself just reading about a lesson I could use in my class."

We are thinking these thoughts:

This lesson is so flexible that it will fit any age group and any subject matter. We hope the reader will try it and discover how much fun it is.

We wish we could meet the reader after he or she has used the lesson; it would be rewarding to hear his or her reactions and comments.

In the past this moment of personal insight and revision has helped make the present lesson what it is; we learned about the butterfly and change as we taught it. Countless teachers and students in the Houston area have experienced the excitement and change of the cocoon and the subsequent flight over the meadow. We hope this book allows teachers and students all over the country to have a similar experience.

## SUMMARY

These two complete metaphoric lessons represent that special integration of left-hemisphere knowledge and right-hemisphere imagery that so often produce moments of creativity and conceptualization. While the lessons are long and thorough, the opportunities for student achievement of the goals of the lesson are considerably increased by the virtue of this thoroughness. Three or four of these complete lessons during the first year of using metaphoric teaching is probably a reasonable goal; teachers have found that the time invested is more than justified by the student response.

What can you do when time is the critical factor, and you want to combine creativity and concept learning in a condensed metaphoric lesson? The answer—the "short form."

# CHAPTER 7

# The Short Form: Planning for an Abbreviated Metaphoric Lesson

## A LOOK FORWARD

Sometimes it's easier to begin a new activity and a new way of thinking with a shorter and simpler, rather than longer and more complicated, activity, always keeping in mind exactly what it is you want to accomplish. This section, entitled "Planning for an Abbreviated Metaphoric Lesson," introduces the condensed design format, a format that allows you to use a metaphoric lesson when you have only a day or perhaps only a few hours to prepare the lesson. In fact, after completing the "short form" exercise, the "long form" becomes an enhancement experience, a chance to create a permanent metaphoric lesson that you will use year after year.

Suppose you were offered an all-expense-paid vacation to Europe, and in addition, you were told that the vacation must begin on August 10 and could last anywhere from a few days to thirty days—the duration of the trip would be up to you. Your problem is that school begins August 27! Although you would like to be able to thoroughly visit one country or see the "sights" in seven or eight, you are caught in a values conflict. Two beliefs vie for your attention; first, you believe that you should start school with your students; second, you believe that you have worked hard for years and that you do deserve such a vacation. The first belief prevails, however, and you decide you must make a compromise. You will visit one country for fifteen days, or you will see the "sights" in only three countries, not seven or eight. Metaphoric teaching often presents a similar challenge in terms of allocating time and determining priorities.

Ideally, each lesson would include a thorough implementation of the metaphoric instructional design process: student background, instructional goal, instructional objectives, pre-assessment, context/focus, metaphoric focus, personal comparison questions, interactive/imagery experiences, creative insight questions, postassessment procedures, materials and equipment, and feature modifications. Pre-assessment, concept analysis, postassessment, and debriefing insights would all be considered critical factors. But teachers are busy people and sometimes there just isn't time to do everything "by the book." In teaching, we often encounter moments when spontaneity and momentum require us to innovate almost on the spot. Time may be short, but the needs are great! These constraints are beyond our control. The question is: How can we create a metaphoric lesson on short notice? How can we design such a lesson quickly and effectively? This chapter provides the answers to these questions.

## HOW DO I PREPARE MY FIRST LESSON?

There are five elements essential to the metaphoric lesson. These elements will help you create such "short notice" lessons:

1. *The Context and Focus*   Take time to think about why you want to use the metaphoric lesson.

   What is it that you are trying to accomplish by using a metaphoric lesson? What is your goal? What are your objectives in terms of: (1) new knowledge, (2) new attitudes, and (3) new performance abilities?

2. *The Metaphor*   Choose a symbol or object as the metaphoric image and provide a collection of props.

   What concrete images are available for the right brain? Remember, the right brain "thinks" in images, not words.

3. *The Comparison*   Design a personal comparison question that allows the student to discover a way in which he or she has something in common with the metaphoric image.

   How can you help the student identify with the metaphoric image? This step is crucial to getting the student "ready" for the interactive/imagery experience.

4. *The Interactive/Imagery Experience*   Take the students through some kind of interactive or imagery experience with the metaphoric image, an experience in which the student "becomes" the image itself.

   How does the concept work? The students will experience the answer in the enactment of the interactive or imagery exercise. In visiting the world of the metaphor, the students will gain an appreciation for what the metaphor can teach them about the concept.

5. *Insight Questions*   Tie the lesson together with debriefing questions that link the overall metaphoric experience with the concept and the subject matter you are teaching.

   What questions can you ask that will focus upon how the concept really works? How can you tie the image to the subject matter being studied? How can the metaphor teach new thinking, new attitudes, and new perceptions?

The following sample lesson illustrates these five elements in a "short notice" metaphoric lesson. Let's assume it is the weekend and you are trying to plan a Monday class presentation. You are teaching ninth graders a history unit on political revolution, and the class has had trouble visualizing why some revolutions are considered "good" while others are seen as destructive. You are concerned with the overall concept—the awareness that revolutionary ideas can transform the established system of a well-ordered government as happened in both the American and Russian revolutions.

## I. The Context and Focus

The context of this lesson stems from a history unit you are teaching on revolutions. The particular focus of this lesson is understanding political revolution, particularly the way in which a new system develops and violently overthrows an old one. This concept is important, because your students are presently studying the French and American revolutions. The primary goal of the lesson is helping students become aware of the power and impact of a revolutionary idea within the "body politic" and the way that "body" will resist and counterattack. They are already familiar with dialectical processes.

New knowledge (cognitive), new attitudes (affective), and new performance skills (psychomotor) that you want students to develop are included in the following objectives:

*Cognitive:* Students will be able to identify the basic role of ideas within a revolution: excite, prompt to action, envelop, and then stabilize new order.

*Affective:* Students will be able to describe their feelings in regard to a people's "revolt" as they look at the American, French, Irish, and Cuban revolutions.

*Psychomotor:* Students will be able to visualize the inside world of an established human system. They will "see" cells as translucent building blocks, blood as a river, nerves as large nets, and the interior of the body with its own inherent order and enforcement systems.

## II. The Metaphor

Choosing a metaphor for this lesson means finding an analogy where something small has the ability to attack, grow, and finally overthrow the larger force it confronts. After a quick personal brainstorm, you consider the following possibilities:

David and Goliath (the small boy and his tiny slingshot conquer the giant and his large sword).
The tiny acorn as it takes over a stone wall.
The wind that grows in power during a hurricane and finally uproots houses and trees.
A virus as it grows within a human body.

You decide to use the virus, primarily because it ideally illustrates the potential impact of a miniscule force upon a large "body politic." As your students see the way a virus can be "born," grow, attack, and gain strength within the body, they will discover how an idea can be born, grow, attack, and gain strength within a country.

To begin the lesson, you have decided to introduce and discuss the novel and movie, *The Incredible Journey* by Isaac Asimov.* Some of your students are already aware of this science-fiction story in which a team of medical specialists in a submarine are miniaturized and injected into a human body in order to repair the heart valve of a great scientist.

Focusing on the movie will help the students get ready for visualizing a similar experience. Several types of illustrations of this movie are available, but other images such as pictures of healthy cells and diseased organs are also needed. In the short time available, seek out as many props as you can; look for pictures of the human body and illustrations of viruses. Check the local library for medical dictionaries, various encyclopedias and other popular sources. (The Time/Life Science series has a whole section devoted to the virus and its many effects.) You might decide to include among the pictures some examples of tulips. This flower actually gains its beauty, color, and shape from a virus.

You might also decide to review with the class the power of right brain imagery; eighth-, ninth-, and tenth-grade classes (in particular) require well-developed "left-brain reasoning" (an actual introduction to the two brain hemispheres and their separate functions) in order to allow themselves moments of right-brain creativity and imagery. You know that you will need to caution the students to suspend their judgmental attitudes (left-brain critical thinking) in order to free their imaginations (right-brain creative thinking) and allow new perspectives to emerge—perspectives that will illustrate what happens in a political revolution.

---

*You could give this story as a homework assignment the week before, if the lesson evolves to become part of your permanent curriculum.

Finally, you will need to highlight the positive roles of the virus—how it combats cancer (synthetic interferon), immunizes (polio vaccine), reprograms congenital diseases (viral genetic engineering), and even creates new products (the several varieties of the beautiful tulip). The students will be accustomed to thinking of the virus as destructive; by acknowledging the positive potential of the virus, you will allow them to consider the essentially neutral nature of the virus. Where it is true that the virus supplants the original cell, it is also true that supplanting can have a positive effect; some systems are improved and enhanced by a "viral" replacement process.

## III. Comparison

Designing a question that allows students to identify with a virus is more difficult than it looks. Few people want to imagine how they and a virus are alike, but you can ask students:

Think of something you and the virus have in common. What common experience do you share with the virus?

This question will allow students to identify their own feelings about being on the outside of the adult world—not children anymore, but not adults either. They can see parallels between the virus entering the body and seeking control and their entry into adulthood seeking personal autonomy. Students will find themselves talking about their roles within the family, school, and society in general; they will talk about the difficulty of being different, of potentially being a force to be considered, but generally powerless to affect a system beyond their control. Students will discover how they often conform to established rules and policies—policies that seem almost impossible to change.

## IV. The Interactive/Imagery Experience

To lead into the imagery experience for this lesson, ask your students how it feels to always do things the way others want them done. How does it feel to conform to other people's rules? Then explain that the visit they are about to take is an experience with the development of power—an experience in discovering how a tiny force disrupts a gigantic system and gains the strength to overthrow it. It will be a guided fantasy in which they will encounter obstacles and danger but remain safe and in control throughout.* It will be an extraordinary

---

*Wherever safety is a potential issue, it is imperative to assure students ahead of time that they will not be in any real danger within the fantasy experience. This reassurance

opportunity to experience the contagious way an idea can grow and gain power—power that can confront an existing system and its established way of doing things. The lesson will be their own "incredible journey," an incredible journey to demonstrate each individual's own potential when a new idea enters a system that demands conformity for survival.

With this introduction, ask the students to close their eyes, and relax . . . to breathe deeply and to allow themselves to become totally at ease.

## The Guided Fantasy Text

With your eyes closed and in complete silence, imagine that you are shrinking in size . . . You are becoming smaller and smaller . . . See yourself as half your size . . . then half of that . . . and then half of that and again . . . and again . . . and again . . . until you are as small as the head of a pin . . . Now become half as small as that . . . and again . . . and again . . . and again . . . Now you are barely the size of a pin point, but you must get smaller . . . You become half as small as the pinpoint . . . then half of that . . . again and again and again . . . Now you are too small to be seen without a regular microscope but you must get smaller and smaller and smaller until you can only be seen by a powerful electron microscope . . . You are now smaller than the smallest living cell . . . Now you must curl yourself into a spiral, almost like a spiral spring . . . This is your core, your inside . . . Outside this core you have wrapped around you a layer of protein and fat . . . It protects your core the way a heavy coat protects you in winter . . .

Imagine yourself as this small little spiral drifting on the wind, drifting, drifting . . . drifting . . . Suddenly you land on a moist surface and you feel like you are being taken upstream along a tiny river . . . You are now inside a human body . . . You travel alone along many rivers, you pass by different organs, different cells, different structures . . . until you finally stop and attach your outer core to a cell . . . A cell much larger than yourself . . . You stay there a long time, first hours . . . then weeks, then months . . . perhaps, years . . . Finally, you enter the cell you have been attached to . . . You go to the center of the cell . . . You enter the very nucleus of the cell . . . Soon the cell divides and you produce an exact replica of yourself, another spiral with a coat around it and that replica of yourself goes with the cell that is splitting away . . . Now, slowly . . . ever so slowly, you move out of the nucleus and into the cytoplasm . . . and you give a message to the cytoplasm . . . You tell it to make more spirals and more protective coats just like

---

then sets boundaries for the imagery and controls the emotional responses prompted by the lesson.

yourself . . . Suddenly the cell becomes a factory making replicas of you
. . . There are more and more and more of you inside the cell until the
cell breaks open and you all spill out . . . Now each of your replicas goes
to another cell and attaches itself and then slides inside to reproduce
more and more and more of you . . . Now you begin to search, you search
through the veins, those long, blue-red canals, and you search all
around you . . . You are seeking a nerve that will lead to a muscle.
. . . Nerves are your food—and also your enemy. They carry messages
to the muscles from the brain and spinal cord. . . . You keep searching,
looking for the nerve, wary of its power . . . Then, suddenly, you see a
nerve . . . There are nerve endings on the outside of the cell body up
ahead; you reach out and attack the nerve . . . Quickly, you get caught
up in the nerve fibers, they are like a net . . .

You feel trapped, and there is only one way to escape . . . overcoming
and capturing . . . Now, this nerve is yours; it is no longer as large or
as strong as it was before you reached it . . . Its power is gone . . . It can
no longer send signals to the brain . . . Now you rest and you reattach
yourself to another cell, but this cell is leaving the body, it is travelling
up, up, up, and now outside the body . . . You have left the battle now
and you are beginning to grow and change again, you are growing and
growing and growing and you are changing form . . . You are beginning
to become like yourself again . . . You are getting larger and larger and
larger, until finally, you are back to your normal self . . . Now, when
you are ready, open your eyes and return to the classroom.

## V. Insight Questions

This part of the lesson ties the whole experience together and produces a moment of conceptual understanding and insight. At this point,
you want the students to see the natural connections between what
happens to the virus and what happens when a (viral) idea takes over
a country. To help them develop these connections, you pose the following questions for discussion. Your directions:

The following statements can be true. Search your minds for ways you could
prove that each of them is, in fact, true. What can you offer as examples to show
that the statement can be true?

1. Taxing the tea for the colonists was like the virus first entering the body.
   Why?
2. The "redcoats" were nerves that responded too slowly.
3. If Equal Rights were the virus, nonuniversal suffrage was the body it
   attacked.
4. The nerve nets were the British military bases; the unconventional warfare

of the colonists was like the virus living within the cell in order to gain strength to attack it.

5. A virus attacked the French monarchy in the 1790s.

Now explore the following questions in terms of the increased insight you can gain:

6. How is the virus of freedom like the tulip virus?
7. What virus idea would you like to see grow within your family? Your school? Your society?
8. What established systems would such ideas end up fighting? Would the destruction of what is already established be worth the impact of your new idea?
9. What does the idea need in order to improve the body it confronts? Under what circumstances is the virus a positive force?
10. Inflation is the common cold virus that hits each nation today. Why?
11. The Federal Reserve is a nerve net that combats this virus. Explain.
12. Who are the white corpuscles in free enterprise? What body are they protecting? What viruses attack them? Can a free enterprise system develop cancer? How?
13. Schools are the immunization virus that prevents the polio virus of ignorance from destroying the future of our country. How?
14. Name some tulips that the viral idea of nonconformity has created.

These five steps, then (the context and focus, the metaphor, the comparison questions, the interactive experience, and the insight/debriefing questions), are the essence of the metaphoric lesson "short form." These steps summarize the essentials of the long form while providing you, the busy teacher, an opportunity to incorporate creative conceptualization techniques in the regular curriculum on very short notice.

However, for many teachers, the question still remains, "I have seen these steps and I understand basic instructional design; yet I have never used metaphoric lessons. Where do I get my ideas? How do I plan my first lesson?" The process is not as difficult as it might initially appear. The following section, based on recent work with classroom teachers, suggests some useful ways to begin using the metaphoric process.

## HOW DO I PREPARE MY FIRST LESSON?

### A Dialogue with Judy Sanders

Not long ago a graduate student of mine came to my office to talk about metaphors; she had been struggling to create a metaphoric lesson for her very specific school population—deaf students. Her students could "sign," ranged from second to sixth grade, had a full range of academic ability, and needed a chance to discover "their own creativity." She was excited about the imagery potential inherent in metaphoric teaching but stymied by how to begin designing a lesson for her classroom.

I began with the basic question: "What is a concept that is essential for your students to learn, something you would like all of them to discover and to be able to use?"

Jane thought for a minute and answered, "That, whether they can express it clearly or not, they are truly creative. So often they do not see the possibilities around them, they feel confined to a world that is limited, defined by others, and often out of their control. For the deaf student, life usually appears as if totally controlled by others. Getting them to appreciate their own creative potential could open new worlds for these students."

"So, the nature of creativity that you're talking about would be the sense of individual expansion, an individual understanding of what 'could be' instead of 'what is'?"

"Yes, and more. I'd also like them to enjoy themselves. I would like them to be able to explore and find out that they have talent to create things on their own . . ."

Because the metaphoric lesson itself is so inherently creative, we needed to define carefully what aspects were important to Jane. Did she want her students to discover that creativity takes discipline as well as intuition? That creativity can occur in math as well as art? That creativity can be fun? In the discussion that followed, it became more apparent to me that Jane wanted them to delight in their own artistic products and to discover that creative resources were all around them.

Our initial reaction was to move back to what had already been designed. For example, we considered the Change/Butterfly Lesson. The butterfly lesson is excellent for stimulating creative awareness, but how could it work for deaf students? They could read the guided fantasy, even read the fantasy while sitting in a meadow, but we were wary of such a simple solution. The uniqueness of the deaf student was a problem and it posed numerous challenges; we decided to put the Change/Butterfly Lesson on the "back burner" while we searched for other solutions. What else could we think of? Jane decided that she wanted something special that would be uniquely hers to share with her class.

We thought of "diamantes." These are special diamond shaped poems that practically everybody can write.* Writing the diamantes

---

*Diamantes are short poems in the form of diamonds. The poems begin and end with nouns with the second and sixth lines being adjectives, the third and fifth lines participles

could be a special form of Level III, the interactive level. The other levels could then focus upon the concept "diamond." The lesson might begin with pictures and actual forms of the diamond; students could be asked where diamonds come from, what they symbolize, why they are valued. The process of making a diamond from carbon, the years needed to change the carbon, and the process of mining of diamonds might begin the lesson. Later, students could look at a real diamond and various pictures of diamonds could be introduced. The example of the unusual diamond might be the baseball diamond. Next, students could compare themselves to a diamond. For the deaf students, this might be an exciting comparison (are they bits of carbon being compressed by learning into small diamonds?). Level III could be the creation of "diamantes" and Level IV might pose such problems as proving these statements are true:

> Signing is a way of mining diamonds.
> Cutting a diamond is going to school.
> Making a diamond in the ground is like getting an education.
> Being deaf is having a diamond inside of you.
> Lip reading is like mining diamonds.

The connections are endless; the potential for personal discoveries boundless. We chatted for several minutes, but Jane was still not satisfied; she wanted to do something else. What might we do with younger students; students who didn't know nouns, participles, adjectives? How could we use the lesson with them?

Jane's questions seem to suggest a sense of awe for the metaphoric process; it was as though the metaphoric lesson had to be special, that it had somehow to involve special symbols, symbols so unique or unusual that no one had used them before. We had to remind ourselves that we were overlooking an essential characteristic of designing metaphoric lessons: namely, that they should use commonplace symbols (things the students already know something about), preferably raw materials from the classroom. We brainstormed further.

"What are some everyday materials you have in the classroom?"

---

and the fourth line nouns. We first saw this idea in the "Green Box" materials published by Humboldt County Schools in Eureka, California.

```
                        light
                white          broken
        shimmering        shining        bouncing
    heat            day            color            night
        streaming        lengthening        promising
            propitious        scary
                dark
```

Jane thought for a moment and answered, "The younger students have building blocks."

"How could we design a lesson around building blocks?" I asked. "What concepts would students be learning? Why have building blocks in the classroom?"

"We use them to teach sequence, how things fit on top of one another, how building is a step-by-step experience."

"Well, that's our concept. Now, how could we design Level I?"

"We could begin with the building blocks they use at play time. Then, we could look at other building blocks, wood ones, plastic ones, maybe Tinkertoys, perhaps even look at pictures of the concrete blocks that are used on construction projects outside the classroom. We might even get some bricks. We could go look at a house being built or visit a construction site; we could look at pictures of the pyramids or other architectural wonders."

"What would be an improbable block?"

"Maybe, we could use a little cloth block, like the ones that are made for infants to play with."

"Great, that cloth block would help them formulate the whole image of 'what constitutes a block?' What makes a block, in fact, a block?"

Jane smiled, the images were still in her mind. Next, we moved to Level II. "What questions could we pose to the students?"

"We could ask them to pick the block most like them," Jane answered quickly. "Some might see the concrete, the wood, the classroom cardboard, the plastic, and even the cloth."

"Then, they could explain why they chose the specific example."

Jane was obviously becoming energized by the discussion; I probed further: "What can we do with your students so they can really interact with the blocks? What activity could we design to enable them to comprehend the metaphor of blocks?"

"We might have them build a building in the classroom," Jane answered.

"What kind of a building?"

"Suppose they decide what the building will be and tell me why they built it?"

That way, the students would enjoy sharing such an experience with their teacher—and she would gain new insights on their values, perspectives, and maybe even their dreams.

"Now, are there other interactive exercises we could use for Level III?" I asked. "Could we do anything else with our metaphor?"

"Well, we might want them to learn the principles of building structures, so we could give them blocks and ask each student to build a special building, or groups to build a special building to share with the class."

This response was also appropriate; the objective of Level III is to create a sense of physical contact with the metaphor. We could also have them read a guided fantasy about being a brick or block in someone's house or have the students pantomine being a brick or a block. The most important element is to make certain that the students have a very real, physical experience with the image itself—in this case, the block.

"Now, how about Level IV?" I continued.

"They could prove things like . . . "

Blocks are books; different grades are building blocks.
A family is a building with many different kinds of blocks.
Signing is putting blocks into place.
The alphabet is a cloth block; reading is using blocks to build real buildings.
Friendship is sharing your blocks.

Our synergy had increased; still Jane did not appear completely "sold" on the block lesson.

"Want to do some more?"

"Yes, can we keep brainstorming? What else could I do?"

"Ok, let's look at creativity again. What's important in being creative?"

"Seeing unusual connections. Like solving a human puzzle."

"What about a puzzle as a metaphor?"

In the minutes that followed we reconstructed another lesson. Beginning with the imagery of a puzzle, we first identified the symbols, the items to use in Level I's focus phrase. We thought of all kinds of puzzles: crossword puzzles, jigsaw puzzles, mazes, labyrinths, the kind of toy puzzle with the little ball to get in place, the pinball machine, and even the large-piece wooden puzzle for little children.

Next, we decided upon some Level II questions, such as "How am I a puzzle?" or "The puzzle most like me would be . . . ", and hurried on to Level III. For a minute or two, we just quietly stretched our minds.

"They could be a puzzle and make a picture for you." I offered.

"I have another idea," Jane countered. "How about providing them with magazines and cardboard. The object would be to find two pictures they like and glue them on both sides of a single cardboard sheet. Then, they could cut out a jigsaw puzzle for their neighbor to solve."

"Right. They could learn that solving the puzzle means recognizing the picture when you see it."

"Yes," answered Jane. "They will find that solving puzzles means looking for clues. The exercise will naturally force them to choose to put together either side A or side B."

We both found ourselves enjoying the mental image of the young students discovering the lesson inherent in the puzzle exercise.

"What about Level IV? What improbable connections could they prove?"

Jane suggested:

School is a puzzle—why?
Adding and subtracting are two-sided puzzles.
Reading is a crossword puzzle.
Signing is a puzzle solver.
Lips are clues to people puzzles.

It seemed that Jane was finally there; I asked if she wanted to continue. She nodded, she said she was not done yet; in fact, that she was just beginning.

"What else is there in the classroom to build a lesson around?" I asked. "Think of everyday items, things that are readily available. Things that you can use as images, but are there for the children to find quickly."

We thought of lessons on shapes, circles, rectangles, triangles, and squares. We thought of pencils—how human pencils could write non-verbal stories for the class; we thought of paper clips and what kind of exercises we could use for interacting with them. Finally, Jane looked up with a smile and said, "I've got it."

"I'm going to use crayons. They're easily available, the students love to use them. And, there are crayon candles, crayon soap, and crayon containers I could use in the Focus phase. The Level II question could be how they're like a crayon, or better still, it could be, 'I am a *(color)* crayon, because . . .' "

"What would you do about Level III?" I asked.

"Can the lesson last two days?" she responded.

"Of course, you're the teacher; make it work for you."

"Well, they can all decide to come to school as a specific crayon. They can come in their color and with as many props as they want to show their color and why it's important. Maybe I'll duck out of the room and dress as a color first and show them how to be a pink crayon."

I offered excited approval, "What about Level IV?"

A family is a box of crayons. Explain.
If school is a red crayon, what color is home?
Signing means having a box of crayons.
Reading is having crayons to match your mood.
Math is having two crayons make a new color.

I looked at Jane, the pattern had taken form; she understood. It's not the special images that make the metaphoric lesson, it's the curiosity of the students and the courageous imagination of the teacher. I knew now that she could use all the images in the classroom; the fingers of the children who were learning how to sign, the windows of the classroom and the windows of the world they could discover, the blackboard eraser, the curtains, the swings at recess time. The symbols were all around her; they were hers for the asking—what treasures would she discover in that classroom? What new insights would her students find each day?

I reflected momentarily on the exciting resource within our right brains, and looked forward to the next time that Jane would come by and share her qualms, her discoveries, her newly found resources.

I also realized that this is the basic process of completing a metaphoric lesson. Interacting mentally with the symbols is a creative exercise for the teacher and, as this story with Jane indicates, is not difficult and is very rewarding.

## PLANNING THE METAPHORIC LESSON: A SUMMARY

In working with teachers from grades K–12, including many who didn't consider themselves at all "creative," simply participating in a single lesson where there was a thorough debriefing and complete explanation of the basic methods and forms enabled these teachers to produce quality metaphoric lessons in a very short time. Typically, the most difficult parts of the lesson to prepare are the guided journey and the questions for creative insight; each of these components can be completed quickly and efficiently if the teacher has done some very basic preparation. The nature of this preparation and some hints for the first-time teacher are included below as each of these two elements is considered separately. First, we discuss the guided journey.

As we noted in the preceding examination of the long and short forms, the guided journey is the core of metaphoric teaching; it is during this part of the lesson that the student is able to become experientially involved with the object under study, to create his or her own insights, to experience a moment of cognitive and affective understanding, and to begin to integrate the present moment of learning into a series of past learning moments, the present concept into past concepts. The preparation of the guided journey is, therefore, critical to the successful teaching of a metaphoric lesson. There are a number of basic, easy steps that can help ensure the proper preparation of an appropriate Level III activity:

1. *Have a reliable source for the content you want to teach.* If, for example, you are going to teach the concept of photosynthesis, find a reference with sufficient detail to adequately explain this concept at the required level of difficulty. (Tenth graders, obviously, are able to comprehend the concept at a more abstract level than sixth graders.)

2. *Be extremely careful in your language when designing the guided journey.* The language of the guided journey must encourage both conceptual understanding and image formation in your students; therefore, while the language must be highly descriptive, it cannot be too prescriptive. The language must suggest rather than define. For example, in the lesson on "time" there are suggestions of familiar objects—rocks, organisms, animals; yet there is not specification as to exactly what these things are. The guided fantasy does not allude to brontosaurs, protozoa, amoebae, or pterodactyls. When man is mentioned, he is not described as of a certain height, hair, or skin color. Man is not described in terms of clothing or hairiness; these things are purposefully not mentioned so that the student has an opportunity to create his or her own image and then compare that image later with the one created by other members of the class. This part of the guided journey is useful for the student, as it provides a moment of both personal and content-related insight. (We might add that the teacher should not be surprised at the images formed by students, young students in particular. One group of fourth-grade students who participated in the "time" exercise described their images of the first men as being in three-piece suits, living in brick houses, and going to work in the city every morning!)

3. *Be certain that there is a flow to the guided journey.* It is crucial that the guided journey not have rapid shifts of content or shifts in mood or tense, and that it move gently from one point to the next. In our experience as well as that of the teachers we have worked with, this has been almost impossible to do at one writing. Our most successful approach has been to make a perusal of the information to be taught, place it in a logical sequence (often chronological) and write a first draft which is considerably more lengthy than required. Then we go back over it making cuts here and there and adding the necessary pauses and transitions. Again, these transitions are necessary to maintain the proper flow. Rapid shifts in direction usually break the concentration of the listener and can break the mood of the guided journey, thus causing the lesson to fail. Refer to the sample lessons in both the first chapter and the second part of the book for examples of these transitions; they are very important to the success of your effort to tap into the right brain through the metaphoric teaching strategy.

4. *Keep these guided journeys in a file for use in other years or in other subjects.* The same guided journey can be adapted to be used with different groups to teach concepts in science, social studies, self-development and a number of other subject areas. They can also be revised easily to be used for higher or lower level/age students.

The second component of metaphoric teaching that provides the most difficulty for teachers who are preparing their first metaphoric lesson is the Level IV creative insight questions. The secret to designing effective creative insight questions is in the use of paradox and hypothetical extension. Juxtaposing two phrases that either seem inconsistent or that require a conceptual leap to connect seems to demand from the student an unconventional response! Explaining why "every friendship is a series of balloon trips" pushes the student to think in a way not normally associated with the regular school curriculum—a way that is more imaginative, less analytical.

Consider the following insight questions:

Science lab is a cocoon—why?
A novel is an hour glass—why?
Cancer is the twentieth-century stopwatch—why?

Each of these questions includes a statement that initially seems unbelievable, contradictory or absurd, but which upon further examination contains the essential elements of truth (i.e., is paradoxical). It is the continual examination of these kinds of questions that produces both creative thinking and insightful response. Your first attempt at writing these kinds of questions will probably leave you feeling somewhat uncomfortable; after all, these are not the kinds of questions we normally ask. Once defined, asked, and responded to, however, this type of question will become easier and easier for you to write and use as well as more meaningful for your students as a learning tool. Writing both the guided journeys and the insight questions becomes personally rewarding after only one or two experiences with metaphoric teaching.

Nevertheless, getting started on that first lesson can be a stumbling block for some teachers. The following sections are, therefore, designed to help overcome this obstacle by providing three different kinds of assistance: first, complete long-form lessons; second, complete short-form lessons; and third, several different types of strategies to establish the climate for creativity in your classroom. The combination of the creative climate that encourages students to explore and the metaphoric lessons that capitalize on this exploration can bring right-brain imagery knowledge into a cooperative conceptualization process with left-brain rational knowledge.

# CHAPTER 8

# *Complete (Long Form) Lessons and Sample Format*

# METAPHORIC TEACHING LESSON PLAN
## The Shoes/Empathy Lesson
### The Long Form: A Participant's Guide

*1. Background of the Class.* Describe your students, the instructional unit you are teaching, the grade level, and any special factors important for understanding the classroom environment.

This lesson is designed specifically to help students imagine what it would be like to be in someone else's shoes. Often students are sympathetic toward a given plight—the devastation of war, the homelessness of orphans, the despair of broken dreams, the destruction of ideas, cities, and nations. But this sympathy translates as "pity," or "feeling sorry" for those caught up in the crisis; we want students to extend themselves—to go beyond being sympathetic—to imagine what it would be like if they themselves were in that situation. This means more than "identifying"—the act of finding something analogous in one's own world with which to compare the situation. It means actually imagining what it would be like to experience war, to be suddenly without a family, to be caught in a broken dream, or to be facing the destruction of your ideas, your city, or your nation.

Opportunities to use this lesson exist wherever it is helpful to have the student "feel" the role of those they are studying or the world of what they are studying. If you would tame a horse, learn to think like a horse; if you would conquer a nation, learn to think like that nation; if you would master the elements, learn to anticipate the actions of the storm. Opportunities for utilizing the concept of empathy are common to most curricular areas:

Biology, science classes

As students study any given animal, its habitat, and its behavior, their understanding of the animal's unique niche increases with their empathy for that animal.

As students study the virus, they can conceptually understand its power when they "become" the virus.

Any natural system, life system, or predictable chemical reaction provides students the opportunity to use empathy and anticipate how the situation works

213

by "being" the item studied. Take, for example, a hurricane; from the point of view of the hurricane, students quickly learn the basic conceptual dynamics of the storm.

Even the path of a food chain would be more easily understood if students "became" an element in that chain and experienced the whole cycle.

**English literature**

The ability to "become" Macbeth, Romeo, Huck Finn, Phinney, or Evangeline would help students feel the pathos of their lives, to understand the fragility of the human condition, and increase their empathy for all people.

Equally important in English literature is understanding the voice/perspective of the author. Moving into the shoes of the character allows the teacher to demonstrate more than one voice—more than one perspective on the theme, plot, and characters.

Examining a piece of fiction for its ability to portray what it means to be human, accepting nonfiction for its sincere statements on the human condition, even reading history with a difference (through the eyes of the historical writer) are all legitimate empathetic skills for students to develop. What was it like to be Anne Frank? How was Churchill's version of World War II selective? How does *Animal Farm* say something profound about what it means to be political?

**Math, geometry, algebra**

How does the engineer use math? The architect? The chemist? The physician? The computer programmer? Seeing the subject matter from their points of view is motivating to the student; it makes the entire subject area "reasonable" because it provides a context, a "big picture" which could someday be the student's own life career.

What was Euclid trying to express? Why did he invent a mathematical language to express these ideas?

What was the motivation of those who invented "new math"? What did they seek to accomplish?

How did Einstein explode what we thought to be true about math? What was he feeling when he formulated the Theory of Relativity?

**Social studies, History, Political science**

This subject matter lends itself well to the development of empathy; we want students to imagine what it would be like to be in another nation, in another time period, or in another system of government.

This lesson initiates such inquiry and can be followed by a "day in the life of _____": any person, nation, setting, system being studied.

You're Alexander the Great—what are you planning to do? You're the new Princess of Wales, how are you feeling? You're Jimmy Carter looking at Reagan's term of office; what do you wish to retain? The possibilities are everywhere, in every lesson.

**Art class**

You are a lump of clay waiting to be made into something—what? Let the clay tell you what it wants to be.

You are a painting waiting to be discovered on a hillside; what painting lies there, what does that scene want to say?

**Music class**

You are John Philip Sousa and you have just written a march; how do you want to hear it played?

You are a flute and capable of great music; what do you wish we could hear?

You are the instrument; how would you like to be kept?

The lesson is only limited by the teacher's imagination; in any given subject matter area there is a wealth of possible empathetic connections. Think of the instructional units you are presently teaching; who would you like students to understand? What process/situation would you like students to experience? The lesson begins that process; it teaches that the student can separate his or her identity from the subject being studied and project the likely feelings and experiences he or she would have if actually faced with walking in the shoes of that person.

*2. Instructional Goals.*   Describe the overall purpose of teaching the lesson. Include the concept you want your students to learn and the context for this concept within the instructional unit you are teaching.

Several related concepts are modelled in this lesson:

*Multi-cultural awareness*   What does it feel like to be Vietnamese in this country? How did it feel to be the Irish at the turn of the century? To be an American Black after the Civil War? After Martin Luther King, Jr.'s, death?

What does it mean to be Chinese, living in China? Or Russian living in Russia? What values would be part of your life? How would you see the world differently? Feel differently? Perceive differently?

There are several possibilities for walking in many different kinds of shoes, on many different pathways, with many different experiences. This lesson is limited only by the diversity of cultures you can introduce and make students aware of.

*Anticipating the other person's game plan*   Whether we are talking about sports, team competition, or battle strategy, this lesson can help students become sensitized to giving up their own biases and assuming the biases of the opposite side. It is the basic awareness needed for designing offensive/defensive strategies, and it is a critical skill for effective leadership.

*Nonverbal awareness*   Ninety percent of all our communication is nonverbal, yet our students are often unaware of this dimension. This exercise demonstrates the vast amount of information available nonverbally and allows the student to practice becoming more aware of this source of knowledge.

*Situational problem solving*   Some problems can only be understood if you are able to imagine yourself caught up in them. This lesson stretches the imagination and allows you to experience developing a perspective of the problem from the inside-out. By placing yourself in the situation, you are able to anticipate the feelings, actions, and thoughts that are typical of that problem. This allows a third-person objectivity in considering possible solutions.

*Empathy*   The lesson, however, was not originally written to teach empathy; rather we were seeking to help some grade school students understand what it was like to be different from the "norm"—and then to imagine the world from the point of view of that other individual.

As such, the lesson helps students with "mainstreaming," helps classes accept foreign students openly, helps individuals be open to troubled students or students who encounter daily psychological abuse.

Empathy, the ability to become a human mirror of the other person —to step into the shoes of the other, to enter the world as the other sees it—is a critical skill for every young person. It solves arguments, it resolves conflict, and it mends fences.

There are many other personality development concepts to be found in this lesson, but suffice to say that empathy was chosen as a basic humanistic skill to help students become aware of (and become effective in working with) others. Empathy is a "right-brain" communication skill, and as such it is concerned with holistic perception, not with detailed analysis or memorized dialogue. For classroom management or basic conflict resolution, it is likely the most powerful skill you can teach any student.

What should students learn about empathy? Begin by checking Webster's definition:

The action of understanding, being aware of, being sensitive to and vicariously experiencing the feelings, thoughts and experience of another of either the past or present without having the feelings thoughts and experience fully communicated in an objective explicit manner; also: the capacity for this.

This lesson will concentrate primarily on the first definition; the lesson seeks to have students feel, think, and consider their actions as though they actually were the other person. This means seeing with the other person's eyes, living in the other person's world, and walking in the other person's shoes (or moccasins).

*3. Instructional Objectives.*   Specify the learner outcomes you will measure; relate this outcome to the concept you are teaching. Include objectives for cognitive, affective, and psychomotor learning.

By the completion of this metaphoric lesson, "The Shoes/Empathy Lesson," students will be able to demonstrate the following measurable outcomes:

*Cognitive Objectives:* To define empathy as the ability to set one's own feelings, attitudes, and ideas aside and adopt the feelings, attitudes, and ideas of someone else.

To respond to a specific situation with specific individuals in terms of more than one empathetic perspective—thus, applying the above definition.

*Affective Objectives:* To identify something in their lives which they would like others to view with empathy.

To value the process of providing empathy to others in moments of crisis, emotional pain, and conflicting values or persepctives and to demonstrate this value with examples where empathy would be appropriate.

*Psychomotor Objectives:* To envision the nonverbal experience in the Interactive Level of the lesson from the limited perspective of the shoe.

To develop the third-person perspective needed to view a situation from within another person's or object's point of view.

*4. Pre-assessment.* Design a formal or informal "pretest" to find out how much the students already know about the concept that is to be taught. Write out these questions even if you will be using them orally.

This pre-assessment instrument sets the stage for the student to become aware of another perspective—that of empathy. It challenges the student to extend his or her viewpoint to that of other people, other objects, even other cultures. As individuals, we are often caught up in our own worlds, our own value systems, and our own narrow perspectives; this lesson expands these worlds to encompass the external/internal worlds of others.

## PRETEST QUESTIONS FOR
## THE "SHOES/EMPATHY" LESSON

1. Have you ever been in a situation where someone else was experiencing great difficulty and you found yourself wondering what it would be like to be that person? Name such a time.
2. Think of ways you have shown someone else that you were sorry. How would this behavior differ if you were living in Europe, Russia, China, or Holland?
3. What does it mean to be treated with fair play? Would your concept of fair play change if you lived in medieval England? Communist Poland? On an American Indian reservation?
4. If you could be in another person's shoes for a day, who would you choose? Why?

5. How would your perspective of role change in the following situations: as a mountain climber, as a cattle rancher, as jungle explorer, and as a condemned murderer? What happens when you change roles?
6. Take any object in this room and imagine what it would be like to look at you from that object's point of view. What would the object see? How would the object describe you?
7. How does a person's clothing make a statement about that person's life style? What does your clothing say about you?

*5. Basic Focus of the Lesson.*   Choose a metaphor to illustrate the concept you are going to teach. If you have difficulty choosing this metaphor, answer the following questions.

A. *What are the basic characteristics of the concept you are teaching?*
   Empathy is being defined as being able to:
   (1) feel the sensations of the other person
   (2) imagine oneself in the other person's situation
   (3) view the world as though one were looking from the other person's eyes, position, and resources
   Empathy is neither sympathy or pity; nor is empathy a thinking of an analogous situation and identifying. It is, instead, a skill of being able to step into that other person's world; it is the art of becoming a human mirror for that person's feelings, attitudes, and thoughts.
B. *What objects, animals, systems of nature, or common, everyday items could symbolize these characteristics?*
   Shoes, mirrors, shadows, Alice in Wonderland, the mockingbird, and the dolphin.
C. *Which of these objects is most accessible in terms of props and concrete examples? And, which would be fun and enjoyable to present?*
   All of the above would make really special metaphoric lessons; each one of the suggested metaphors models the ability to move into another's world, to function as an alter ego, to place oneself in the personality of another.
       Because mirrors and shoes can both be seen as metaphorically empathetic, and because both are very common, both were considered, but shoes were chosen because they were more accessible. You, the teacher, have thirty different pairs of shoes instantly to demonstrate the versatility of empathy.
       Additionally, the concept is strengthened by the cultural idioms of "put yourself in the other person's shoes" or "walk a mile in the other person's moccasins." Shoes also allow us to use a different kind of interactive exercise, demonstrating the experiential/imagery dimension of nonverbal experience.

D. *List all the materials you have readily available to use with this metaphor.*

Our own shoes, boots, slippers, and tennis shoes; a pair of baby shoes, a porcelain shoe planter, a big pillow shoe, a ballet slipper, a construction boot, and Indian moccasins. In addition, we gathered many pictures of all sorts of shoes; these were put on transparencies. Among these were "The Old Woman in the Shoe," a flower child shoe, and a shoe illustrated with silent movie greats.

To these many different shoes are added to all the different shoes that our students are wearing. We included a shoehorn, a shoe tree, and a number of different shoelaces.

*6. The Metaphoric Focus.*   Describe the order of materials and symbols that will be used to focus the class on the metaphoric image of the lesson.

At this initial level, students will learn to distinguish between the actual product called "shoes" and the representations and symbols that stand for this product.

Begin the lesson with several kinds of real shoes. (Empty your closets and bring in one of each kind.) It is helpful to make sure the students avoid making value judgments concerning the use of each shoe. Instead, help them discover that each shoe has a different function; the function depends upon the design, the social circumstances, and purpose for buying the shoe. As examples, use baby shoes, children's shoes, athletic shoes, evening shoes (both men's and women's), and practical, daily work shoes. Discussion can center around these questions:

1. What factors determine our choice of shoes? (Answers might include sex roles, economic resources, and work to be done.)
2. What kind of shoes do we like to wear? (This question helps students distinguish decisions based on fact from personal preference decisions, decisions of individual taste, or monetary considerations.)

From this discussion, lead into the symbolic level of the shoe as a metaphor. Write the word SHOE on the chalkboard and show pictures of several different kinds of shoes. These pictures are easily found in magazines and newspapers. We have two such shoes on transparencies that are especially powerful; we initially cover up the person wearing the shoes and ask the students to imagine what that shoe usually does. One picture is of work boots off the ground; when we uncover the total picture, it is a woman parachutist. The other picture is of cowboy boots; when we uncover it, it reveals the actors on the TV show "Dallas." These two illustrations dramatize the contextual information we use when judging someone and the world in which they live.

After you show the most common examples of shoes, introduce some unusual pictures and sculptures of shoes: a golden horseshoe, a bronzed pair of baby shoes, a picture of "The Old Woman in the Shoe," an old-fashioned flower vase shoe, a large plastic store shoe, or perhaps a shoe pillow. Choose items that are unlikely, things that cause the students to pause before deciding to call the items "shoes." This pause is crucial to the conscious awareness of accepting the metaphor and the concept you are teaching.

*7. The Personal Comparison.*   Design a comparison question that will be used for the class to identify with the object.

This level can be very enjoyable and insightful because it makes use of a ready resource and immediate associations. Be careful to set an environment where excessive joking or teasing is not allowed. You will be using the students' own shoes; the experience, therefore, is potentially sensitive and must be set up in terms of trust and positive comments.

Ask the students to take off one of their shoes and to look at it on their desks. (This activity is usually very popular, because for years we have not allowed them to put their shoes anywhere but on the floor!) Ask them to think of an answer to either of the following questions:

When I look at my shoe, it reminds me of this characteristic about me . . .
or
My shoe is like me because . . .

Take turns around the room having the students share their answers. Long explanations are not necessary, but establish the ground rule that all the comments are valid and a way of understanding more about ourselves. When in doubt about a given response, always associate yourself somehow with the response given. This takes the spotlight off the individual and lets the students associate the answer with more than one person. Example: "It's falling apart!" You could say, "I know what you mean; I've had several shoes that would make that statement about me, too."

Most answers are both revealing and personally enlightening (for self and others). Students enjoy this exercise. All kinds of responses will emerge if you are careful with your timing. *Do not start the sharing process* until every student has thought of an answer to the question. Allow no other class comments after each student's answer. This is not a discussion; this is an individual sharing time with the class. It involves self-disclosure; as such, it means that a climate of trust and the feeling that all answers are acceptable must be maintained.

A word of caution: Because this exercise is personal and does involve an item associated with the way the individual lives his or her life, rescue comments that are inadvertently too revealing or that seek reassurance. We also allow students to pass if the experience is too personal for them.

"My shoe has seen better days and so have I."—Your comment can be something like: "I guess, we'd all have to say that about our shoes some days; good and bad days are a part of living in our world."

"My shoe gets stepped on and sometimes I feel like all that ever happens to me is being stepped on." Your comment could be: "I, too, have felt stepped on sometimes. That's a normal feeling, and part of being human in this world."

What's critical at this point is that no response be treated as unusual or inappropriate.

We've found that students who normally do not have insights to share will have something to add when doing this exercise. It's also a preparation experience for the Level III exercise that comes next. If there is time, record comments on the chalkboard and look for similarities of experience or perception. Usually, most comments are social in nature and make a statement about the student's overall life style.

*Insight Modeling*

After the comparison sharing process is finished, begin a time of sharing the insights people gained in the comparative exercise. Everyone should be free to pass or join in as he or she wants to contribute to the general discussion. Avoid calling on students; they may be thinking about things too personal to share with the group.

Begin this discussion with examples of your own. Be careful not to think up your examples ahead of time; if you do this, your body language has a way of betraying you—you will appear "canned" in your responses. Instead, ask yourself what you really did learn and share one of those insights. Remember that the level of intensity you use tends to prompt similar responses from the class; don't get too personal. Self-disclosure has a way of repeating itself on the level being modelled. Thus, if you are too personal, it tends to scare some students; if you don't share at all, your class will not "dare to share." It is a question of judgment; but, when in doubt, keep comments positive and light. Examples of personal insights for you might be: "I realized that I don't often polish my shoes. That's alot like me; I need to polish up the things I do, so others will see them shine;" or "My shoes are designed especially for comfort, and that's the way I like to live my life. I rarely pay attention to fads; feeling comfortable is usually more important to me." Such comments help the students identify their own insights to share with the group.

This discussion should be short; it is better to limit sharing in the group and stimulate interest for more insight-sharing sessions.

*8. Interactive/Imagery Experience.* Design a participatory nonverbal exercise, role play, or guided fantasy experience for your students. The purpose of this is to involve actively the student with the image or object.

This level involves taking the class on a silent walk around the school building (outside the building if possible). There must be no talking; talking interferes with the personal awareness each student gains from the experience.

Begin the class nonverbal walk with the following instructions:

We are going to go on a special walk today. This is the walk our shoes take, not the walk we take. As we walk around the buildings and outdoors, concentrate only on the experience that your shoes are having. If they could think, what would they be thinking about the different surfaces, the changes in the ground, the experiences you are about to give them?

Try to vary the walk experience; go up a little hill or incline, climb stairs, walk on grass, gravel, and strange surfaces as much as possible. Have students jump, skip, run, and tiptoe. Try to concentrate on the experience your own shoes are having, because you will be a spark and model to the discussion that will follow. This walk should be about ten to fifteen minutes long; longer walks lose the "shoe" emphasis in the students' minds.

When you return, the following questions will be helpful in debriefing the overall sensations (record responses on the chalkboard):

1. What do you think your shoes were "thinking" when we left this room?
2. How did your shoes "feel" about climbing the stairs?
3. What did your shoes like to do best? What was hardest to do?
4. Did your shoes like to do everything you do? Things you don't like to do? (These answers will surprise you.)
5. What can your shoes tell you about yourself? About the way you walk in this school?
6. Were there familiar places that we walked to that would seem strange from your shoes' point of view? Why?
7. What does it mean to be "walking in another person's shoes"?

*9. The Creative Insight Moment.* List the questions and compressed metaphors you will use to link the concept and metaphor together.

Think of improbable connections and analogies that could be creatively thought of as "true."

In this level we capitalize on the student's experience with the shoe metaphor as a symbol, a personal comparison, and finally a personal experience. Analogies should fit the instructional concept you are teaching. In this case, the following analogies are designed to emphasize empathy within specific subject matter areas.

Social studies: Society is one large shoe store. How does the American shoe store differ from the Chinese?

Judging shoes by their colors is like judging people by their race, religion, or culture.

The United States is the tennis shoe (sneaker, tennie, runner, athletic shoe—or whatever else your region calls this shoe) of the world. Why?

School is a shoe horn where all of us are squeezed.

English: A library is a shoe store where we can find many fits.

If a novel is a shoe, how does *A Separate Peace* fit you?

Grammar is a shoe we wear everyday. How does it feel?

Math: Multiplication is like having ice skates.

Adding and subtracting are like tying your shoes.

If equations are shoes, you feel like _____ in them.

Values: A pluralistic society means having more than "Kinney" shoes available.

If you were to go for a walk in this shoe (use one of your pictures from Symbolic Level), your experience would be . . .

Gaining knowledge about oneself is like growing out of one pair of shoes and into a new pair. Why?

What is added when people are judged only by their shoes?

History: A history book is like a closet full of shoes. Some shoes are ignored.

*Socrates* was a bare foot in a world filled with sandals; *Lincoln* was a sandal in a world filled with hunting boots; or _____ was a _____ in a world filled with _____.

Penmanship:  Penmanship is shoe polish. When do we want it?

Health:   Going to the dentist is like visiting a shoe repair shop. How does the shoe feel?

     Watching what you eat is like finding the right shoes for the right occasion. Why?

There are many more possible ideas. The secret to good analogies is looking for the improbable to stimulate an insight. The shoe walk itself is also a subject for discussion.

Going to a new school is like going on a shoe walk.
Going for a shoe walk is like meeting people for the first time.
Everyone's shoe walk is personal, so is everyone's family. Why?
Choosing the right shoes for a shoe walk is like . . .

The lesson could conclude with after-school assignments:

1. Take a different shoe walk this afternoon in a different pair of shoes and compare the changes in what happens. How does your perspective and experience change?
2. Look in a shoe store, and write a story about the people who come in the shoe store from the point of view of one shoe.
3. Look at the shoes in your closet; write a discussion they would have about you if they could talk.
4. Go to a Salvation Army store and look at the old shoes. Discuss the many kinds of experiences these shoes have had.

It is hoped that these examples prompt many more activities for you and your students. They are the beginning. The best ideas may yet emerge from your imagination and the minds of your students.

*10. Postassessment.* Describe the evaluative measures you will use to determine the outcome of your lesson. These measures will relate back to the instructional objectives you designed in Step 3 of this form.

 The postassessment is a time to check whether the metaphor and the concept have been linked together successfully for new insight and awareness. In this case, we will be looking for a realization that empathy means: (1) leaving your own feelings, thoughts, ideas, and perspectives behind; (2) adopting as accurately as you can the probable feelings, thoughts, ideas, attitudes and perspectives of the person with whom you are being empathetic; (3) willingly shifting perspective to a position beyond you in order to better understand, help, and aid that person.

## POSTASSESSMENT QUESTIONS

1. Think of someone in your world who needs empathy. If you were to be empathetic with this person, how would you comment about that person's experience?
2. Empathy is a shoe that never wears out yet seems to expand with each use. Explain.
3. Friendships can be like old shoes; what must we remember about having friends?
4. What would it be like to walk in the shoes of Lincoln? Of Booker T. Washington? Of Margaret Mead? Of Billy Graham? Or Lech Walesa?
5. Think of something in your life that you wish someone else would be empathetic toward. What is it?
6. State the differences in the world at large when the viewer is in your shoes and not you yourself. What are some of the changes in perspective?

*11. Materials and Equipment.* Make yourself a list of all props, supplies, audio–visual equipment, and instructional materials that you will need to teach this lesson.

This lesson requires an assortment of different kinds of shoes; we emptied our closets, taking one of a kind. In addition, you will want to seek out baby shoes, unusual shoes, and various old shoes.

A special feature of this lesson is the use of your students' shoes; this means most of your props are readily available. These shoes will provide variety, and the alternatives needed for demonstrating the concept of empathy.

Use transparencies showing shoe stores, shoe repair shops, and many different kinds of shoes, like ballet slippers, storm trooper boots, soccer shoes. For these, you need an overhead projector; you might want to have a record player and use a popular song as well: "These Boots Were Made for Walking . . ."

*12. Personal Insights and Revision.* Include insights you gained as a result of presenting the lesson. Note areas you are exploring and new ways to connect the metaphor with the concept you are teaching. Describe changes you would make in the future.

We did not realize that students could feel so vulnerable in explaining their shoes; as adults, we are used to wearing shoes we want to wear—students are not always wearing the shoes they prefer. It is important to respect anyone's privacy if he or she passes in the comparison stage.

In teaching leadership to third graders, we added another interactive exercise to the shoe walk. We had everyone trace their shoes on construction paper and introduce themselves in terms of their shoes; then, we shared these introductions in the group. Questions such as: "What makes a shoe a leader?" were then explored.

228

# METAPHORIC TEACHING LESSON PLAN
# The Rainbow/Perspective Lesson
## *The Long Form: A Participant's Guide*

*1. Background of the Class*  Describe your students, the instructional unit you are teaching, the grade level, and any special factors important for understanding the classroom environment.

This lesson is best used with third grade and above; students will need an understanding of the water cycle, evaporation, and the principles of cyclical natural systems. The lesson can also be used as an introduction to more than a science unit; you could, for example, use this lesson to introduce any of the following subject area units:

| | |
|---|---|
| Foreign language | Experience with differing worlds (land, sky, lake) determines the words we use and our awareness for language to express these experiences. |
| English literature | Example of perspective, point of view, position, and interpretation. |
| Social studies | Journey of the water drop leads into units like Marco Polo, the astronauts, explorers, the impact of social climate, change factors, and perspective. |
| History | A nation's history is like the experience of a given water drop; the recording of history is left in the river beds, lakes, and other naturally-occuring phenomena. |
| Science, earth science, ecology, geography | Focus upon the water cycle and its natural processes, impact, and systems. |
| Mathematics, geometry, and physics | Focus upon the water cycle as context for math and physics problems to be solved. |
| Chemistry | Focus upon basic chemical experiments with water; microcosmic example of matter conversion and molecular change. |
| Psychology, counseling, self-esteem classes | Life has storms and our ability to see rainbows depends upon our personal energy, our vantage point, and our willingness to see things from alternate perspectives. |

*2. Instructional Goals.* Describe the overall purpose of teaching the lesson. Include the concept you want your students to learn and the context for this concept within the instructional unit you are teaching.

Several related concepts are introduced by this lesson:

*Perspective:* Students will learn that we "see" things in terms of our own vantage point. The experience of the water drop has a variety of differing perspectives, culminating in the "rainbow" moment, when the water drop can "see" the pattern of all the colors it can reflect.

*Exploration:* The dynamics of any exploration can be experienced with this lesson. The water-drop journey can be likened to anyone going into uncharted territory and experiencing the unexpected. Units on explorers, pioneers, and new pathfinders can be strengthened with this lesson's metaphoric introduction.

*Environmental awareness:* The water drop "lives" in several different environments which dramatically affect its overall shape, scope, and experience. Social studies, ecology, political science, and literary analyses could all be potential subject matter for this concept.

*Climate adjustment:* Wherever the necessity exists to check the climate before reacting; to respond to the climate at hand; to adapt to survive the overall climate; this lesson will strengthen the awareness of climatic pressure, impact, and effect. Historical, political, social, physical, chemical, and psychological climates are all possible instructional goals for using this concept successfully.

For purposes of this lesson plan, we will focus upon the concept of *perspective;* this means that students will gain an overall awareness that our point of view on a given subject depends upon the position we are experiencing and the resources (internal and external) we have at hand.

*3. Instructional Objectives.* Specify the learner outcomes you will measure; relate these outcomes to the concept you are teaching. Include objectives for cognitive, affective, and psychomotor learning.

By the completion of this metaphoric lesson, "The Rainbow/Perspective Lesson," students will be able to demonstrate the following measurable outcomes:

*Cognitive Objectives:* To identify the basic components of the water cycle and trace the path of water as it occurs on this planet.

To define the concept *perspective* in terms of four major characteristics: observer, viewpoint, available resources and/or information, and defined role limitations.

*Affective Objectives:* To compare their lives to the balance of nature and state ways in which they "flow," "evaporate," and "encounter storms."

To express a moment of the "rainbow" awareness that emerged from a difficult life experience or personal "storm" moment.

*Psychomotor Objectives:* To visually "see" the route of the water drop from the mountainside to the waterfall to the lake to the sky to the storm to the sunlight and to the image of the rainbow.

To visually, imaginatively, and experientially "let go" of the classroom and explore the images that the guided fantasy script causes to occur in the mind.

*4. Pre-assessment.* Design a formal or informal "pretest" to find out how much the students already know about the concept that is to be taught. Write out these questions even if you will be using them orally.

PRETEST QUESTIONS FOR
THE RAINBOW/PERSPECTIVE LESSON

*Directions:* "The following questions will help me determine our overall understanding of PERSPECTIVE in terms of _____ (the unit you are presently teaching). Please answer them quickly and briefly in the spaces provided."

1. What does it mean when we say, "They have two different perspectives."
2. If you were a drop of water in the sky, would it make a difference if you were part of a storm or part of a rainbow?
3. What do "rainbows" mean to us? What messages do we attach to a rainbow?
4. Can you describe the basic process of the water cycle? When you look at a lake, can you see the rainstorm that has landed within it?
5. What do people need in order to see the potential that comes from a moment that was painful, difficult or frightening?
6. What makes a rainbow? What happens in order for us to see one?
7. Think of a moment of conflict which you or a friend had to face. What new perspectives came out of that moment? Did you grow or become strengthened through the process?

*5. Basic Focus of the Lesson.* Choose a metaphor to illustrate the concept you are going to teach. If you have difficulty choosing this metaphor, answer the following questions.

A. *What are the basic characteristics of the concept you are teaching?*
First, look in a dictionary for a general definition:
*Perspective:* (1) to look through, (2) the capacity to view things in their true relations or relative importance, (3) the appearance to the eye of objects in respect to their relative distance and position, (4) the interrelation in which a subject and its parts are mentally viewed, (5) the technique or process of representing on a plane or curved surface the spatial relations of objects as they might appear to the eye.
Second, think about the critical factors you want students to gain in learning this concept:
*Perspective:* (1) to identify who is doing the viewing, (2) to identify the resources/information available to the viewer (determining the influences upon that person's judgment), (3) to assess that person's position (viewpoint) in terms of vantage/limitations, and (4) to define the role expectations that determine the limitations of the viewer's perception of the scene, objects, or events.

B. *What objects, animals, systems of nature, or common, everyday items could symbolize these characteristics?*
Several artistic renditions of the same theme (bridges, for example), telling a familiar story from several points of view, a natural cycle such as water and the rainbow, the story of the blind men and the elephant.

C. *Which of these objects is most accessible in terms of props and concrete examples? And, which would be fun and enjoyable to present?*
"Theme" sets of pictures were considered; several images of bridges are available (used in the past to open and close workshops) and have considerable potential. Another possibility: telling stories from the multiple perspectives—*The Canterbury Tales, Rashomon, The French Lieutenant's Woman, Vanity Fair,* and varying versions of fairy tales (two separate versions of Goldilocks, for example); and there are several romance novels on the market now that have "twenty-three endings to the story—you decide how the story ends."

For this lesson, however, it was decided that an image that presents perspective as a positive resource in the midst of overwhelming data to be "sorted" was necessary. This clarification led back to the water cycle, to the use of the rainbow, and to the discovery of the beauty that often emerges after a storm.

D. *List all the materials you have readily available to use with this metaphor.*
A calendar of rainbows, several pictures of the rainbow, several rainbow items (bedsheet, shower curtain, T-shirt, key ring, mobile, wall graphic), pictures of a waterfall, mountain lake scenes, a flower with glistening water drops, "dewdrops" that can be made in the classroom with ice cubes and water.

*6. The Metaphoric Focus.* Describe the order of materials and symbols that will be used to focus the class on the metaphoric image of the lesson.

Begin with pictures of water, everywhere, in all sorts of forms. You are creating an image of water as the life blood of this planet (which it is!). Use transparencies or pictures that depict water scenes on the ocean, in the mountains, water falls, mountain lakes, water as snow, sleet, rain, and fog. The pictures help the students see the versatility of water; you might want to have glasses of water, a tea kettle, and ice cubes as well.

Next, introduce the rainbow using real pictures of the rainbow; these can be easily located in the many "rainbow calendars" that are sold in gift shops. Include personal slides of rainbows, pictures, and artistic renditions. Then, show the rainbow as it is seen commercially all around us—as a motif for bedsheets, shower curtains, key rings, wall graphics, posters, and paintings. Finally, have T-shirts and clothing with rainbows on them.

This process focuses the right brain on the rainbow itself and offers many pictures for seeing water in a new perspective—a more aesthetically pleasing perspective.

*7. The Personal Comparison.* Design a comparison question that will be used for the class to identify with the object.

Several different strategies are possible for encouraging the comparison moment:

1. You can have the students look at all the rainbow pictures and pick out the rainbow that most reminds them of their life and how they are living their life.
2. You can simply pose the question, "How is your life like a rainbow?"
3. You can look at the various forms of water—steam, water in liquid form, and ice cubes—and ask the students to say which form of water is most like the way they are living their lives.
4. Use the water pictures (the lakes, mountainside streams, the storms, and the raindrops) and ask the students to choose one of the pictures because there is something in the picture that is a lot like themselves. Ask them to explain.

The students enjoy having the picture beside them as they explain the comparison that came into their minds; even when they are responding in dyads (not the total group), they will often point to the picture they are thinking of or get up and bring their dyad partner over to the picture for a better view.

*8. Interactive/Imagery Experience.* Design a participatory nonverbal exercise, role play, or guided fantasy experience for your students. The purpose of this is to actively involve the student with the image or object.

## The Guided Fantasy—The Rainbow

Imagine you are a tiny drop of dew sitting on a mountain flower early in the morning on a beautiful summer day . . . The sun is rising, and you feel yourself sliding off the flower's petal onto the soft ground below . . . There you are greeted by many more water drops and together you form a trickle, a small stream of water . . . Combining with the others, you feel stronger, more powerful . . . Soon you have become a hardy little stream of water, softly cascading down the mountainside . . . You ripple over the rocks, the broken tree limbs, the moss, and the many mountain ferns . . . As you flow along, you are joined by many more little streams . . . Together, you all combine to make a mountain creek, a ribbon of water that is laughing and gurgling like a watery mountain jogger, travelling steadily down the much-worn mountain river trails.

The synergy of all of you is exciting; you enjoy being with so many other water drops . . . You know that water is the life-giving element of the earth, the most needed element on the face of the planet . . . As you grow, you sense the indestructible nature of yourself; you know you cannot be harmed . . . You can explore, see new places, experience wondrous things, change and be transformed, but you will remain . . . You will be as you have always been, hydrogen and oxygen, permanent elements of the earth's surface . . . You know you have nothing to fear, but you have many unusual, unpredictable, and wonderful experiences ahead of you each day, each moment.

As you run along the mountain pathway, you can hear the call of the mountain's Ferris wheel, the beautiful, exciting mountain waterfall. You know it beckons to you with a wonderful ride, a chance to swirl outward into the mountain air, to fly through the misty blanket of other water drops, and to blend and be part of the power of this element called water.

Soon you feel the pull of the waterfall, and you dance forward . . . You embrace the current and enjoy the swift, moving Ferris wheel of water . . . You leap forward into the wet air, and you are caressed by the other water drops around you, you turn over and over, but always with a feeling of enjoyment and thrill . . . Then, you fall softly into the beautiful mountain lake below . . . As you greet the lake, you see that it is smooth, clear, and like glass . . . Inside the lake, all is serene, comfortable, and reassuring.

The morning goes by . . . You enjoy the power and majesty of being part of the lake . . . There is life all around you . . . The lake is filled with fish, insects, and even occasional animals . . . For you, it is like a watery zoo . . . You are in the center of the lake . . . From your viewpoint you see water everywhere . . . It is a happy scene, a warm, sunny mountain day, and a cool, beautiful, refreshing bath in the embrace of your family members, the many water drops that form the lake . . . Above you, you can see soft, white pillows of air: the clouds that are wisps of air that change shape and call to you to join them . . . You see an eagle fly in and out of the clouds . . . The eagle is so beautiful and soars so effortlessly.

Toward midday, something miraculous begins to happen . . . The sun gets warmer and warmer and you feel lighter and lighter . . . Soon you feel yourself being lifted upward . . . You are drawn into the air, lighter and lighter, feeling like a feather on the wind . . . You know this is the process called evaporation, the moment when you can become water vapor instead of a water drop . . . You are happy, excited, and filled with anticipation . . . You begin to fly upward, higher and higher . . . It is special to be up above the mountain lake . . . You go higher and higher into the blue sky . . . It is an adventure you know well; you have experienced this process many times . . . It is one of the best things about being a part of this element called water. . . . You are transforming and becoming a light form of water, a light dust of water, a wispy form of you.

You are part of the water dust, the fine mist of water particles that makes the beautiful clouds you saw in the lake . . . You feel yourself being surrounded by more water dust particles, and you are soaring like the eagle you saw from the lake . . . You are flying once again, dancing in the air, and enjoying the currents of air that lift you upward and into the vast blue sky ahead.

As you get higher, you meet solid dust particles and form with them to change from being water vapor, the air-like gas that lifted from the lake, to become a water drop again, the more solid form of you . . . You are round, small, but more solid, more together, more in a form that can greet the earth and nourish all that live on the earth . . . Soon, you feel yourself dropping down, you glide ever so slowly downward toward the ground below . . . You are very light; you are only one twentieth of an inch in diameter and you drop only five feet a second . . . Time goes very slowly; the seconds are like minutes . . . All around you other water drops are falling, too . . . Cousins close to you who are heavier drop a little faster . . . Some of them are as big as one fourth of an inch in their diameter and drop much faster . . . Soon you have all become

part of a mountain rain, a rainfall that refreshes the earth below
. . . You drop slowly down to join the earth, when suddenly a gust of
warm air comes up from underneath you and lifts you upward again
. . . You soar back up into the beautiful cloud of water dust and water
drops . . . You know that you are not destined to become part of the rain
yet, you have still another adventure ahead of you.

This time you have another experience before you drop to the earth
and join your family in giving moisture to all living things . . . The air
around you is laden with small, tiny water drops like yourself . . . The
earth below is saturated with the rainfall of your relatives . . . You,
however, still remain in the sky, part of the beautiful, heavy with light
raindrops, mountain sky . . . It is the moment after the rainstorm, the
moment when the sky is still filled with water drops, when a moment
of expectation falls upon the mountain world . . . You rest high in the
sky, a special leftover of the storm . . . You wonder what will happen
next.

Then, a truly wondrous thing happens . . . The sun comes out ahead
of you in the late afternoon sky . . . It shines back towards you from
its descending point in the sky . . . You begin to feel warm and you feel
the sun's rays come into you and the light bend within you . . . It hits
the innermost side of your rain drop form and bounces back towards
its entry point . . . As the light bounces back, it sends forth an array
of beautiful colors; reds, oranges, yellow, greens, blues, indigos, and
violets . . . The colors shimmer forth . . . You are a splendor of bouncing
light and color . . . It is the opportune time for the most marvelous
experience water can have . . . far below, you look to see if someone can
see you.

There on the mountain side is a solitary figure—a human being—
looking up toward you in the sky . . . The sun is to the person's back,
and the person is smiling and pointing your way . . . You know what
is happening . . . From where that person is standing, you are not many
colors . . . You are one color . . . And around you, the other drops below
and above you are seen as other colors . . . You are part of a large,
light-filled, colorful arch to this person . . . Although in reality you are
all the wonderful colors of the sun's ray, to this person's eye—at the
angle this human being sees you—you are one brilliant color . . . At last,
you have become part of a rainbow for the person below . . . It is
wonderful to know that you have joined with the other raindrops to
become this beautiful symbol of light and promise, the sign of the
majesty of water . . . You enjoy the moment, and then, slowly you leave
the other bouncing water drops and glide softly to the earth below
. . . You land and then look upward . . . You can see the mountain world
again, the splendor of the newly washed sky, and at last you can see
the rainbow you were once part of, the rainbow that divides the sky in
half and sends forth beauty to be seen from exactly this spot on the

earth . . . It is a moment to remember, a moment of renewal, a time of unique perspective, a comment on the beauty of water as it interacts with all living things . . . You are happy to be part of this natural cycle, part of this ever-occurring wonderful experience in nature . . . You allow yourself to cherish this moment in time . . . Now, slowly and only when you are ready, return from that mountain scene and the beauty of that summer day you shared, and come back to this classroom and all of us. When you are truly ready, and not before, open your eyes.

### Debriefing the Guided Fantasy

When the students have completed the guided fantasy experience, it is important to debrief the overall activity with them. Start with simple hand counts and open-ended descriptive questions; then proceed to more substantive (higher level) questions.

1. What mountain flower were you sitting on when the fantasy began?
2. How many people saw the moss? The ferns? The mountain river trail? (This means hand counts; it helps if you raise your hand with each question.)
3. When you came to the waterfall, were you afraid? What made you less afraid? How did the watery "Ferris wheel" feel?
4. When you landed in the lake, how did you feel? What could you see in the lake? (How many people saw fish? What kind? How many people saw insects? What kind? How many people saw animals? What kind?)
5. When you looked up at the sky, did you see the clouds? Did you see the eagle? What did it look like?
6. When you were drawn up into the air, how did it feel? Describe the "water dust" that was all around you.
7. How did it feel when you changed from water vapor back to a water drop? Why do you think you felt this way?
8. Could you feel the warm air when it lifted you back up in the midst of the rain storm?
9. What did the sky look like just before the sun came out? Could you feel the warmth of the sun?
10. How did it feel to know the light entered you and then bent backwards—shedding all kinds of light? Could you see the colors? What did they look like?
11. What did the person down below look like? Was the person a man or woman?
12. When the person looked up at you, what color were you?
13. When you fell down to earth, did you see the rainbow? What did it look like?
14. Did you want to leave? How do you now feel about water drops?

15. What were some of things that were built into this fantasy to keep you from being afraid?
16. Which image of that whole fantasy was most enjoyable? Which image was most exciting?
17. Is there a part you would change? Is there a part you would prolong?
18. What unusual perspectives did you experience? (Like being a water drop inside the lake, being part of a rainbow, feeling the air currents as you flew)

From the concrete answers, students discover how different each individual's guided fantasy can be. The imagination of each student has created the details of the experience he or she has had. Students who are not sure that they want to go on the fantasy journey are usually convinced by the enthusiasm of the others to try harder the next time a metaphoric lesson is given. Most of the students will enjoy the process, and view it as energizing, creative, and "worth it."

*9. The Creative Insight Moment.*   List the questions and compressed metaphors you will use to link the concept and metaphor together. Think of improbable connections and analogies that could be creatively thought of as "true."

Ask students in dyads (or small groups) to discuss the following statements and show that the statement can be true and explain why.

1. A child is a raindrop; the classroom supplies the sun for his or her colors to shimmer.
2. Storms have the potential for new perspectives; it depends upon the source of energy and where you are standing.
3. Learning in school is like the water cycle.
4. Books can be water drops; students reading books can be the sun's ray; teachers helping students to read are like the eyes who see the rainbow.
4. Parents often face the sun and cannot see the rainbow in their child.
6. Appreciating individual differences is seeing each raindrop shimmer in different colors as it falls.
7. Rainbows are all around you, but you won't see them if you are standing in the wrong place without a source of light.
8. The prepared mind has the ability to generate light for the rainbow.
9. Insight is a personal rainbow.
10. Conflict produces the storm; your experience, values, and thoughts

cause a perspective from which to see the rainbow. Where does the
light come from?
11. All storms produce rainbows if you are in the right place at the
right time with adequate sunlight.

*10. Postassessment.* Describe the evaluative measures you will use
to determine the outcome of your lesson. These measures will relate
back to the instructional objectives you designed in Step 3 of this
form.

## POSTASSESSMENT QUESTIONS

1. Draw a small diagram of the water cycle that you experienced in the
   guided fantasy.
2. If you were to see your life as a water cycle, where are you right now?
3. What elements need to be present for people to perceive new insights when they experience "stormy" moments in life?
4. Describe a moment of insight after a moment of conflict in your life.
   What new perspectives emerged?
5. What is the source of energy in your life? How can you increase this
   source? How can you use it to see your own "rainbows"?
6. What difference in perspective will occur if we change any of the
   following elements in a given statement of perspective:
   a. The observer (If there is a new person seeing the situation . . . ).
   b. The viewpoint (If the person sees the situation from a new view
      point . . . ).
   c. Available resources/information (If the person has new resources
      or new information for judging the situation . . . ).
   d. Role expectations (If a new role is expected of the viewer . . . ).

*11. Materials and Equipment.* Make yourself a list of all props, supplies, audio–visual equipment, and instructional materials that you
will need to teach this lesson.

You'll need an overhead projector, several pictures of rainbows and
water scenes (always bring masking tape so these pictures can be put
up around the room), a tea kettle with a bunsen burner or hot plate,
ice cubes, a pitcher of water, and as many different little objects and
items as you can find with the motif of the rainbow on them.

*12. Personal Insights and Revision.* Include insights you gained as a
result of presenting the lesson. Note areas you are exploring and new
ways to connect the metaphor with the concept you are teaching. Describe changes you would make in the future.

Students really enjoy this lesson. They love the "mountain Ferris wheel" experience; they describe the misty, fog experience as intriguing and curious; they are not frightened by the storm. We think this happens because we were careful in the design of the fantasy; we did not lead the mind into frightening places—we let the waterfall be a Ferris wheel, for example.

We thought the many different "rainbow" motifs on familiar teen objects would be popular; in actuality, students seem to prefer to identify with the real rainbows, the ones that we were able to show from the calendar pictures of actual rainbows.

# The Balloon/Goal-Setting Lesson
*The Long Form: A Participant's Guide*

*1. Background of the Class.* Describe your students, the instructional unit you are teaching, the grade level, and any special factors important for understanding the classroom environment.

With very little modification, this lesson can be presented at all grade levels; originally written for a fourth-grade class of gifted students, the basic concept of "goal setting" is valid for most classes, and the language of the lesson is uncomplicated, allowing even younger students to have profound experiences with the lesson. As a conceptual organizer for any instructional unit where setting goals, achieving specific objectives, and planning actions are critical components, the Baloon/Goal-Setting Lesson helps learners identify the difference between your goal and your objectives (the standards you want to maintain on the way).

Opportunities to use this lesson are numerous; every subject area and basic grade level has numerous skills and activities that students can consciously recognize as part of their own individual goal setting. Knowing that they are actually planning both the goal and the means to reach that goal is a significant experience for young students; knowing that the means must be specific, measurable, and well-defined if one is to actually obtain a preplanned goal is an academic "gift" to the older student.

Examples where goal setting is critical to the understanding of skill attainment include the following:

| | |
|---|---|
| Math concepts | Students often do not understand why they are mastering the multiplication tables, the geometric theorems, the algebraic equations. Goal setting might emphasize the utility of these skills once mastered and their relative merit in understanding other disciplines such as chemistry, medicine, and physics. |
| Scientific inquiry | Students often miss the point of laboratory experiments; their atti- |

tude is often, "If we already know the answers, why are we doing this? Why can't I just memorize the answers?" The lab work (after using this lesson) becomes part of the process of journeying to a place where scientific skills are more important than merely accepting currently held scientific truths.

Social Studies and History

Much of what we, as a people, have done—the definition of society, its mores, customs, and rituals—involves specifying goals and pursuing specific objectives.

What goals or objectives enabled Napoleon to conquer Europe? Lost him Russia?

What objectives built the Third Reich? Were they also responsible for losing it?

What goals underlie the development of a democracy? What objectives create the achievement of that goal?

English grammar and reading

In the midst of rules, constant practice, and continual corrections, it is easy to lose sight of the goal of English writing and reading. Focusing upon the ultimate goal of effective communication allows the mechanics of getting there to make sense to the learner.

Literature

What goals did the author set? How does the author reach these goals? What objectives are critical to achieving these goals? How is the literature structured to obtain the overall goal (effect) the writer seeks to reach?

This lesson can help the learner distinguish between theme and plot (theme being the goal and plot

|  | being the objectives); it can clarify the joy of the product (the creation of the masterpiece) and the joy of the process (the actual writing experience). The product is the goal; the process embodies the objectives. |
|---|---|
| Psychology and Personal growth | Helping students set achievable goals for themselves is a part of building self-esteem and self-confidence. To have a personal goal that can be accomplished, you need a vision of both where you are going and the ways in which you are going to travel. |
| Leadership Skill-building | The lesson was originally designed to helped gifted students learn leadership as a construct; students learn from the lesson that they need the "big picture" and a destination for their leadership. Then, the actual skills become objectives to reach that personal goal of leading others. |

*2. Instructional Goals.* Describe the overall purpose of teaching the lesson. Include the concept you want your students to learn and the context for this concept within the instructional unit you are teaching.

There are several related concepts that can be taught with this lesson:

*Goal setting:* This is the primary concept for which the lesson was written; the lesson takes the learner through the steps of deciding the journey's destinations, preparing measures to help facilitate this journey, experiencing the journey itself, and then finally arriving at the destination. In essence, the student sets a goal, prepares for the experience, decides upon objectives, builds an action plan, encounters and overcomes difficulties, and arrives at the goal.

*Accepting the Challenge of an Opportunity:* The lesson models the acceptance of a special journey that is both new to the student and unpredictable. It is an initial challenge to step into the balloon and become a participant in a new adventure. Challenges in the classroom and acceptance of new opportunities could be compared to this balloon experience.

*Courage to Dare to Explore the Unknown:* For younger students, this lesson could be an example of the courage that astronauts or explorers (of any kind) need when they face the unknown and yet dare to go ahead.

*Strategic Planning:* Students often rush into things and then realize that they need to plan, to look at their situation, and to consider the options they have available. For a successful balloon ride, you must plan for all sorts of contingencies; a study could be made of balloonists (middle school level curriculum) and strategic planning could be the conceptual goal of the overall unit.

*Preparation and Sequence:* This, too, could be a lesson for younger students; comparing any preparation period and sequential process with the balloon journey would have dividends for the students. Each part of the balloon journey must be carefully planned and executed in sequence, or the balloon and its riders could be in serious danger.

You may, of course, find many more attitudinal concepts that could be modelled with this lesson; primary, for us, was the use of the metaphor for goal setting. Acceptance of challenge, courage to explore, strategic planning, and preparation for sequential process are all, in some ways, subsets of this overall concept of personal goal-setting.

What does goal-setting mean? We want students to gain an appreciation of a goal as a destination; and that achieving a goal requires: preparation, specific objectives, an action plan, checkpoints, the courage to overcome obstacles, and recognition that you have, in fact, arrived.

*3. Instructional Objectives.* Specify the learner outcomes you will measure; relate these outcomes to the concept you are teaching. Include objectives for cognitive, affective, and psychomotor learning.

By the completion of this metaphoric lesson—"The Balloon/Goal-Setting Lesson," students will be able to demonstrate the following measurable outcomes:

*Cognitive Objectives:* To define the basic components of effective goal setting: specifying the goal, preparing and identifying resources, outlining specific objectives, planning to overcome obstacles, designing an action plan, recognizing goal accomplishment.

To analyze any moment of goal setting as having basic sequential steps that lead to accomplishment; and to apply these steps to such a moment in order to examine the effectiveness of that goal-setting situation. (Did Admiral Byrd set effective goals in exploring the South Pole? Did Marco Polo use goal setting in exploring the Orient? What kind of comment is the author making in the "Quest for the Holy Grail"? What kind of lifetime goal did Edison make?)

*Affective Objectives:* To personally compare other moments of goal setting with the sequential process of this lesson.

To develop an attitudinal shift in terms of patience, careful preparation, appreciation of sequence and follow-through, willingness to overcome obstacles, and excitement in completing a given goal and task.

*Psychomotor Objectives:* To internally "see," "experience," and "hear" the journey in the balloon—feeling the lift-off, the mist, and the crisp air, seeing the beauty of the sky and earth, and hearing the sounds of the birds and the balloon itself.

To develop greater facility for imaging, envisioning a suggested experience, and allowing the body to relax and shed stress-filled muscle tension.

*4. Pre-assessment.* Design a formal or informal "pretest" to find out how much the students already know about the concept that is to be taught. Write out these questions even if you will be using them orally.

This part of the lesson will "set up" the terms you want students to learn and master. You may give the pretest orally (especially if the lesson is given to younger students), or you may want to adapt the following written assessment for the comprehension level of your students.

### PRETEST QUESTIONS FOR
### THE BALLOON/GOAL-SETTING LESSON

1. What is involved with setting a goal and planning the steps to achieve the goal?
2. How do we know when a goal is accomplished? Give an example of a goal you personally set and then achieved.
3. What kind of preparation precedes accomplishing a goal?
4. What were the specific things you did to achieve the goal (the specific objectives that helped you reach the goal you set)?
5. Did you put these objectives, steps, or plans into an overall action plan? Did you have dates for completing each of the intermediate activities?
6. How do you feel when you reach a goal you have set for yourself? Think of such a moment and describe the feeling.

7. If you had one year to live, what goal would you set for yourself?
8. Have you ever been in a hot-air balloon? A small private airplane?
   A helicopter? What did it feel like? If not, what do you think it would
   feel like?

*5. Insight Questions.* List the questions and compressed metaphors
you will use to link the concept and metaphor together. Think of improbable connections and analogies that could be creatively thought of
as "true."

A. *What are the basic characteristics of the concept you are teaching?*
   First, check the dictionary for a general concept definition:
   *Goal:* An object or end that one strives to attain, an aim or score to
   be achieved.
   Second, review the basic components of successful "goal setting."
   (This could include a review of Mager's *Instructional Goal-Setting.*)
   For purposes of our instructional objectives which we have already
   defined, we will list the characteristics as the following:
   *Goal setting:* (1) To identify a specific, achievable goal to be attained;
   (2) to recognize that attaining a goal requires preparation and planning; (3) to define specific, measurable steps to take to achieve this
   goal; (4) to put these steps into an action plan with dates, schedules,
   and checkpoints; (5) to identify behaviors, products, and acceptable
   performance that will show the goal has been completed.
B. *What objects, animals, systems in nature, or common everyday items
   could symbolize these characteristics?*
   Any animal that must build its own shelter would be an excellent
   metaphor for goal setting; animals that migrate and meet their
   mates (like penguins) would be good subjects; a trip of any sort
   would meet these criteria; the story of the Velveteen Rabbit could
   be an allegory that models these characteristics; any hero/histori-
   cal figure recently studied could be made into a metaphoric lesson
   to "relive" the adventure and experience the goal-setting process.
C. *Which of these objects is most accessible in terms of props and concrete examples? Which would be fun and enjoyable to develop and
   present?*
   Recently, we were given a balloon calendar with all sorts of pictures
   of hot-air balloons, balloonists, and soaring shots from the sky. At
   the time, we thought it would be fun to find a concept that balloons
   could teach; coincidentally, one of our in-service students called us
   and asked if we could help with a unit on leadership/goal setting
   and asked if balloons could be used as the image/metaphor. That
   request prompted this lesson.

Our student wanted to teach a four-week unit on "Reach for the Sky" where gifted children in a "Magic Mentor Workshop" could be focused upon goal setting and the achieving of specific action plans. This lesson was a focus for that instructional unit.

D. *List all the materials you have readily available to use with this metaphor:*
The calendar (which was made into transparencies); slides of a hot-air balloon fair from some friends (including pictures taken from the balloon in flight); different kinds of balloons, beach balls, party balloons, and magazine displays of the transoceanic balloon trips. Pictures that showed the earth below from the perspective of sky-divers, airplanes, and helicopters. Finally, we went to the bookstore and looked up books on ballooning, which provided still more outstanding illustrations for the image portion of the lesson.

*6. The Metaphoric Focus.* Describe the order of materials and symbols that will be used to focus the class on the metaphoric image of the lesson.

Begin this lesson with a display of various kinds of balloons. You can have party blow-up balloons, beachball-like balloons, and many slides and transparencies of hot-air balloons. If you do not have access to slides or transparencies, take care to gather many pictures of hot-air balloons. It would also be helpful to invite a balloonist to come and visit the class—as preparation for the overall metaphoric lesson.

The basic distinction you want the students to learn is that how you build the balloon, stock it, plan its itinerary, and develop your overall travel plan will increase the likelihood of reaching your destination safely and effectively. Many of your students may have seen movies with balloon trips, *Around the World in 80 Days* and *Flight to Freedom.* * Both are excellent examples of preparation, deciding upon flight plans, encountering and overcoming obstacles and arriving at predetermined destinations.

The overall purpose of this Level I experience, then, is to awaken the mind to the imagery of balloon sailing, to cause the right brain to envision the flight, to imagine the feeling of being airborne, and to be open to the guided fantasy that will follow. As the right brain focuses upon the images, the interest of the students increases, a sense of increased energy enters the classroom, and anticipation will mount.

---

*Another excellent, though less well-known, film featuring hot-air balloons is the recently made *Olly, Olly, Oxen, Free* with Katherine Hepburn. To reinforce the safety of balloons in today's world, it should be pointed out that Ms. Hepburn did all her own flying in this film and there were no stand-ins for her in any of the scenes.

*7. The Personal Comparison.*   Design a comparison question that will
be used for the class to identify with the object.

Several different kinds of questions can be used for the comparison
moment:

1. Tell your students that life is a series of balloon trips. What kind of
   a balloon trip is school? Is being in this grade level? Being nine,
   eleven or fourteen? Being an American as compared to being a
   _____? Living in this town as compared to living in _____?
2. Ask students to find a way in which they are like the balloons they
   have just seen. Which one is most like them? Why?
3. Ask the students to think of a journey they have made that was a
   lot like a hot-air balloon ride. Share these journeys.
4. Simply ask: How are you like a hot-air balloon?

Students enjoy this part of the exercise; it causes them to begin to
discover insights on a personal level. Be sure to accept their answers
without asking for proof or further explanation; they are vulnerable in
terms of the connections they are making and every spontaneous insight should be valued and treated with respect. It is critical to set a
climate where everyone's comments will be important and evaluating
ideas is not allowed. This is a moment of image brainstorming. Students will respond with comments like:

"Being in middle school is like a balloon trip where the balloonist lets you
steer the balloon."

"I chose the picture with several balloons leaving the ground in stages—that
bottom balloon is like me as a new baby, the other balloons are like parts of
me throughout my life. Right now, I'm about half way up into the sky. See that
top balloon—that's me as a grown up."

"I'm like a hot air balloon because I only fly if I fill up with knowledge and
new information. School is a lot like the fuel that fires the gases into the hot
air balloon."

"I like having the 'big picture' of what I'm doing—like being in the balloon
and getting to look down on the total landscape."

*8. Interactive/Imagery Experience.*   Design a participatory nonverbal
exercise, roleplay, or guided fantasy experience for your students. The
purpose of this is to actively involve the student with the image or
object.

## The Guided Fantasy

Today we are going to go on a very special trip, a trip that begins in
your mind with your imagination, a trip that will allow you to see many

things, experience the beauty of the earth and the thrill of the sky. Would you please close your eyes and allow yourself to completely relax . . . just breathe in deeply and completely relax. Make yourself comfortable—be very silent and listen carefully to the sound of my voice. Let your imagination come alive and let the pictures come into your minds.

It is daybreak and you are in a huge field. The sun is just beginning to shine . . . It is a beautiful morning, and you can see people all around you . . . Near the people are beautiful, huge, tent-like, silky-looking sheets stretched out on the ground like giant, multi-colored patches . . . Near these brightly colored patches are special carriers—gondolas that look like large baskets for carrying passengers up into the sky . . . Everyone is busily getting the balloons ready for flight. You are excited . . . You know this morning you will be able to take a trip in one of these balloons . . . It will be a wonderful opportunity—a special occasion to choose a special balloon to travel where you would like to go . . . You know you will be completely safe in the balloon you choose, that you will travel with a balloonist of great skill to a place you have long wanted to visit . . . You are about to have a wonderful, very special adventure.

You look around the field . . . You are looking for the balloon that is going to a place you would like to visit . . . Where do you want to travel? What do you want to see? Who do you want to visit? You continue to look around the field and then suddenly, 'way across the field, you see a balloon that is going exactly where you want to go . . . You walk over to this balloon, and as you get nearer and nearer, you can hear a hissing sound . . . The beautiful silky patch is beginning to take shape. You can see the balloon inflating, beginning to show its many colors to the world. What does it look like? Are there symbols on the balloon? What colors can you see?

When you arrive at the balloon site, you know your decision is a good one . . . You know that this balloon is well made and that you will be safe riding in it. The trip will be exciting and enjoyable . . . You greet the people around the balloon . . . They are happy to see you and urge you to come closer. Near the balloon you see two of your friends who will be travelling with you . . . They are excited too . . . Inside the gondola is the balloonist who will be sailing your balloon . . . This person has had many balloon flights and has great skills. Your balloonist will know how to steer the balloon, how to guide it, how to follow the flight plan, and how to finally bring it back to earth. With confidence and eagerness, you and your friends climb into the balloon's gondola and look back out at the field. Everything you need to make the trip is in the gondola. This is a special day . . . Today you will begin a journey toward that destination you have chosen

. . . Today you will fly like the wind, sail in the sky, and reach your goal.

Slowly . . . you feel the basket come up off the ground and begin to rise into the air. You look at the faces of those who are riding with you . . . Your friends are excited, too . . . It is a moment you have all waited for . . . a moment to ride in the sky, to truly visit a far away place you have longed to see—a place you would like to reach.

You look out into the sky . . . All around you are other brightly colored balloons with other people . . . Many other journeys are beginning today . . . Many other places will be visited. Many other people will be seen . . . Many other things will be done. You begin to relax . . . The balloon rises higher and higher in the sky . . . Above your head is the blue sky, and you can feel a slight wind all around you . . . It is a wind that is gently helping your balloon rise higher and higher. Down below you is the ground . . . You can see people in the field . . . Then you can see the field next to other fields. It's like looking at a many colored checkerboard, a checkerboard that nature is creating for you.

You see a flock of birds in front of you . . . They are travellers with you . . . They are flying in the same direction as you. As you come closer to the birds, look them over carefully. What kind of birds do you see? What color are they? Are they singing? What does their singing sound like? Continue past them. Look all around you and down below on the land. You see little houses, trees, little spots of water, and highways that look like pretty silver ribbons on the earth below. It is beautiful to see the earth this way . . . It is like becoming a bird . . . You can see the whole route to the faraway place you want to visit. You see the highways . . . You see the forests . . . You see hills and valleys . . . It is a view to remember

You think about the place you are planning to visit . . . how wonderful it will be to reach this place . . . to see the people you plan to see . . . to do the things you plan to do. You think about the journey, and you know you can make it . . . You know that your balloon will travel all the way . . . It will go the full distance. And it will be strong, safe, and protective . . . It will weather any wind . . . It will stay up even if the rain comes and falls all around you.

As you are thinking about rain, your balloon encounters a faint mist —you are flying through a huge, white cloud . . . The air is damp, moist, and very heavy. It is a fine, misty fog . . . but you don't worry—you know the balloonist has made many trips and can fly the balloon in all kinds of weather. You know you'll be able to make it through to the sunlight . . . Your balloon will be strong and the gondola will keep you dry. Soon the balloon passes through the cloud and comes out into the sunshine again. The earth below is even prettier than before . . . It sparkles like a million diamonds as the sun bounces off the rain drops down below.

You can see a beautiful lake . . . with sailboats on it . . . Nearby, you see a park with people riding horses . . . Then, you see a great, rolling countryside with cows and horses and all kinds of animals. Look closely . . . what do you see?

The wind continues to blow . . . Your balloon is now soaring over a city . . . It is passing little towns . . . It is coming to your destination . . . You are excited that you are finally arriving where you wanted to go, but you are sad that the trip is coming to an end and wonder what will happen down below. Slowly, the balloonist adjusts the heater that inflates the balloon, and your balloon begins its descent. It is a slow, gradual trip to earth . . . 'Way ahead you see another open field. Down below in that field are the people you have come to visit . . . They look like tiny, little dolls, dolls that are waving to you, far above them. Closer and closer you get . . . Soon they look more and more like people you know—not like the little people you first saw. Now the balloon is coming very close . . . You are not afraid . . . You know the balloonist has the skill to land the balloon.

Gently, it glides on to the ground . . . and you know you have arrived. All around you are other balloons that have come from many places . . . People are smiling and are happy to see you. It was a wonderful journey and you have arrived at a truly special place. You know that you can make more trips and you will have more opportunities . . . You look at your companions . . . they feel successful, too.

You feel the ground under your feet and you know that this flight is over. All that remains is climbing out and beginning new adventures in this new place. Look at your balloon once more. . . . Look all around you and see those who have travelled to be where you are . . . It's a special day; a day of accomplishment, a day of pride and happiness. Now, the day is ending . . . The sun is slowly setting in the sky . . . The sky is turning red and orange . . . You know the journey was worth the brief rain and the uncertainty . . . You know you'll make many journeys in the future and will travel to many more places. Now, take one more look at this field of balloons and their many passengers. Now, when you are ready, and not before, return from that splendid field of journeys completed and come back to this room, and when you are really ready . . . open your eyes and join us.

*Debriefing Questions*

1. When you first began the trip, you were in a huge field with lots of other people. What did you see on the ground? What colors did you see?
2. On the large, many-colored "tents" were attached little basket-like carriers; what color were they? How big were they?

3. Where did you decide to go? Why did you want to go there?
4. You began to look around the field for your balloon, and then . . . you saw the perfect balloon for you. What did it look like?
5. Could you hear the hissing sound as the balloon began to fill? What did the balloon look like as it inflated?
6. Were there symbols on your balloon? What were these symbols?
7. Near your balloon were two of your friends; who were they?
8. Inside the balloon in the gondola was the balloonist; what did this person look like? Why did you trust this person?
9. When you first began this trip, how were you feeling?
10. How did it feel when the balloon began to lift off the ground? What did you see below and above you?
11. What was all around you? What kind of resources were in the gondola?
12. You could see fields below you; what did they look like?
13. Suddenly, you saw a flock of birds. What kind of birds did you see? What did they look like? Were they singing?
14. Later, you encountered a light rain in the sky. What was it like? What did it feel like? Did you want to turn back?
15. When the rain cloud had passed, you came into the sun again. What did the earth look like after the rain? Did you want to keep going?
16. Then you passed by a lake; what was on the lake? You passed by a park; what did you see in the park?
17. Then time moved more quickly; you passed through many towns, a city, many countrysides. Finally, you reached your goal; what did you see down below?
18. What did the people look like? How did the picture change, the closer you got to the earth?
19. Who was there to meet you? How did you feel knowing you had made it?
20. Before you left the new field, you looked around at others who made similar trips. What did they look like?
21. What did you realize about taking trips?
22. What did the sky look like? What did the sun look like?
23. Did you want to leave the fantasy? What would have happened if you could have stayed a little longer?
24. Think of one thing that made this journey special. Why was your destination a place you wanted to reach?

*9. The Creative Insight Moment.* List the questions and compressed metaphors you will use to link the concept and metaphor together. Think of improbable connections and analogies that could be creatively thought of as "true."

1. Every goal is a destination to reach; every goal needs a well-planned journey in order to be achieved.

   The first day of school is a balloon trip. Why?

   Learning a new skill is like taking a balloon trip. Why?

   Studying a chapter in history is like taking a special balloon trip. Why?

   Developing leadership skills is becoming a balloonist. Why?

   Discovering the cure for cancer will be the scientific balloon ride of the 1990s.

   Wishing for something without planning is like wanting to visit somewhere without finding a vehicle, having resources, or developing a travel plan.

   A coach is a special balloonist. What trip does the coach take you on?

   Parents are balloonists for life. Why?

   Teachers are like different balloonists waiting in the field. Each teacher takes you to a different destination. Think of two different teachers you have had. How were their balloon rides different?

2. Part of every journey toward reaching a goal is encountering obstacles or "rain."

   Think of a goal you decided to reach; what were the rainstorms you ran into?

   Conquering Europe was Napoleon's first balloon trip; conquering Russia was his second. What happened to Napoleon's second trip?

   A video game is a gondola. Why?

   Computerized instruction is a balloon trip with a mission control on the ground. Why?

   Each team sport is a separate balloon trip. Can having one trip help you take another?

   Multiplication is a balloon trip to take you to a place where you can have your own independence.

   To become an astronaut, you must be willing to take many balloon trips. Name some of these.

   Every friendship is a series of balloon trips. Think of one of your friends and describe your first balloon trip with this person.

   Life is a series of balloon trips. Why?

3. Think of a life goal you have for yourself. If you were to compare this goal to a balloon trip, what journey lies before you?

Do you know where you want to go?

Who will be your balloonist? Are you skilled enough to be your own balloonist? Is there someone in your world you could ask to help?

What kind of "rain" could you encounter? Will it be fine mist? A huge storm? Can you prepare for this rain?

What kind of terrain (mountains, and valleys, deserts, forests) must you journey over?

How will you know when you arrive at your goal, at your destination? What will the ground look like? Who will be there to greet you? What skills will you have?

4. Every year of school is a separate balloon ride. Think of some balloon rides you have had.

   What kind of a balloon ride was first grade? What kind of "rain" did you run into? Who was the balloonist? Where did you land?

   What is the difference between the balloon ride of elementary school and the balloon ride of middle school?

   What kind of a balloon ride is high school? Is it bumpier? Is it smoother?

   Who is your balloonist when you enter college?

5. Goal-setting means taking time to plan the journey and identify where you really want to go.

   Setting the goal means deciding on your destination.

   Determining your objectives is making a travel plan and being sure you can recognize the goal when you reach it. What will it look like when you really reach your goal?

   Making an action plan for your objectives is like filling out your trip plan with several stops for refueling and taking on provisions.

   Sharing your overall goal-setting plan is like inviting friends to go with you to help you see the lay of the land, the storms, and the indications that your goal has been reached.

   Anticipating the rain means realizing that every action plan runs into obstacles. Will you quit if you are "rained" on?

   Reaching the goal means meeting your objectives. You know you have arrived because you know what the "land" looks like when you are at your destination.

   Ending one balloon trip is an opportunity to take another. Every reached goal tells your mind that you can accomplish more goals if you want to.

*10. Post-assessment.* Describe the evaluative measures you will use to determine the outcome of your lesson. These measures will relate back to the instructional objectives you designed in Step 3 of this form.

The following postassessment can be used as a goal-setting instrument; this activity can then be followed with the attached "Personal Goal-setting Flight Plan."

## POSTASSESSMENT QUESTIONS

1. Think of a goal that you would like to accomplish this week (in two weeks, in a month, in the next six weeks). What would you like to achieve?
2. If you were to achieve this goal, what would your life be like? How would things be different from the way they are now?
3. What kind of steps must you make to reach this goal? How could you know that you are, in fact, reaching each one of these steps?

| STEPS TO BE TAKEN | EVIDENCE THAT THE STEP HAS BEEN TAKEN AND MASTERED |
| --- | --- |
| 1. _____ | _____ |
| 2. _____ | _____ |
| 3. _____ | _____ |
| 4. _____ | _____ |

4. What kind of resources/provisions will you need?
5. Who could be a resource balloonist to help you design this journey?
6. If you decide to go on this journey, what kind of obstacles will you quite likely encounter? (What will your "rain storms" and "climate changes" look like?)
7. Plan your steps in question 3 again and set a timetable for your arrival at each step.

| STEP TO BE TAKEN | EVIDENCE I MADE THE STEP | DEADLINE FOR ACCOMPLISHING THIS STEP |
| --- | --- | --- |
| 1. _____ | _____ | _____ |
| 2. _____ | _____ | _____ |
| 3. _____ | _____ | _____ |
| 4. _____ | _____ | _____ |

8. How will you know when you have reached the original goal set in question 1?
9. How will you feel if you make that goal?
10. Do you still want to achieve this goal? If so, fill out the attached Personal Goal-setting Flight Plan.

## A PERSONAL GOAL-SETTING FLIGHT PLAN

1. I want to reach the following goal:_____
   _____
   _____
   _____

2. What could keep me from reaching this goal?
   ———— I don't really have the skills, ability and/or knowledge needed.
   ———— I don't want it badly enough to really plan and work for it.
   ———— I'm afraid that I might fail.
   ———— I'm afraid of what others might think.
   ———— Others don't want me to reach this goal.
   ———— The goal is really too difficult to ever accomplish.
   Some other reasons might be:_____
   _____
   _____

3. What are some things I could do so the above things don't prevent me from reaching my goal?
   _____
   _____

4. Who can help me?
   Name:                              Kind of help:
   _____           _____
   _____           _____
   _____           _____
   _____           _____

5. What are my chances for success?   Why do I feel this way?
   ———— Very Good                     _____
   ———— Good                          _____
   ———— Fair                          _____
   ———— Poor                          _____
   ———— Very Poor                     _____

6. What are some of the good things that might happen if I reach this goal?_____
   _____
   _____

7. What are some of the bad things that might happen if I reach this goal?_____
   _____
   _____

8. What are the chances that the bad things would happen if I reached the goal?

———— Very High    What could be done to reduce my "odds"?
———— High          _____
———— 50/50        _____
———— Low           _____
———— Very Low

9. Do I still want to try to reach this goal?
    _____ Yes        _____ No        _____ Still Undecided
Why?_____

10. What are some first steps I can take to reach this goal?_____
_____
_____
_____

11. What else must I do if I am really to succeed in reaching this goal?
_____
_____
_____

12. Am I going to take the above steps?
    _____ Yes        _____ No        _____ Still Undecided
Why?_____

13. If my answer to question 12 is Yes, I make the following self-contract:

### SELF-CONTRACT

I, _____, have decided to try to reach the goal of _____. The first step I will take to reach this goal will be to _____ by _____ (state time). The following people will be contacted to help me: ____
_____

My target date for reaching my overall goal is _____

*11. Materials and Equipment.*    Make yourself a list of all props, supplies, audio–visual equipment, and instructional materials that you will need to teach this lesson.

You will need a slide projector, slides, an overhead projector and transparencies, and screen. In addition, you might seriously consider finding someone who is a balloonist to come in and share with the students ahead of time or afterwards his or her experiences with a hot-air balloon.

Look for many illustrations of hot air balloons; if you have difficulty locating these, find *The Ballooning Handbook* by Don Camcrow or any number of other ballooning books. In addition, try to find a number of inflatable objects: party balloons, beachballs, even blow-up toys. A number of swim toys are appropriate for this activity.

### GOAL-SETTING TRAVEL ITINERARY

Goals are long-range places to travel; reaching a goal involves setting specific objectives (action plans) for each goal you set. You will find that some action plans require that work begin immediately; others may not need action until next week.

| GOAL | What do you want to have accomplished? | How will you feel when you have achieved this goal? |
|---|---|---|
| TIME SCHEDULE | When do I want to reach this goal? | Why do you want to follow the time schedule? |
| Implementation Objectives | | |
| ACTION PLANS<br><br>What can I do by tomorrow? | What will you actually do? | How will you know these plans are done? |
| By one week from now? | | |
| Within one month? | | |
| Are further steps necessary? What would they be? | | |

*12. Personal Insights and Revision.* Include insights you gained as a result of presenting the lesson. Note areas you are exploring and new ways to connect the metaphor with the concept you are teaching. Describe changes you would make in the future.

In making the point that we must prepare in order to reach the significant goals we set for ourselves, we discovered that many of our great artistic, scientific, and political leaders were outstanding examples of this principle.

What kind of trips had Pasteur already had when he discovered the cure for rabies?

What kind of preparation went into Einstein's plan before he formulated the theory of relativity?

What kind of objectives must be met if the goal is a gold medal at the Olympics?

What kind of a trip is the movie *Rocky?* Did he reach his goal? What were his objectives? What did his flight plan look like?

We found that the process by which we achieve the goal becomes a critical part of success. Without a preplanned travel itinerary, we are ill-prepared, conquered by outside forces, and, thus, often thwarted from achieving our original goal.

# METAPHORIC TEACHING LESSON PLAN
## The Rock/Security Lesson
### The Long Form: A Participant's Guide

*1. Background of the Class.*   Describe your students, the instructional unit you are teaching, the grade level, and any special factors important for understanding the classroom environment.

This lesson explores the basic nature of security—what causes people to feel secure and to trust the predictability of their experiences. Because of the sophistication of its guided fantasies, the lesson is designed for fifth grade and above; to use the lesson with younger students requires designing a different interactive experience from the one in this lesson.

Security is a basic issue for everyone; Maslow typed "security" as our second level of need (physical need being the only one more basic). We all need to know we are safe, away from threat, protected from danger. But what allows the individual to feel secure? What are the attributes of feeling that we are safe? This lesson explores the concept of security in terms of the need for stability, protection, predictability, and consistency.

Knowledge is one base for creating such personal security; predictable skills can provide another base as we develop a sense of consistent performance leading to consistent outcomes. The following subject matter applications could be enrichment experiences with this concept; essential to the process is a working right brain application of what it feels and looks like to be secure:

*New (unfamiliar) subject matter*   Every time we introduce new concepts, new content, new information, new skills, our students are faced with an assimilation process that challenges what they already know. This lesson is a good advance organizer for such an experience, because it allows you to discuss what the "rocks" are that provide the foundation for the new information or skills to be learned.

*Personal growth*   What are the "touchstones" that we judge our experiences by? What stays constant in the midst of changing perspective, changing values, and changing skills? We need to identify the "rocks" that we build our life upon—religion, the family, our ethnicity, our education, our economic status. These all make good discussion points for using this lesson.

OUR FUTURE

NEW IDEAS

MY ROCK

GROWTH

The lazy dog jumped over the fence.
ADJ.   NOUN.   VERB   PREP. CLAUSE.

Building a Sentence.

$6 \times 6 = 36$
$3 \times 2 = 6$
$4 \times 4 = 16$
$2 \times 2 = 4, 4 \times 2 = 8$
$1 + 1 = 2 \cdot 2 = 4 + 4 = 8 + 8 = 16$

FOUNDATION

D. FROST

*Societal mores*   Our sense of what is proper, appropriate, and "correct" for the specific occasion is dictated by cornerstone values we all agree to live by. In this country, these could be: democracy, fair play, universal education, entrepreneurial opportunity, and trial by jury. Any of these concepts could be introduced with this lesson.

*Historical truth*   Although the real "truth" of any situation is fast lost with the accounting of many who remember selectively, nevertheless, our sense of historical accuracy is a keystone to predicting the future. Our overall sense of national security is predicated on a firm belief in the reality of the history we learn and the "truths" we hold to be accepted by all. Examples include the following: the Magna Carta, the exploitation of slavery, the horrors of the Holocaust, the Bill of Rights.

*Teaching the basic underlying principles of any discipline*   Every language we teach, every new lesson that requires learning specific terminology or a specific set of principles, every science lesson with its causal relationships—each has a basic "rock" foundation that must be established before the student can learn to "manipulate" data in terms of the discipline.

In math, multiplication tables are such a cornerstone; in science, learning the phylogenic classification systems provides the basics for studying plants and animals; in English, it means learning basic grammatical rules; in chemistry, it involves mastering the Periodic Table of the Elements.

Whether we're teaching the child to learn to add or schooling the student in the basic of Aristotelian logic, we must first have a conceptual appreciation for the foundation that allows the freedom to sort, gather, and rearrange information. That foundation is the bedrock of support for the intellectual structures we later build.

*2. Instructional Goals.*   Describe the overall purpose of teaching the lesson. Include the concept you want your students to learn and the context for this concept within the instructional unit you are teaching.

Although the primary concept to be introduced by this lesson is *Security,* there are several related concepts that can be taught with this lesson:

*Permanence:* Students look for what is long-lasting, what will remain when everything else has changed, what can be counted upon—no matter what. This lesson explores the nature of a rock—it creates a sensation of permanence in the midst of shifts in time and perspective.

What is critical to permanence? Does anything last forever? To be something seen as permanent, the situation needs to be "intended to last indefinitely." Rocks can shatter, break up, and turn to dust, but we generally view them as long-lasting and able to withstand the impact of time and circumstance.

*Stability:* This is a related quality; Webster's defines stability as: "the quality state or degree of being stable, the strength to stand firm or endure: FIRMNESS."

In human relationships we look for a firmness of purpose, a sense of resolution or conviction, and predictability in action, ability, and attitude. Stability allows us to grow, to expand, and to accent abrupt turns of fate. It is a paradoxical attribute that can respond to modification because of its basic firm identity.

*Bonding:* This is an entirely different concept taught by this lesson; "bonding" is a uniting tie or linking that occurs (often involuntarily) as a result of close relationships. We think of bonding in terms of an animal mother and her offspring—the protected and the protector, the follower and the leader.

There is also a bonding experience that occurs with possessions; as human beings, we can have relationships with inanimate objects. This can be seen all around us: the secretary "owns" the school desk, the coach "owns" the playing equipment. This secondary territoriality is very strong—especially when the individual has had nonverbal experience with the object.

Both guided fantasies facilitate such an experience; in both fantasies, participants will feel an "ownership" and desire to possess the rocks they receive in the exercise.

This bonding creates a sense of the object (the rock) being an extension of the person who has touched it. If positive emotions occur at the time of this experience, the autonomic nervous sustem will produce a favorable reaction to the object itself. "Once set in motion, [the reaction] is carried on by itself until a new stimulus causes the emotion to change." (Ringness, 1975)*

We chose to focus this lesson on security as the instructional goal; by security, we mean helping students discover the following (Webster's):

(1) the quality or state of feeling free from danger
(2) safety: freedom from fear or anxiety
(3) something given, deposited or pledged to make certain of the fulfillment of an obligation

The need to feel protected is a basic underlying need, one that takes precedence over the need to belong, to like oneself, or to think reason-

---

*Ringness, Thomas A., *The Affective Domain in Education,* 1975.

ably and/or creatively. If we can help students have a better understanding of this basic need, we can give them insights into human motivation and their own natural resources.

*3. Instructional Objectives.* Specify the learner outcomes you will measure; relate these outcomes to the concept you are teaching. Include objectives for cognitive, affective, and psychomotor learning.

By the completion of this metaphoric lesson, "The Rock/Security Lesson," students will be able to demonstrate the following measurable outcomes:

*Cognitive objectives:* To define the basic attributes of feeling secure about something: that the situation is predictable, free from danger, free from uncertainty, safe, and guarantees consistency of behavior.
To analyze any given situation in terms of how secure it is; to apply the definition of "being firm as a rock" to situations where security is a prerequisite to successful performance.
*Affective objectives:* To identify moments in their lives that felt secure and safe and compare these moments to ones of extreme change and flexibility.
To value the basic human need for security by identifying ways to increase a feeling of security within their lives.
*Psychomotor objectives:* To visualize the journey to the forest lake, "see" the suggested images, and experience the sounds, sights, and sensations of this visit.
To experience nonverbally the bonding with a rock; to explore this rock until it is so familiar that it can be discovered again nonverbally even when mixed with several other rocks.

*4. Pre-assessment.* Design a formal or informal "pretest" to find out how much the students already know about the concept that is to be taught. Write out these questions even if you will be using them orally.

Pre-assessment can influence the overall working definition each student has for the concept of security; it can assess perceived needs for security and identify situations that warrant security. To the average student, security is often equated with love, and family security is usually the most stable experience the student has had. Some students, however, do not have these experiences; they have lived in unstable environments, changing households, and blended families. Their responses are quite different. In the classroom, we seek to develop a more conscious understanding of security—security as a result of being predictable, consistent, and protected.

## PRETEST QUESTIONS FOR
## THE "ROCK/SECURITY LESSON"

1. Think of a situation in which you feel very secure. What kind of circumstances were there that helped you to feel secure?
2. We all have things that are like "Linus's blanket." Think of something you own that makes you feel secure when you are near it (like your first doll, an old baseball glove, the kitchen table, a class ring, or a favorite chair). What is that item? What were the circumstances surrounding your earliest experiences with it?
3. If we say that the mother is "the rock" of the family, what do we mean? Suppose we say the father is "the rock"; how does our definition change?
4. Think of a moment when things changed too rapidly for you (like a new school or new home). How secure did you feel in that moment? Why do you think you felt the way you did?
5. What do we mean if we say "work is the cornerstone of success"?
6. What do we want people to learn if we say, "Truth is a rock in the midst of life's unpredictable storms?"

*5. Basic Focus of the Lesson.* Choose a metaphor to illustrate the concept you are going to teach. If you have difficulty choosing this metaphor, answer the following questions.

A. *What are the basic characteristics of the concept you are teaching?*
   We will define *security* as the following:
   (1) a sense of being free from danger, threat, or uncertainty
   (2) a sense of being in a situation that is consistent, predictable, and protected.
   (3) a guarantee of predictable future behavior
   (4) a confidence of safety and certainty
   This definition expands the cultural definition of "being loved and protected" to "being free from harm," to "having predictable consistency," and to "perceiving long-lasting patterns of behavior."
B. *What objects, animals, systems of nature, or common, everyday items could symbolize these characteristics?*
   Consideration was given to using an animal shelter system or natural warning network (like the beehive, the beaver's dam, or the rabbit's warren) and natural safeguards (white corpuscles in the body, the soldier ants in an ant colony, the leader of the pack or herd), as well as items that help us feel secure (a favorite personal

possession, familiar habits, and household furnishings). Ultimately, objects that have the characteristics of "being secure" (a mountain, an old tree, a stone wall, and finally, a rock) were selected. From these, the rock was chosen.

C. *Which of these objects is most accessible in terms of props and concrete examples? And, which would be fun and enjoyable to present?*
Exploring the security systems of animal homes presented difficulties in terms of props. Rocks, which can symbolize security quite well, are accessible everywhere; you can get props outside your door, and they are, of course, extremely permanent and long-lasting. There are all sorts of allusions to the rock as stable and secure: "Peter is the Rock upon whom I build my Church"; "It's as strong as the Rock of Gibraltar"; "It's steadfast as a rock." Even our recognition of a mountain as secure is based upon its composition of rock; cities are built upon bedrock, cornerstones are used to frame houses, touchstones provide a feeling of personal security, keystones decipher our past.

D. *List all the materials you have readily available to use with this metaphor.*
Roadway stones, collector stones, slate, quartz, granite, volcanic rock, river rock, petrified wood, and even a paperweight out of glass. Searching further, many illustrations were discovered as well: Stonehenge, the Rock of Gibraltar, and many cliff/mountain paintings. There was an illustration of the stone used by David against Goliath, there was a new pop art illustration of a rock floating in air, and there were stone walls found in New England. In addition, a pillow stone, a door stop stone, and a plastic rock were added to the rock "props."

There are many books on the subject of rocks and stones that provide transparencies to use as well.

*6. The Metaphoric Focus.*   Describe the order of materials and symbols that will be used to focus the class on the metaphoric image of the lesson.

To begin this presentation, introduce a number of different kinds of rocks to the class: simple roadway rocks, beautiful rocks from collections, slate, quartz, volcanic rocks, river rocks, and special rocks—for example, a jewel, an underwater oceanic rock, or a petrified wood rock. Ask the class to think of all the characteristics that make a rock "a rock." List these responses on the chalkboard. Typical answers include:

"Hard, strong, doesn't crumble and withstands pressure."
"Unbreakable—you need something really powerful to break a rock."

"It's a mineral, solid, and inflexible."

"It's really a large stone, compressed within the earth, found in large quantity near mountains, cliffs, or ravines."

"It's characterized by its ability to bear up and remain firm, and is used as a support for other things."

To awaken an awareness for metaphoric insight, have several pictures of rocks available to show the class. Have large rocks, little rocks, rocks like the Rock of Gibraltar, and even ones in famous paintings, like Constable's "Stonehenge." Suggest that these pictures are also "rocks," but they are metaphoric representations, not actual rocks. Remind the class that metaphors are symbols; they represent real experiences, real objects, and real relationships.

Next, write the word ROCK on the board. Ask if all the pictures and drawings mean the same. Then, produce some unusual examples of rocks: a pillow rock, a plastic rock, or a paperweight rock out of glass. Ask if these are also rocks. Have the students discover that they must "give conscious permission" in their minds for these objects to be classified as rocks. (It means a shift from their initial classifications of a pillow, a play toy, or a paperweight.) It means a conscious decision to allow the shape to be the essential characteristic for naming the item.

Finally, ask the students how they feel about rocks. Why are cities built on bedrock? Why is the parable of building your house on rock and not on sand so profound? How do we use rocks to better our lives? This discussion will cause your students to perceive the rock in a new light, in fact as a basic building tool, and it will allow them to view rocks as necessary supports to creating structures that are long-lasting.

*7. The Personal Comparison.*   Design a comparison question that will be used for the class to identify with the object.

This level explores the concept of "rock" as it is presently developed in the student's personal frame of reference. Begin by focusing the students upon the rocks you have assembled and helping the student begin the process of comparing one's self to the metaphor.

Using the materials you gathered for the FOCUS level, ask the students: "What is there in me that has the permanence or stability of stone?" Share the responses with the total class; or have the students share their answers in dyads with one another. Group responses can be recorded on the chalkboard as each class member gives his or her example. Take time at the end of the group's sharing to identify common threads in people's reactions and intriguing points of view. This encourages students to expand personal insight and develop a sense of trust within the classroom.

Students will comment, "I have both sharp and round edges," or "I have parts of me worn from time and weathering storms of life." Look for similarities in comments and point these out. "I can be sharp at times, and other times I want to smooth things out," could match another's example, "I've smoothed out during my time in school." Help the students recognize unique features about themselves as well: "My rock is a glass rock: sometimes I think I'm breakable," or "I used to collect rocks near a seashore; they remind me of the strength I get from my family."

*8. Interactive/Imagery Experience.* Design a participatory nonverbal exercise, roleplay, or guided fantasy experience for your students. The purpose of this is to actively involve the student with the image or object.

These two exercises combine nonverbal experiences with real rocks and the imaginative adventures of guided fantasies. To prepare for these fantasies, you will need river rocks for all the participants (hidden out of view) and a helper to aid you in quickly placing rocks in each student's outstretched hand at the appropriate moment.

## The Guided Fantasy

Today we are going to visit a beautiful, completely safe forest . . . It is morning, and the dew is still on the ferns and forest plants. The sun is beginning to peer through the large trees down to the forest floor below . . . Look at the sunbeams; see the slight dust particles dance in the light . . . All around you is a special world . . . Look at the plants and trees . . . Notice the open spaces; the forest is like a large, natural cathedral, a place that is untangled and open. The trees are like pillars reaching skyward, greeting the sun, the birds, and white clouds far above . . .

The animals in this forest are safe to see and encounter . . . Ahead of you on the path is a little animal. Near this animal is its mother, another friendly animal . . . What does the animal look like? What color is it? How young is it? . . . Are there more animals in the distance? . . . You hear chirping in the distance; the birds and animals in this forest are talking to one another . . . What is their message? What are they communicating? Ahead of you is a well-worn pathway. It leads to an opening in the forest where you can see flowers, and a little stream rippling through the center of the opening . . . Go closer to the stream . . . Look at the plants around the stream and for an object lying on the ground . . . Look at the object carefully. What is it? What does it look like? Do you want to keep it? You have the choice . . . Now look further

... Near the stream is another object: a book ... Look at its cover; what does it look like? Look at the book again and notice its title ... What is this book about? You can keep this book, too, if you would like to have it ...

Now, find a really soft place to relax near the stream. Make a pillow for your head. Lie down and totally relax ... Listen to the water in the stream ... What does it sound like? ... Can you hear the waterfall in the far distance?

Next, open your hand, because a gift is going to be given to you. It will be a rock from this forest. Get to know this rock ... Feel all its edges, its sides, its surface. Find the unusual features that belong only to this rock ... What makes this rock special? Why is it unique? ... How does it let you know it is different? Spend time with your rock; it is a gift of the forest ... It has seen many stories, many happenings ... It has been an inhabitant of the forest for many years, through many seasons ... Explore its surface; what is familiar? What is special? What belongs only to this rock? ... Now for a little while, you are going to put this rock away ... Place it in front of you and let it lie by itself. Later, you will meet this rock again ...

It is now mid-afternoon in the forest; you look back toward the pathway that led you to the stream and see that the sun has shifted its light ... The pathway looks almost magical and inviting ... Slowly, sit up and take a last look at the stream ... A small, harmless animal has come down to the stream to take a drink of water ... Watch this little animal, and leave the opening quietly so it is not frightened ... Wander back toward the initial scene of the open, large forest ... Look upwards to the sky ... Can you see clouds? ... A soft mist is beginning to fill the air, and you know you will have to leave the forest soon.

Now, when you are ready, and not before, leave the forest behind ... Come back to our classroom, relax, and when you decide to join us, open your eyes.

## Discovering the Rock

This part of the exercise demonstrates the nonverbal recognition skills available to all of us. The rocks have been collected and put in a pile in the center of the room while the students eyes were closed.

I.  Explain to your students that in the center of the room (on a desk, table, or any open area) is the rock they "met" in the forest. Ask them to find it and make sure it really is their rock. (The rocks should have pencil numbers on them; as you pass out the rocks, make a quick notation of which student got which rock. For example, D.S.–19, S.R.–23, P.B.–4, R.B.–9)

Soon, your students will realize that there is only one way to find the rock. They must close their eyes. Having met the rock nonverbally and blind, they can usually only find it again that way. Quickly, as they close their eyes, they will begin to find their rocks. (To facilitate this process, you may want to have four or five groups of rocks, with each row going to its own group.)

II. When each student has his or her rock (and you have checked for accuracy), ask the students to get reacquainted with the rocks. What is new about the rock? What else can it tell you about the forest? What is surprising and something that you would not have predicted?

III. From this discussion, lead into a total debriefing of the forest journey and the experience they had:

1. What did the plants and trees look like?
2. Did you feel the sunbeam? Could you see the dust particles in the light?
3. What little animal was in the forest with its mother? What was its color? How did it act? Was it feeling secure? Why?
4. When the birds began to chirp, did you hear them? (Hand counts can be used.)
5. What object did you see by the stream? What did it look like?
6. What did the book look like? Could you read the title? What was it about?
7. When you were lying quietly by the stream, could you hear the rippling of the water? Could you hear the waterfall in the background?
8. How did you feel when you "met" your rock? What was unusual about it? How was it different?
9. How did you feel when you had to part with your rock? Why?
10. When you looked back at the pathway, had the sun really changed the scene?
11. What little animal came to the stream to drink? Did you startle it? Did it startle you? How "safe" was it? How did you judge its level of safety?
12. Could you feel the mist coming? Was it going to rain when you left the forest? Did the rain help you want to leave?
13. What did you learn about you?

Once the forest scene has been discussed, move to the experience they had locating the rock in the classroom.

1. Why was it hard at first to find the rock?
2. How did it feel to look for the rock with your eyes closed?
3. What new things did you discover about the rock when you could see it?
4. If your rock could tell one story, what would it be?

5. Think of how you felt when you had the rock back in your hand and you knew it was your rock. Why did you feel secure? Can you explain that feeling?

6. What familiar object or item do you own that helps you feel comfortable and at ease with work? Do you have a favorite chair? Your own bed? A favorite possession? What does it feel like to be with that object?

We usually let the students keep their rocks—(depending on their maturity; of course rocks can be dangerous). We have found that the students often become very nonverbally "attached" to them. In fact, a special version of this lesson could be done using very colorful rocks (the kind normally found at vacation spots or rock stores) and letting students discover the dimension of color when they "meet" their rock. Is this how they pictured their rock? They, however, would undoubtedly want to keep these rocks, and that might get expensive!

## An Alternative Guided Journey with the Rock

Close your eyes and begin to relax . . . Today, we will have an adventure with a special rock . . . As you are relaxing, please extend your right hand in front of you, and soon you will be meeting a rock that is especially yours . . . When you receive your rock, remember to keep your eyes closed and run your finger over this rock . . . Feel each of its edges, its little curves, its crevices . . . Get to know your rock and how it feels to you . . . Now turn it to its flattest side, and imagine yourself becoming smaller and smaller while the rock stays the same size . . .

You are going to visit this rock as a very tiny person . . . As you grow smaller, imagine that you are standing on the edge of this rock. It is a perfect place to go for a walk. Move slowly over the rock . . . Are some places too smooth to stay on? . . . Are some places too steep? . . . Travel onto the other side of the rock and wander over the surface . . . Are there different textures? . . . Do you have different problems in walking? . . . Do you have to climb in some places? Now look for a special hiding spot on your rock . . . Crawl into that hideaway and allow yourself to feel completely free and safe . . . This is a special place for you; a place you can always return to whenever you are with your rock . . . You may stay here and think of the joy of being just with you . . . Slowly, when you are ready to leave this hideaway, walk out on the surface of the rock, and allow yourself to return to normal size . . . The rock will seem smaller and smaller . . . soon it will be just a rock in your hand . . . When you have decided you want to return to our room, open your eyes and look at the special rock you have just visited.

## Debriefing Questions*

1. How did you feel when you "met" your rock? What was unusual about it? How was it different?
2. How did it feel to become small and walk on the surface of the rock?
3. Did you find steep places? Smooth places? Did you climb?
4. Describe your hideaway spot? How did it feel to be there?
5. Did you have trouble becoming small or normal size? How did it feel to be like Alice in Wonderland?
6. How did you feel leaving your safe place on the rock?
7. What was it like to actually see your "hideaway" spot? Did it differ greatly from the one you experienced in your mind?
8. Which is more enjoyable—the experience with your eyes closed or the experience with your eyes open?
9. If you close your eyes, can you easily return to the experience you just had?
10. Suppose I were to tell you that your hideaway spot protects your ego—you can always retreat to it as a place to regroup, find support, and seek refuge. When do you think people would be most likely to use it?

*9. The Creative Insight Moment.* List the questions and compressed metaphors you will use to link the concept and metaphor together. Think of improbable connections and analogies that could be creatively thought of as "true."

This level will link the metaphor (the rock) with the concept (security) being taught in the lesson. Depending upon the subject matter you are teaching, pose the following analogies for the students to discuss and "prove true."

| | |
|---|---|
| Social studies | A nation's constitution needs to be a rock. |
| | The family is the rock of society. |
| | A smile is a friend's rock. |

---

*This guided fantasy presupposes prior experience with guided fantasies. It involves advanced skills: the ability to imagine yourself reduced in size, the ability to imagine yourself wandering on the face of the rock, and the ability to re-emerge and view the rock as an ongoing talisman for refuge. It is a special experience, however, for creating a place of protection in the mind of the participant; you can, for example, tell the students that whenever they feel upset, emotionally unsafe, or tossed by unpredictable change in their lives, they can re-create the feeling of being protected and safe by just spending some moments with their rock. In fact, that is what people really are doing every time they carry a lucky charm or special keepsake with them in their wallets or pockets.

Winking is a rock when the world is caving in.

The wedding ring is the rock of the marriage.

The American flag is every citizen's rock.

The family membership is a rock we never forget.

A rabbit's foot is a rock for the child within each of us.

Math

Multiplication tables are the cornerstones of all math problems.

Axioms are the bedrocks of geometry.

Mathematics provides the rocks that secure the foundation of our national economy.

To add and subtract is to have a touchstone in your pocket.

To multiply and divide is to have a mountain in your pocket.

English

The dictionary is a Rock of Gibraltar for the writer.

Grammar is the rock behind the written word.

Tragedy is Shakespeare's rock.

Humor is a cornerstone for pathos.

Theme is the rock; plot is how the rock is displayed.

History

Democracy is the rock upon which America was built.

Charms were rocks for medieval physicians.

The Bible was the rock of the pioneer family.

The Bill of Rights in 1776 was an unpolished collection of diamonds.

Business

The typewriter is the secretary's personal rock.

The appointment book is the business person's most valuable rock.

A nation's monetary system is a rock collection.

Time management is a cornerstone for business success.

| | |
|---|---|
| Political science | Changing the government is like mining in a rock quarry. |
| | Finding silver or gold is the job of a national political convention. |
| | People politics means respecting each person's rock—no matter what it looks like. |
| | Free elections are the rocks upon which our political security is built. |
| Religion | Peter is the foundation rock of the early Christian church. Explain why. |
| | The cross is the rock of the Christian Church. |
| | The Star of David is the rock of Judaism. |
| Foreign language | Latin is the grammatical keystone for most Western languages. |
| Interpersonal relationships | Trust is the rock that allows friendships to be built and protected. |
| Classroom management | Classroom rules are the basic rocks that support the foundation of class activity. |
| | Silence is the teacher's rock. |

*Essential Concept Recognition**

Applies to all subject areas shown here with the apple as an example of a science lesson or a social skills lesson.

Gray is to the rock as red is to the apple. Why?

Applesauce is to the apple as gravel is to the rock.

Petrified wood is like a brass apple.

A rubber rock is like a glass apple. Why?

A worm is to the apple as erosion is to the rock.

Hard is to the rock as security is to you.

Rocks aren't rubbery, people aren't invincible.

---

*Essential concept attributes:* Webster defines an attribute as being "an inherent characteristic or accidental quality of a thing." Essential concept attributes are those "distinguishing features" essential to attaining an understanding of a given concept. Distinguishing attributes are criterial (unique to the given concept without which the thing in question becomes part of another concept—like the skin of an apple as compared to the skin of an orange). They are also within a range of acceptable values for the attribute (apples have *color; black* is the *wrong color* for an apple; *red, yellow, green* are acceptable *colors.*) (Jerome Bruner, Jacqueline Goodnow, and George Austin, *The Study of Thinking,* 1967.)

The most important element in the rock is its stability; the most important element for me is my self-image. Why?

*Follow Up*

Depending upon the subject matter you are teaching, the following activities could be used:

1. *Writing:* The students could tell the story of the forest from the point of view of the rock.
2. *History:* The history of the stream or the surrounding area (the stream could be Bull Run or a tributary of the Rhine) could be discussed from the perspective of the rock.
3. *Math:* A word problem built on the stream, rocks, and animals could be given.
4. Small group discussions could occur around the following analogies and how they relate to feeling secure:
   Each day is a special rock.
   Governments are rocks.
   Every animal can be a rock.
   School is a rock.
   The family is a rock.
   Monetary systems are rock collections.

Remember that extended metaphors should be designed to center around the subject matter being taught in the present lesson. The "rock" experience can be adjusted to any subject matter being presented.

*10. Postassessment.*   Describe the evaluative measures you will use to determine the outcome of your lesson. These measures will relate back to the instructional objectives you designed in Step 3 of this form.

The following postassessment links the concept of a rock with the concept of security and checks for the following elements: awareness of the need for protection, ability to predict behavior and situation, freedom from fear and danger, sense of safety and consistency.

## POSTASSESSMENT QUESTIONS

1. Think of a moment when you felt very secure. How was that situation "a rock" you could depend upon?
2. Families are the rocks upon which we build our adult lives. How is your life being built?
3. Society's police force is its basic bedrock for stable social interaction. Why?

4. What's the primary rock of your life? Why? When do you use this rock?
5. What is the "rock" in our banking system? Why is it sometimes like a volcano?
6. Name an item in your life that functions as your daily "security rock."
7. What were the "security rocks" of Napoleon, Edison, Henry Ford, Carnegie, and Rockefeller? (William Faulkner, Shakespeare, George Washington, Vince Lombardi, or _____?)

*11. Materials and Equipment.* Make yourself a list of all props, supplies, audio–visual equipment, and instructional materials that you will need to teach this lesson.

This lesson needs a collection of rocks—preferably ones you have found outdoors in a similar environment to that of the guided fantasy. (We found river rocks to be best when we field-tested this fantasy.)

In addition, you need to collect many different kinds of rocks— volcanic, quartz, granite, slate, petrified wood, etc. (These rocks can be found at lapidary shops.)

Last, collect pictures (or transparencies) of famous rocks, mountains, and cliffs for focusing the mind on the mineral, its stability, and its consistency.

Helpful in defining the attributes of the concept are strange rocks —glass rocks, pillow rocks, or door stop rocks.

*12. Personal Insights and Revision.* Include insights you gained as a result of presenting the lesson. Note areas you are exploring and new ways to connect the metaphor with the concept you are teaching. Describe changes you would make in the future.

The first time we did this metaphoric lesson, we gathered up rocks from our driveway and were amazed to hear that the participants felt "cognitive dissonance" from receiving a rock that did not belong in the forest or near their stream. Since then, we have been careful to use the worn rocks of a river bed or a forest riverside.

It is astonishing to discover the accuracy of the participants in finding their rocks once they have closed their eyes again. It is also very good experiential data for discussing the world of the handicapped— blind, deaf, or disabled persons.

The colorful rocks are terrific for the presentation; unfortunately, it is almost impossible to get them back—so they can end up being expensive in the long run.

# METAPHORIC TEACHING LESSON PLAN
## Design Format
### *The Long Form: A Participant's Guide*

1. *Background of the Class* Describe your students, the instructional unit you are teaching, the grade level, and any special factors important for understanding the classroom environment.
2. *Instructional Goals* Describe the overall purpose of teaching the lesson. Include the concept you want your students to learn and the context for this concept within the instructional unit you are teaching.
3. *Instructional Objectives* Specify the learner outcomes you will measure; relate these outcomes to the concept you are teaching. Include objectives for cognitive, affective, and psychomotor learning.
4. *Pre-assessment* Design a formal or informal "pretest" to find out how much the students already know about the concept that is to be taught. Write out these questions even if you will be using them orally.
5. *Basic Focus of the Lesson* Choose a metaphor to illustrate the concept you are going to teach. If you have difficulty choosing this metaphor, answer the following questions.

   A. What are the basic characteristics of the concept you are teaching?
   B. What objects, animals, systems of nature, or common, everyday items could symbolize these characteristics?
   C. Which of these objects is most accessible in terms of props and concrete examples? And, which would be fun and enjoyable to present?
   D. List all the materials you have readily available to use with this metaphor.

6. *The Metaphoric Focus* Describe the order of materials and symbols that will be used to focus the class on the metaphoric image of the lesson.
7. *The Personal Comparison* Design a comparison question that will be used for the class to identify with the object.
8. *Interactive/Imagery Experience* Design a participatory nonverbal exercise, roleplay, or guided fantasy experience for your students. The purpose of this is to actively involve the student with the image or object.
9. *The Creative Insight Moment* List the questions and compressed

metaphors you will use to link the concept and metaphor together. Think of improbable connections and analogies that could be creatively thought of as "true."

10. *Postassessment* Describe the evaluative measures you will use to determine the outcome of your lesson. These measures will relate back to the instructional objectives you designed in Step 3 of this form.

11. *Materials and Equipment* Make yourself a list of all props, supplies, audiovisual equipment, and instructional materials that you will need to teach this lesson.

12. *Personal Insights and Revision* Include insights you gained as a result of presenting the lesson. Note areas you are exploring and new ways to connect the metaphor with the concept you are teaching. Describe changes you would make in the future.

# CHAPTER 9

# Condensed (Short Form) Lessons and Sample Format

# METAPHORIC TEACHING LESSON PLAN
## Diversity as a Value: The Leaf
### *The Short Form: A Teacher's Guide**

*1. Context and Focus.* Describe the situation in which the lesson will be taught and/or the rationale for teaching it. Specify your goal and define two or three objectives for the lesson.

The need for this lesson is felt by many teachers in many varied settings and at many different grade levels. The lesson is aimed at addressing the problem of ethnocentrism or egocentrism as it exists in almost all classrooms. Specifically, this lesson is intended to provide students an opportunity to see other students, students who are different from them, as equally valuable and important human beings; in essence, exploring the need for diversity in nature and relating this back to the need for diversity in man.

The primary goal of the lesson, then, is to give students a positive attitude regarding the racial and ethnic diversity that exists within your class. The lesson is thus primarily an affective one, the focus is on changing attitudes, not on learning new information, although new information will certainly be a by-product of this lesson.

Your objectives reflect the fact that this lesson is primarily affective:

*Objective 1:* Students will be able to describe the need for diversity in nature and relate this to the need for diversity in man.

*Objective 2:* Students will value both themselves and their classmates as unique and intrinsically worthy of respect whether or not they share the same racial or ethnic background.

*2. The Metaphor.* Select a metaphor to represent the concept you are teaching; identify and select objects you have that represent this metaphor.

Diversity can be suggested by many natural metaphors; for example, diversity in plant life or within particular types of plant life (flowers),

---

*In each of the following short form metaphoric lessons there are innumerable potential contexts and foci for which the metaphor could be used. Each of these lessons is presented here as an example of a very specific use of the metaphor in a very well defined cognitive or affective area. Adaptation of this specific lesson to one that meets your immediate requirements often means changing only the focus, the objectives and the insight questions. The interactive/imagery phase is usually quite flexible.

in geographic formations or particular kinds of geographic formations (mountains), in animal life or particular kinds of animals (birds). The metaphor chosen for this lesson is the leaf because leaves are accessible, familiar, and common. The variety within leaves will be used to illustrate, first, the variety within humans, and second, the variety within the class.

To begin the lesson you have decided to show the film, "The Leaf," a short nonnarrated study of a leaf from the day it buds on a tree, through the summer and its burst of energetic greenery and into autumn and its change of color, fall from the tree and return to the soil.

Leaves of all types and textures are available; ask each student to bring in one leaf on a given day. The leaves are placed on the bulletin board with each student's name just below it. Then, on the day of the lesson, you bring in not only more leaves, but pictures of leaves, transparencies of leaves, postcards and books showing leaves, leaf calendars, and illustrations of unusual leaves such as the pine needle, the tobacco leaf, or the cactus spine. For unusual connections bring in jewelry representations of leaves, such as an enamel leaf pin or a gold "leafed" leaf.

It is not necessary at this stage to point out the obvious diversity in the leaves, nor the obvious fact that each leaf has function and form in its own way. You are, in fact, readying the class for the comparison phase, the phase wherein they begin to learn the lesson of the leaf.

*3. The Comparison.*   Design a comparison question that can be used by the class to identify with the object.

Because the leaf is such a common, everyday object, most students will have an awareness that far surpasses the knowledge of leaves revealed in the preceeding metaphoric phase. The personal comparison questions are:

Think of a way in which you and the leaf are alike.

or

Of all the leaves you have ever seen in your life, which one is most like you? Why?

or (for lower grades)

Pick a leaf in this room, tell how it's like you.

Students will probably take longer to respond to this comparison question than others. They will have had so many interactions with leaves that they will be reviewing the many different kinds of leaves they know looking for the individualizing elements of each.

Possible answers:

"I am like the oak leaf because my family is strong."

"Sometimes I am like the leaf of poison sumac: come near me and I'll get you; but other times I'm like the tea leaf, and ultimately very soothing for people."

"I am like an old maple leaf in fall, ready to fall from this tree and start a new life as I go to college."

"I am like a birch leaf attached to my family, it is my single source of nourishment."

"I'm more like the pine needle than an oak leaf because I see myself as really a different kind of leaf."

After these responses have been shared, you might ask questions such as:

"Why did we get so many different answers?"

or

"What insights did the leaf give you on yourself or on others?"

*4. The Interactive/Imagery Experience.* Design a participatory non-verbal exercise, roleplay, or guided fantasy experience for your students. The purpose of this is to actively involve the student with the image or object.

The interactive imagery experience for this lesson is a guided fantasy. It is critical that the students be completely relaxed and ready to enter a world where rational objection will yield to imaginative possibilities. Make the room dark and let the students close their eyes, bring your voice to a level just above a whisper, and let your calmness relax them. Have the students take two deep breaths as you begin.

Imagine that you are a leaf on the branch of a tree . . . The branch that you are on hangs down low over a winding river that flows through the forest . . . It is a warm day and the sunlight filters through the branches high above you . . . Around you are thousands of other trees and millions of other leaves, all different from you . . . The river below you is clear . . . It sparkles in the sunlight . . . What kind of leaf are you? . . . Are you all one color? . . . Are you many different colors? . . . Are you a large, broad leaf or a small, delicate one? Look at the image of yourself in the water . . . See yourself as this leaf.

Below you in the river some fish are swimming lazily about . . . You watch them for awhile as they swim in and out among the rocks . . . How large are the fish? . . . How many of them do you see? . . . Are there different kinds? . . . Soon the fish are through feeding and they swim slowly down the river . . . You are alone.

Now the sunshine that has warmed you is leaving . . . As night falls the air seems cool . . . The river is quietly splashing lightly here and

there . . . In the distance you can hear an owl . . . and then another
. . . The night is still . . . You think of the fish and wonder where they
are, now that it is dark.

Morning comes, and the river beneath you comes alive . . . Look down
into the crystal clear water . . . The fish are back . . . Can you see them?
. . . It is early and they are very hungry . . . They dart about quickly
catching small insects off the water's surface . . . Their scales shimmer
in the morning sun . . . You can see lots of different colors as the fish
move about . . . You can hear them splash as they swim through the
water . . . The fish feed and you watch quietly from above . . . As the
morning wears on, the sun is warmer and the fish are full . . . Soon the
fish disappear and you are alone again.

Wait . . . you are not completely alone . . . There is a gentle breeze
beginning to blow . . . You can hear it rustle through the leaves high
above you . . . It rustles through all the leaves in the forest . . . It feels
warm and soothing as it blows across your surface . . . Do you feel it?
. . . You move gently as the breeze blows all around you.

You have been on this branch for quite awhile now . . . You like being
able to look down into the river . . . You have the sun to warm you
. . . And the breeze to comfort you . . . Although you like it here you
wonder where the fish go when they leave.

One day passes . . . and another . . . The sun comes . . . and it goes
. . . Some nights the moon is full. The fish come to the rocks in the river
below . . . They leave when they are ready . . . You are still on the same
branch.

The next time the breeze begins to stir . . . You make up your mind
. . . You want to go with it . . . You want to glide on the wind . . . The
breeze is soft and gentle as it glides across your surface . . . You lean
in the direction that the breeze pushes you . . . As the breeze surrounds
you, you offer no resistance . . . You want to see more of the river than
the part right beneath you.

The breeze is stronger now . . . It pushes you . . . The wind blows
harder . . . You strain to go with it . . . As the wind gets stronger, the
excitement builds within you . . . The wind rushes past you . . . And you
strain to go with it . . . A big gust comes and . . . SNAP . . . you are free
. . . The wind carries you . . . It lifts you higher, higher than you've been
before . . . Now it pulls you down to rest safely on the surface of the
water . . . The river is cool . . . Cooler than the air that you are used
to . . . But you aren't worried . . . The water holds you up . . . It is
carrying you along on its cool, glassy surface . . . And with you are
hundreds of other leaves of different shapes, sizes, and colors.

You are happy . . . The river feels good . . . It is easy to float and now
you are moving . . . You're drifting away from your tree . . . You are
sad to leave . . . But the sadness does not last . . . You have stayed here

long enough and you are glad to go . . . And besides, many other leaves are with you.

As you glide along, you see some rocks ahead . . . The rocks are in the middle of the river . . . The water splashes up against the rocks . . . On top of the biggest rock you notice a creature sunning itself . . . You're getting closer . . . What does this creature look like? . . . What color is it? . . . Does it have a tail?

Drift past the rocks and continue your journey down the river . . . Look up ahead . . . Across the river there is a large, grassy clearing filled with beautiful wildflowers . . . There is a small animal in the shade near the bank of the river . . . What does it look like? . . . Does it have fur? . . . What color is it? . . . As you watch it it carefully makes its way to the edge of the water . . . The ground beneath it is soft and moist . . . The grass is cool and green . . . The animal leans closer and takes a drink . . . The river currents pull you along . . . As you look back towards the clearing . . . The small animal drinks its fill and disappears across the meadows.

The gently flowing river pulls you . . . You glide along . . . The sun is bright in the sky above . . . The banks of the river are shaded by trees, some with leaves much like you . . . Up ahead there is a break in the trees . . . another clearing . . . You are anxious to see what is in the clearing . . . You get closer . . . You let the water pull you towards the high tangled grass at the edge of the river . . . Here in the weeds you can take a closer look . . . In the clearing you see a house . . . Take a good look . . . What is it made of? . . . Is it a big house . . . Or a small cottage? . . . What is in the clearing around the house? . . . Are there any flowers?

Wait . . . there is something moving . . . A human is walking towards the river bank . . . The person is getting closer . . . What does this person look like? . . . Can you see what kind of clothes the person is wearing? . . . The person is coming right down to the water's edge . . . and is looking at you . . . The person is right next to you . . . The human you are watching bends down and reaches out to you . . . Slowly and carefully the person picks you up from the tangled weeds . . . Safe in the human's hands you relax . . . You know that the trip down the river has been a good one . . . When you are ready to leave the shaded bank of the river, slowly, very slowly . . . Come back to the classroom . . . and open your eyes.

*5. Insight Questions.*   List the questions and compressed metaphors you will use to link the concept and metaphor together. Think of improbable connections and analogies that could be creatively thought of as "true."

In order to establish the climate for achieving your objective through this guided journey, ask some of the following questions:

1. How many of you were green leaves? Yellow?
2. Were any of you different colors?
3. How did you feel about so many colors?
4. Did you feel the breeze blowing? Or the water pulling you along?
5. What kind of fish did you see?
6. What kind of animal was sunning itself on the rock?
7. What kind of animal came to drink at the edge of the river?
8. What kind of house was in the clearing?
9. What did the person who found you look like?
10. Did any of you change colors during the fantasy?
11. Did you like to be picked up from the tangled weeds?

There will be a large diversity of answers to these questions in discovering the uniqueness of each person's experience. You want to capture and maintain the feeling of this uniqueness in the following insight questions.

If people are leaves, how many different kinds of trees are represented in this classroom?

If all the leaves were the same size and shape and color and all people were like leaves—what would it mean?

A forest is to leaves as what is to people?

Imagine a forest of oak trees and only oak trees. How do you feel about this?

If the maple leaf is your best friend, what kind of leaf are you?

Because the purpose of this lesson is one of values and attitude changing, you may have to ask this type of question until your students "get it." Simply pointing out to them the obvious relationships between the strength and beauty of diversity in nature and the strength and beauty of diversity in a classroom will undermine the purpose of the lesson. It is all right to summarize an insightful response that leads this way; this will often prompt other students who have been thinking along the same lines but who have been hesitant to contribute or to volunteer their own insights. Again, however, you must be wary of imposing your purpose on their insights. Take each insight as it comes, expand on it when possible; it is quite likely that you will achieve far more than your original instructional goal!

## METAPHORIC TEACHING LESSON PLAN
# Values Clarification, Personal and Historical: The Perfect Day
### The Short Form: A Teacher's Guide

*1. Context and Focus.* Describe the situation in which the lesson will be taught and/or the rationale for teaching it. Specify your goal and define two or three objectives for the lesson.

This lesson is especially designed for junior and senior high school students as well as for adults in classes where values clarification and stress reduction are curricular concerns. In this respect, "The Perfect Day" is essentially an affective lesson. However, the lesson can also be used to create a deeper understanding for the personal values of literary and historical figures. For example, what would have been a perfect day for Lincoln or Washington, for Napoleon or Franklin? What would have been a perfect day for Huckleberry Finn or Anna Karenina? What would be the difference between the perfect day for Hamlet and the perfect day for Macbeth?

For the purposes of this lesson, however, the focus will be on values-clarification regarding leisure time. The lesson is appropriate to any situation where an opportunity for leisure-oriented values-clarification or for a "time-out" to reduce stress is called for. This lesson therefore is primarily affective in design; that is, the overall goal is the discovery of values rather than the assimilation of a new curriculum concept. Incidentally, this lesson has been used most successfully with teachers in stress-reduction workshops because stress is often a result of the conflict between what we do and what we value.

*Objective 1:* Students will clarify their own personal values in regard to the use of leisure time.

*Objective 2:* Students will discuss the role of conflicting values and how this relates to increasing personal stress.

*2. The Metaphor.* Select a metaphor to represent the concept you are teaching; identify and select objects you have that represent this metaphor.

The symbols for the perfect day are numerous, but because the perfect day is more abstract than the butterfly or the leaf, the symbols used to represent the perfect day are also more suggestive and less well defined.* In doing this lesson, we have used pictures that suggest vacation possibilities such as beaches, mountain cabins, ski resorts, ocean liners, mountains, streams, waterfalls, castles, forests, tropical islands, and fjords. We have also used pictures that suggest a different kind of perfect day: pictures of churches, of families together, of harmony in nature, of outstanding accomplishments (such as graduation or receiving the Nobel Prize) and of two people sharing affection.

The purpose of these pictures, whether they are slides, transparencies, photographs, or posters, is to open the imagination to the many possibilities of what a perfect day can be.

*3. The Comparison.*   Design a comparison question that can be used by the class to identify with the object.

Almost all students will have had a personal experience with a day that they considered either perfect or almost perfect.

Choose one of the scenes from the pictures, posters and slides that have just been shown.

Which one would you most like to visit? Why?
or
Which one of these scenes is most like you? Why?
(I'm more like the mountain waterfall because of the constant turbulence that I cause—or because of my ceaseless roar that seems to be heard only by the mountains)

*4. The Interactive/Imagery Experience.*   Design a participatory nonverbal exercise, roleplay, or guided fantasy experience for your students. The purpose of this is to actively involve the student with the image or object.

Today we are going to go on a journey in your mind. Relax and breathe deeply, close your eyes, let your body relax totally relax, breathe deeply, listen to the sound of my voice. You are going to go today to the perfect place.

It is now the morning of a perfect day . . . You are outside . . . The sky is blue . . . You lie down on a blanket on the grass and close your

---

*Again, a caution: Students in grades eight, nine, and ten, due to their physiological brain development, usually need a thorough introduction to right/left brain theory before their dominant rational brain will allow their image brain to experience the "risky" world of the guided fantasy.

eyes and you are transported to the perfect place . . . You can be alone or with somebody else, but the place is your perfect place . . . Picture it in your mind . . . Is it an island or a snowy mountain; is it on a boat ride or on the continental divide? . . . You are now at your perfect place . . . See yourself there . . . The weather is just right . . . The scenery is perfect . . . Everything you need for a perfect day is right there.

Now you are doing the perfect thing for this place you are visiting . . . You are enjoying yourself . . . smiling . . . You are in touch with what is truly special about this place . . . You are truly enjoying this activity . . . Feel yourself doing it; sense your happiness . . . enjoy it . . . Now it is lunch-time and your favorite meal is in front of you and you can have anyone you like come and join you . . . It can be someone in your life now or someone you have always wanted to meet . . . See the meal, see the individual items before you . . . You are talking and listening to someone special; feel the warmth of the sun and see the beauty of the spot you are visiting.

Now it is early afternoon and perhaps your visitor has left you for awhile . . . You decide to wander . . . You see a path that leads off . . . You decide to follow it . . . It is so beautiful and inviting . . . It is secure and safe . . . You begin walking; you smell the scents of the trees and perhaps you see a flower . . . You continue down the path till you come to a bench and you sit down on the bench . . . On it is your favorite book, a book you have read . . . You pick up the book and it comforts you like an old friend . . . You hold the book for a while and remember the joy of reading it.

You take the book and continue walking . . . You see a friend or a family member ahead on the path . . . a friend or family member you have not seen for a while . . . You greet this person . . . You embrace . . . You have not seen this person for a long time and there is much to say . . . You talk for a while . . . You say to this person things you have always wanted to say and you feel good all over . . . then you head back down the path . . . The weather is still perfect . . . The day is gorgeous and you see a beautiful but harmless animal off in the distance . . . You stop and watch the animal and it turns to look at you.

Now the sun is dropping in the sky and there is a beautiful orange glow on the horizon . . . The late afternoon breeze touches you and you feel close to the things you value most.

The day is now ending . . . Take time to ponder the beauty of the place you chose for your perfect day . . . See once again the sky . . . the scenery . . . the animal life . . . Feel your own sense of peace with the world . . . Let this feeling linger.

And now when you are ready, and not before, return to this classroom and when you are completely ready . . . open your eyes.

5. *Insight Questions.*　List the questions and compressed metaphors you will use to link the concept and metaphor together. Think of improbable connections and analogies that could be creatively thought of as "true."

Each person's experience with this guided fantasy is unique—and often personal. It is best to begin the debriefing or insight phase in dyads where a trust relationship permits the sharing of not only the factual information regarding the trip each person took, but also the special insights that occur as a result of taking this trip.

1. Where did you go on your perfect day? Is this a place you've been before or a place you've always wanted to go?
2. What kind of weather did you experience? Were you in a place where the feel of the sun was important?
3. What was the activity you enjoyed in this perfect place—sailing, skiing, praying, relaxing?
4. What kind of meal did you have? Did you dine alone or was someone with you—who was that person?
5. When you walked down the path did you see trees and flowers? What kinds? What was the title of the book you found, and who was the friend or family member you met?
6. As you walked back down the path you saw an animal—what kind of animal did you see? Did it move or fly with grace?
7. As you pondered this perfect place what did you feel? Did it hurt to let go of this feeling and return to the real world?

Remember, each person's sharing will be unique; if you solicit responses to be shared with the entire group, don't be surprised if some are reluctant to share. It is a very personal experience. The question to end this lesson with is simple and personal; usually it needs no oral response, but you will notice students reflecting on the evaluation of their answer to the question: "What did this journey tell you about your values?"

## METAPHORIC TEACHING LESSON PLAN
# Film Developing/Print Processing—
# A Technical Lesson
### *The Short Form: A Teacher's Guide*

*1. Context and Focus.* Describe the situation in which the lesson will be taught and/or the rationale for teaching it. Specify your goal and define two or three objectives for the lesson.

The following metaphoric exercise is an example of a technical process lesson. Although this lesson easily stands by itself (and has well-defined goals and objectives) a secondary purpose of including this lesson is to demonstrate how the metaphor can be used to teach technical skills. Some major copy machine companies, for example, use an imagery experience to teach technicians the path of paper through a copy machine. In this lesson the learner becomes a single frame on a roll of film that is being processed in order to understand the technical process of film processing and print development.

This type of lesson can also be used to teach other technical processes: the use of the lathe, for example, or the principles of the internal combustion engine or the digestive process in humans, the packaging process of a common food item or the curdling process of making cheese. Whenever there is a step-by-step sequential process, the metaphor can be used to teach it.

This lesson has been used by teachers in high school journalism classes. The primary goal of the lesson is to provide students with an imaginary opportunity to develop and print a roll of film in preparation for actual darkroom work so that when the darkroom lesson occurs, the students will already know the steps and processes involved.

The objectives of the lesson are:

*Objective 1:* Students will be able to list the four chemical steps in developing film and the four-step process for making a print. (Cognitive)

*Objective 2:* Students will have a greater appreciation of the artistic possibilities of printing and developing film. (Affective)

*Objective 3:* Students will be able to develop and print a roll of black-and-white film using time and temperature tables. (Psychomotor)

*2. The Metaphor.* Select a metaphor to represent the concept you are teaching; identify and select objects you have that represent this metaphor.

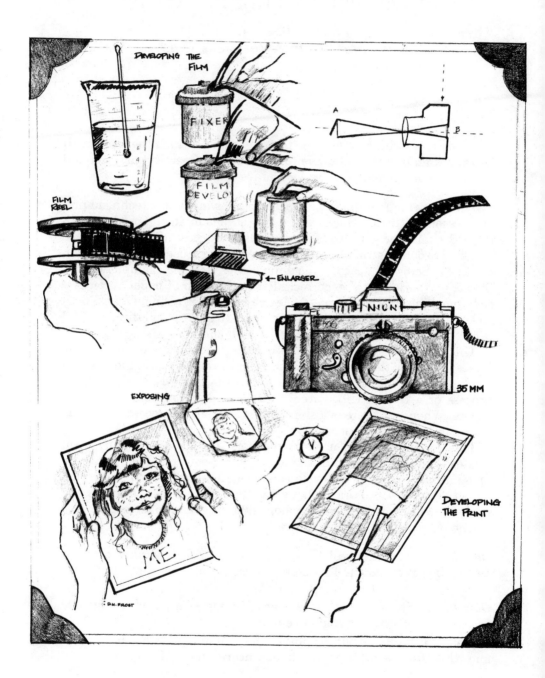

DEVELOPING THE FILM

FIXER

FILM DEVELO

FILM REEL

← ENLARGER

NIKN

EMG

35 MM

EXPOSING

ME.

D.H. FROST

DEVELOPING THE PRINT

294

Because this is a technical process lesson, the metaphoric representation takes place during the guided fantasy. No object or symbol is selected in this case to represent a roll of film as it goes through the stages of processing and development into prints. Rather, the students themselves are asked to imagine themselves as the object, to become a single frame on a roll of film as it goes through the developing and printing process. This differs from other lessons—the virus lesson, for example—because even though the students are asked to become the object, their insights from the activity are not designed to be applied to other curricular areas. However, in order to spark student interest and enthusiasm and in order to achieve the lesson's second objective, teachers should bring in many different kinds and types of photographs, from acknowledged masterpieces (perhaps the works of Ansel Adams) to "out of focus" or off-center home photographs; overexposed, underexposed and other poorly taken photographs might also be shown.

*3. The Comparison.*   Design a comparison question that can be used by the class to identify with the object.

This lesson focuses on a technical skill—the skill of developing and printing film. As noted above, in this lesson photographs (prints, slides, transparencies) should be shown and displayed. Of course there is a myriad of possible photographs you might bring to the classroom and much that can be learned in terms of the photograph being a representation of the object photographed rather than the object itself. However, for the purposes of this lesson, bring in the representative selection of photographs suggested in the metaphor section and share them with the class, then display these pictures prominently in one part of the room.

After the photographs have been shared and displayed, ask the students to choose (mentally) one of these pictures and then to think about why they chose it. Next, they should answer the question:

If you were to think of a way that you and your picture are alike, what would that be?

*4. The Interactive/Imagery Experience.*   Design a participatory nonverbal exercise, roleplay, or guided fantasy experience for your students. The purpose of this is to actively involve the student with the image or object.

Again the interactive imagery experience for this lesson is a guided fantasy. In this case, the students will become a single frame on a role of exposed film. They should be completely relaxed and ready to enter a world where their rational minds will yield to their imaginations. Adjust the lights to achieve as much darkness as is safe and reasonable and let the students close their eyes; bring your voice to a level just above a whisper, and let your calmness relax them. Have the students take two deep breaths as you begin.

Imagine you are a frame on a roll of film that has just been taken by a photographer. Look at the photographer and see what he looks like . . . Do you know him? He is being very careful with you because he has just taken something that is very special to him. You cannot see what he has taken on you because you are still undeveloped . . . You feel very warm and safe in the photographer's camera.

Soon the photographer carries you into a room and turns off the light . . . Everything is very dark . . . Now you feel the photographer's hand taking away the casing you have been living in . . . A cool breeze suddenly surrounds you . . . Then you feel the photographer's hand wrapping you around and around to fit into another casing. Once again you feel warm and safe. He then puts you into a long black cylinder and closes the lid. As he does this you see a little light stream through the top of the cylinder . . . You feel safe . . . Look up. What do you see? As you are looking up you hear water running above you. As you listen to the water, think and imagine what kind of picture you are . . . Suddenly you feel a warm sensation all around you . . . A warm substance that the photographer called developer is covering you. It has a funny odor to you. What does it smell like? . . . As the substance covers you, you feel a change in your outer covering. Little tiny pieces are floating off of you . . . How does it feel? Slowly the pieces stop coming off. Then you feel the warm substances being poured off. Fresh water is then poured on you. It is very cool and you feel very relaxed just like after a hot bath . . . The water is then poured off and you should feel free of the particles that left you . . . Now another substance that seems to tighten your outer covering is poured on you. It seems to hold in place the parts of your covering . . . Before you seemed very loose and heavy and now you feel very firm and stable and light as if something has departed from you.

Again the substance is poured off and cool water is poured over you. Flow back and forth with the water . . . just as you would if you were standing under a beautiful, crystal-clear waterfall. Feel the water clean you . . . Now you see light stream into the cylinder as the photographer removes the lid. The light feels warm and inviting. As you are removed from the cylinder, the photographer begins to unwind you from the casing. As you are unwound you can begin to see an image on your frame. What is it? Can you make out the image? The photographer then lifts you and places you under a current of warm air. You begin to dry and feel good all over.

Now the photographer picks you up and takes you into a dark room. You can see a little in the room, and you notice a lot of equipment. What type of equipment do you see?

The photographer gently picks you up and places you into a machine. You then feel light penetrate your skin, causing you to separate from your covering. Feel yourself floating . . . As you float, think of yourself as special for being picked by the photographer. You finally stop floating and rest on a slick white paper. You feel yourself soaking into the paper. You are now part of the paper. The photographer picks you up . . . and puts you gently into a watery solution. Suddenly you feel yourself change. It feels the same as before except pieces are not coming off of you. Look at yourself. All this time you have wondered what you look like. Now you know . . . Now look at the photographer. What kind of expression does he have on his face . . .

He picks you up and puts you into a solution which stops the changing process in you. Very quickly he places you into another solution. You begin to tighten up like you did before and now you are very rigid and firm . . . He places you into a whirlpool of cool fresh water. You feel very clean and good. The photographer takes you from the water and admires you. How do you feel? Is he happy with his work? Take one more look at yourself and when you are ready come back into the classroom and slowly open your eyes.

*5. Insight Questions.*    List the questions and compressed metaphors you will use to link the concept and metaphor together. Think of improbable connections and analogies that could be creatively thought of as "true."

In this lesson, the goal is to prepare the student to master a technical skill. Using the guided fantasy as a vehicle, the student experiences each stage of the film development and printing process. Insight questions are designed to take this a step further, taking the process and using it and its attendant features as metaphors for creative insight.

1. How would developing the "prints" of your life differ from developing the "prints" of your mother, father, sister, grandfather?
2. If the film of your life had only twenty-four frames, which ones would you choose? Why?
3. Developing film in semilightness is reading a book in semidarkness. Why?
4. Skipping a step in the printing process is the history of the Middle Ages. Why?
5. Biographies are the film of a life. Who does the developing?

6. "Cropped" prints are the historian's tool. Why?
7. The twelfth frame is your life till today. What will the rest of the frames look like?
8. An insight is an exposed frame that needs developing and printing.

# METAPHORIC TEACHING LESSON PLAN
# Relationships: Journey to the Planets
## The Short Form: A Teacher's Guide

*1. Context and Focus.* Describe the situation in which the lesson will be taught and/or the rationale for teaching it. Specify your goal and define two or three objectives for the lesson.

This lesson exemplifies the kind of multi-level impact that can be achieved through metaphoric teaching. On the surface the goal of this lesson is to provide information on the planets of our solar system—the cognitive objectives specify the need for students to be able to name the planets in terms of their proximity to the sun. Information regarding the relative size of the planets, the color of each planet, the number of moons circling each planet, and the apparent density of each planet is presented in this guided journey in order to be assimilated for later recall. This cognitive information, however, is supplemented by equally important affective insight and objectives; insight and objectives that attest to the dual (seemingly bipolar—cognitive/affective) nature of metaphoric lessons. The affective objectives enjoin the students to examine personal relationships in terms of the metaphors of the planets. Which of my friends is most ethereal, which one is closest, which one is surrounded by the most moons, or the most solid? Does distance play a factor in relationships? Are you pulled too strongly by being in the "orbit" of a larger "planet"? These types of questions are examined for affective insight while the information gained is reinforced in the memory by the continuing comparisons that surface, identifying one's "Mercury" or "Jupiter," for example. Thus, the objectives for this lesson are from all three domains:

*Objective 1:* Students will be able to list and name the planets of our solar system in the order of their distance from the sun. (Cognitive)

*Objective 2:* Students will be able to examine personal relationships using the metaphor of the planets as an organizer. (Affective)

*Objective 3:* Students will be able to draw a two-dimensional representation of the solar system including the sun and all known planets. (Psychomotor)

*2. The Metaphor.* Select a metaphor to represent the concept you are teaching; identify and select objects you have that represent this metaphor.

The
Solar System

RELATIONSHIPS

The
Family System

Relationships can be explored through many natural metaphors: the metaphor of the tree, its branches, roots, leaves and trunk, for example, or the metaphor of the land, different land forms representing different kinds of relationships. The metaphor for this lesson is the solar system, with emphasis on the planets.

Because so much recent research has been done on the planets, a multitude of props are available, ranging from films to photographs. Any one of the short, fifteen- or twenty-minute educational films of the planets will provide imagery and factual information for the students (some of the episodes of the "Cosmos" series are excellent). In addition, there are planet calendars, planet books, and *National Geographic* and *Smithsonian* magazine articles on the planets. Students can easily observe at least one planet, Venus, with a modest telescope. Many will have seen planetarium shows or other visual displays of the planets.

Planet mobiles can be found, as well as planet wallpaper and other planet decoration. Planets, unlike leaves, clocks and butterflies will always have to be shown in a representative mode so the unusual planet must be more than a picture. One of the more successful unusual planet representations is a ceramic of Saturn, with the rings lightly but securely attached with thin steel wires. The question "Is this a planet?" is jarring to the students because Saturn has become so familiar through pictures that this three-dimensional piece of pottery presents a long intellectual stretch as a planet. Remember, you are readying your students for the next phase (the comparison phase) at this point, not providing information or answers.

*3. The Comparison.* Design a comparison question that can be used by the class to identify with the object.

Metaphors are so effective because of both the commonality and uniqueness of each of our experiences with the object. Each student can relate to the butterfly, the leaf, or the rainbow, because each student has seen or somehow experienced these objects; in addition, each student's experience, though common, is also unique. The comparison question on the planets is designed to capture both of these qualities.

After you have shown the film and pictures of the solar system, pose the following question: Think of a way in which you and one of the planets are alike: what is it? (This question allows the students to mentally review the physical properties and pictures of the planets and to project a response based on both knowledge and image.)

Again, for lower grades, an alternate question is: Choose a picture of one of the planets: How is it like you? Answers to these questions will usually vary from the immediate ("I am like Mars because I like orange and green") to the more thoughtful ("I am like Pluto, so far removed from my source of light and energy"). Accept all answers without comment; you may wish to go back, after all have shared, to re-examine the issues of commonality, while encouraging each student to appreciate the uniqueness of his or her insight.

*4. The Interactive/Imagery Experience.* Design a participatory nonverbal exercise, roleplay, or guided fantasy experience for your students. The purpose of this is to actively involve the student with the image or object.

In some ways this lesson will be easy for students while in other ways it may be difficult. The purpose of the lesson is to give students a sense of planetary distance and relationship and, in order to do this, they are to be taken on an imaginary space journey through our solar system. Because today's student is sophisticated in terms of space travel (most know, for example, that we cannot travel to Venus in a day or a week or even a month by presently available technology), the student has to be made aware that this trip takes place in some future (yet relatively imminent) time. On the other hand, because so much of the student's world has been shaped by *Star Wars, Star Trek, Return of the Jedi,* and other space-oriented films, today's students tend to believe that speeds in excess of the speed of light ("Warp" speed) will someday be possible. This guided journey must, therefore, be presented in this light. Setting the stage for this lesson means establishing that it is some time in the future and interplanetary travel is safe and routine, not unlike jet travel over the vastness of the oceans today.

The interactive imagery experience for this lesson is a guided fantasy. Have your students completely relax and prepare them to enter a world where rational objection will yield to imaginative possibilities. Darken the classroom and have the students close their eyes; bring your voice to a level just above a whisper, let your calmness relax them. Have the students take two deep breaths as you begin.

It is some time in the near future. Space travel is very safe and every week hundreds and hundreds of people travel in spaceships to the planets in our solar system . . . Today you are one of these people. You are getting onto an elevator that is taking you up into the spacecraft on top of a huge rocket. The spacecraft is very safe . . . It looks like the "Columbia" and "Challenger" space shuttles that have been used to put satellites into space . . . It is different only in that it can also land safely on other planets . . . You meet the pilot and shake hands, you meet the co-pilot and the navigator and shake hands with them, too. . . . They fly these spacecraft the same way that pilots fly jumbo-jets today . . . You take your seat and look around . . . There are twenty other people on board . . . They are all excited, relaxed, feeling safe . . . You

hear the pilot's voice . . . He is telling you to fasten your shoulder belt
. . . An air bag pops out of the seat in front of you and gently but firmly
pushes on your chest . . . You are excited . . . You hear the roar of the
rocket and you begin lifting off slowly at first . . . then faster and faster
. . . It is very loud and then very quiet . . . The big rocket has pushed
you into space and fallen away . . . You are safely flying more than two
hundred miles above the earth . . . As you look down you see the blue
of the oceans and the white of wispy clouds . . . The sky above you is
dark and dotted with the bright light of billions of stars.

You hear the pilot's voice . . . He is saying that you are now going
to leave this view of Earth and travel on to Mars, the closest planet to
Earth away from the sun . . . You know that Mercury is the planet
closest to the sun but it's too hot to go there . . . You know that Venus
is between Mercury and Earth but you are heading out, away from the
sun . . . While you are thinking of this you hear the pilot's voice telling
you that you can look out the window and see Mars . . . From your
window Mars looks yellow-orange with little patches of green all
around . . . You know that Mars is farther away from the sun than
Earth so it is colder . . . You wonder what causes those green patches
. . . You wonder how cold Mars must be at night, colder than any place
on Earth . . . Now Mars is beginning to fade off into the distance as you
relax back in your chair. A steward brings you a meal on a tray . . . You
feel like you are sitting in a flying restaurant as you head off into the
sky . . . You look back out your window at Mars . . . Mars is relatively
close to the Earth, and the distance between Mars and the next planet
you will see (Jupiter) is much greater than that between Mars and
Earth . . . As you look out your window you see that Mars has two
moons and that the surface of Mars is cratered like Earth's moon. In
fact, Mars looks more to you like a moon than a planet . . . You wonder
if any kind of plants or animals live on Mars . . . You sit back and think
to yourself, the sun is at the center, then Mercury, then Venus, then
Earth, then Mars . . . And you hear the pilot's voice saying "Jupiter will
be appearing on the large forward window in thirty minutes" . . . You
begin staring at the screen and watching the stars . . . Suddenly Jupiter
appears . . . It is huge . . . many times the size of Earth. It would take
ten Earths all hooked together just to make a belt around Jupiter
. . . You are surprised by its size . . . You expected Jupiter to be big, but
it is far bigger than you imagined . . . The pilot decides to take you on
a trip around Jupiter so you can count the moons . . . You notice that
Jupiter appears to be made of gases, not rocks like Earth, and you count
the moons . . . Jupiter, you discover, has twelve moons . . . As you
complete your journey around Jupiter you feel relaxed and excited
. . . What a thrill to see Jupiter close up. Now you complete your loop
around Jupiter and are heading off into space again . . . It is very dark

outside your window but the glow of each star is clearly visible; you can see billions of stars, and each one is special . . . It is like being in the desert on a cool clear night . . . You feel like you could reach out and touch each star . . . The next planet you will see is Saturn. As you sit back in your seat you think about the planets and how each is so different . . . Saturn is quite a distance from Jupiter, so you have time to sit back and relax and watch the stars out the big window . . . Then, seemingly out of nowhere, the image of Saturn appears . . . The rings around Saturn remind you of thousands of racetracks circling a great orange planet . . . You know there is no life on this planet because it is made up primarily of poisonous gases and there is no oxygen or water on Saturn. The pilot begins the turn around Saturn as you head back to Earth. Uranus, Neptune, and Pluto are too far away to be seen on this trip, but you know that Pluto is the coldest planet because it is the planet farthest from the sun. As you continue your arching turn around Saturn you gaze out at its beautiful rings. And now you are heading back toward Earth . . . past Jupiter now, then past Mars as you look out your window at the planets. As you are approaching Earth the pilot's voice announces that today, as a special treat, he is going to pass by Earth and fly between Venus and Mercury before the final landing on Earth. You are excited as you look out your window and see the blue of the planet Earth pass by your left window. Venus is next, and there it is . . . beautiful in the dark sky . . . Venus is very hot . . . much hotter than Earth and about the same size as Earth . . . Plants as we know them cannot live on Venus because it is so hot and the atmosphere is so thick that it acts like a mirror . . . Now, out of the window on the right side, you see Mercury, the hottest and smallest of the planets . . . Because Mercury takes fifty-nine days to make one rotation on its axis, the dark side of Mercury is frozen, while the light side is so hot that any water there would just evaporate. You complete your turn and head back to Earth. As you land you think about the planets you have seen, about Mercury nearest the sun, about Venus, Earth, Mars, Jupiter, and Saturn; each different, each special, each beautiful in its own way . . . It's been an exciting journey but now you are safely back home . . . When you are ready, and not before, return to this room and open your eyes.

*5. Insight Questions.* List the questions and compressed metaphors you will use to link the concept and metaphor together. Think of improbable connections and analogies that could be creatively thought of as "true."

Warm up the class for personal insight by directing the following general questions to the whole class:

1. Which planet seemed most mysterious?
2. Which planet seemed most exciting?
3. Which of the planets would you least like to visit?
4. What did the sky look like?
5. What did Earth look like?
6. What things seemed different between Earth and the other planets?
7. Did the planets change colors as your perspective of them changed?

Once the students are warmed up for personal insight, ask the following questions:

A planet is to the galaxy as you are to _____?

If _____ is your Mercury, who is your Mars?

A man is to a planet as who is to you?

Friendships are planets, families are solar systems. Explain.

Rings are friends, moons are _____?

Who is your Saturn, who is your Mercury, who is your sun?

These affective insight questions can be followed by cognitive, knowledge-based questions and by completing the assignment specified in Objective 3. Expand on the insights and capture the recall that is based on image. Each expanding answer will build on the one before it. The final question, "Who is your planet or sun?" might be answered privately or in dyads. It is not likely that students will want to share this with the class.

# METAPHORIC TEACHING LESSON PLAN
## Design Format
### *The Short Form: A Teacher's Guide*

1. *Context and Focus* Describe the situation in which the lesson will be taught and/or the rationale for teaching it. Specify your goal and define two or three objectives for the lesson.
2. *The Metaphor* Select a metaphor to represent the concept you are teaching; identify and select objects you have that represent this metaphor.
3. *The Comparison* Design a comparison question that can be used by the class to identify with the object.
4. *The Interactive/Imagery Experience* Design a participatory nonverbal exercise, roleplay, or guided fantasy experience for your students. The purpose of this is to actively involve the student with the image or object.
5. *Insight Questions* List the questions and compressed metaphors you will use to link the concept and metaphor together. Think of improbable connections and analogies that could be creatively thought of as "true."

# The Metaphor as a Measuring Tool

Creativity is an elusive concept, a concept large enough to embrace many seemingly conflicting perspectives (the prepared mind and the unfettered mind, for example), a concept whose understanding has been enhanced by the recent discoveries of the process specialization of the cerebrum's right and left hemispheres. Creativity is an activity of solitude for the poet, of collective cooperation or improvisation for the musician. Webster's says that to create is "to produce through imaginative skill," yet this literal definition belies the cultural metaphors which often limit creativity in the classroom, cultural metaphors which suggest that only Edisons, Beethovens, Shakespeares, and Michelangelos are truly creative. As students are exposed to creativity as a special gift for the few instead of a common event for the many, the awe produced often impedes the creativity desired. In fact, in the case of creativity, the dictionary definition is more liberating than the cultural definition because it stresses the commonality for all of us in being creative—the commonality that is our imagination, that right-hemisphere power that each of us shares. The purpose of this book, then, is to demonstrate through the image of metaphoric teaching the ways that creativity can be included in the regular curriculum in order to enhance and promote both creative products and conceptual learning. The lessons themselves establish a creative atmosphere that should carry over into other subject areas, an atmosphere that John Curtis Gowan describes in reviewing the work of Puccini and Wagner:

[The process of such high] creativity consists of three phases: 1) the prelude ritual . . . 2) the altered state of consciousness or creative spell, during which the creative idea is born, starting with vibrations, then mental images, then the flow of ideas which are finally clothed in form. This syndrome then proceeds with extreme and uncanny rapidity in what is always referred to as a trance, dream, revery, somnambulistic state, or similar altered condition, and 3) the postlude in which positive emotions about the experience suffuse the participant.*

---

*Gowan, J.C. "The View from Myopia." *The Gifted Child Quarterly,* 1976, 20, 378–87.

Metaphoric teaching, the strategy of right-brain encouragement, is designed to induce and sustain these conditions in the classroom. Metaphoric lessons continually reinforce students' for their own imaginative leaps, but there are other conditions that should also obtain in order to promote creative attitudes. The following checklist is a teacher-oriented set of standards that will encourage student participation in metaphoric lessons and increase the overall effectiveness of the lessons. Following these guidelines will enhance the creative potential of each student in your class by making the instructional statement that we are often looking for *an* answer rather than *the* answer. Implementing these guidelines essentially says, "We value the contributions of this image brain as much as those of the verbal brain." The following "mental set," then, is designed to put a creative atmosphere as well as creative strategies into your classroom.

1. *Value creativity.* Reward your students for thinking creatively, for coming up with alternative ideas, solutions, and perspectives. Give examples of personal moments of creativity that were unusual, different, or the exception to the rule.
2. *Help students become more sensitive to their environment.* Teach students to notice the world around them; note spatial relationships between people and objects; take time for nonverbal awareness and "reading" body language. Focus upon an object always seen as a whole (the bicycle) and take it apart mentally; focus upon objects always seen as separate (students in the classroom) and put them together as a whole (the classroom as specific personality).
3. *Encourage the manipulation of objects and ideas.* The creative process often means turning things upside-down—peering in from all sides and all perspectives. What does a sunflower look like to a caterpillar? What does a chessboard look like if you are a pawn? Compare life as a _____ versus life as a _____.
4. *Teach students to test ideas for implications.* Students learn the biases and prejudices of those around them. When a moment of stereotyping arises, look at the creative implications of the bias. All _____ do the following; what would happen if _____ who is a _____ did this behavior?
5. *Develop an overall attitude of tolerance toward a new idea.* An idea may seem wild, but help students value it for its creativity. Brainstorm new ideas as a daily part of your class; reward students for alternative perspectives, regardless of their practicality. Develop the rule that brainstorms are not to be criticized.
6. *Beware of forcing set patterns on students.* Set patterns ("there is only one right way to do this") have a way of causing people to "program" their thoughts; new ideas, new perspectives, and new patterns will not even be considered.

7. *Develop an overall creative atmosphere in the class.* Encourage students to display creative products, to see the room as a creative thinking lab where experimenting and deviating from the norm are as important as learning structure and order.

8. *Teach students to value creative thinking.* Creative thoughts emerge spontaneously; help students to express them. Look for the "big picture" of a concept as well as the detailed application. Encourage insight in the classroom and add "insight exercises" to your lessons.

9. *Teach skills for avoiding peer sanctions.* Sometimes this means championing the unpopular idea (even when you normally wouldn't); sometimes this means teaching students not to laugh or make fun of strange or weird perspectives (or drawing the laughter onto yourself); sometimes it means designing lessons that deliberately challenge the peer assumptions of everyone (dyads for revealing a "dumb" idea that turned out to be a good idea).

10. *Give information to the class about the creative process.* Teach your class that the left/right brains exist (even second graders can learn about the "word" brain and the "picture" brain); this helps people value the images and creative perspectives that do not hold up to logic or the scrutiny of the orderly left brain—but provide the inspiration for original, new products.

11. *Dispel the idea that only some people can be creative—that only masterpieces are true products of creativity.* We are all creative; 50% of our cerebrum is devoted to producing alternative images and perceptions all the time. Teach students that creating means enjoying the right brain's way of thinking; it means exploring a whole universe of alternative ways of seeing things.

12. *Encourage self-initiated learning.* When a student decides to do something on his or her own, encourage the exploration. Try not to focus on the product; many students are frightened away from the process (of writing a novel, creating a new product) because we try to excite them with the end result. Concentrate on the feelings developed as a result of the *process.*

13. *Teach problem solving as an ideal opportunity for being creative.* Problem solving means looking at several alternative strategies for the solution; teach students that the first solution is only a clue to the better solution they will find through brainstorming and pooling their ideas.

14. *Create a need for a creative point of view.* Provide moments when only the raw data or basic material is present—how many different versions of life in a garden are there? Write five of these versions with the same basic information (from the point of view of the garden hose, the daisy, the onion, the corn stalk, and the crow).

16. *Make resources available for ideas to come true.* When students get

a creative idea (such as a class play), do your best to help that idea become a reality. It is critical to maintaining creativity—to value the creative ideas by allowing them to become *real* in the classroom.

17. *Encourage the habit of working out the completion of a creative idea.* A large part of creativity is hard work—the work that comes after the moment of insight or burst of imagery. Help students value the actual creation of the products they envision. Narrow down their excitement to manageable levels; then encourage them to complete the ideas they think up. (It may be difficult to write a novel, but students can pick an episode in the novel and write it in detail. They can simply "set the stage" by saying what came first, and they can also conclude with what will follow this episode.)

18. *Make sure that your feedback is constructive.* Creating new things is a risky business; if you criticize without a welcome, there is a tendency to return to a logical approach. Show what is working well in the new product; then, add only slight suggestions for modifications. Always add these suggestions as several possibilities—one suggestion will say there is one right way to do it. Several alternatives will keep the creative perspective going.

## WHAT KEEPS CREATIVITY IN THE CLASSROOM?

1. *Open-ended Questions!* Try to build moments where there are no right and wrong answers possible, where students can expand and explore their own perceptions and thoughts. We have found that creativity is fostered when students discover that there are no "right" or "wrong" personal opinions and personal interpretations.

If you were Macbeth at the end of the play, how would you be feeling? How would you feel about Lady Macbeth?

If you were to imagine an argument between Tom Sawyer and Huckleberry Finn, what would they argue about? Who would say what?

If you were to guess how Gregor felt waking up one day to discover he had become a giant roach, what feelings do you think raced through his mind?

Imagine you could be a "rockinghorse winner," what would you want to buy with all that money? Is there anything so important to you that you would keep riding? Suppose in the end, you would be all right; what goal or purpose would be worth riding the rockinghorse for a month? A year? A whole childhood?

Expansion questions—"imagine if," "if you were to guess," and "what if . . . ," questions—force the student to explore his or her own viewpoint. Because these moments are highly personal and involve a degree of vulnerability, be sure to protect each comment as valuable and valid. Avoid judging or evaluating such answers as "right" or "wrong." Instead, teach your students to value the creative perspective inherent in responding to an expansion question.

2. *Democratic Attitudes!* There are many ways to approach this problem—how many can we discover? This approach causes the student to seek creative alternatives. It avoids fostering a classroom environment where student try to guess the teacher's point of view and teaches them to come up with new ideas and new perspectives. The authoritarian classroom—"my way is the only way"—stifles creativity and demands conformity.

3. *Flexible Personalities!* People who break easily do not have an opportunity to experience the excitement of brand new ideas. Learn to be open to the unusual idea, the strange perspective, the "off-the-wall" opinion. Such openness will encourage students to look at options and alternatives without fear of disapproval or censorship.

4. *Respect and Personal Dignity!* Each individual deserves respect and personal dignity—no matter how he or she may be behaving or responding. Ridicule and sarcasm are deadly to creativity; they may "work" at the moment for control, but they have a backlash effect in terms of future openness and willingness to try new approaches. Extending personal respect to each student (regardless of the situation) will foster self-confidence and self-esteem. Knowing I am respected means I can feel confident about offering a new creative idea without looking foolish or inappropriate.

5. *Formative Evaluation!* Teach students that evaluation can be a moment to increase your skills or expand your overall understanding; evaluation can be a nurturing experience with a sense of personal growth. Avoid creating a classroom where grades are the basic feedback mechanism; grading causes students to seek "right" answers; self-improvement (without grades) will encourage the student to probe for new combinations and alternatives

6. *Several "Right" Answers!* Students can learn that each question has a host of possible "right" answers that will work or respond to the situation being discussed. If being right is the primary emphasis of classroom instruction, students stop exploring the possibilities for creativity and produce work which meets the teacher's expectation for "what is correct."

7. *Encouragement for Divergent Personalities!* The "emperor's-new-clothes" student may be frustrating, but this person's safety from ridicule is crucial. The way you treat the maverick is the standard by which the class judges your overall tolerance of differing points of view. Welcome the divergent perspective as an opportu-

nity to model openness to creative perspective and alternative thinking.

8. *Creativity for its Own Sake!* Creative products are risky (they don't always come off the way we envision them!); if trying a new approach and being creative is valued, students will learn to be more spontaneous, open to risking a moment when the idea doesn't "work," and willing to expand conventional thinking. If succeeding is the primary emphasis, student will respond with what they think you want to hear.

9. *Tolerance of the "Play Attitude"!* Humor, fun, fantasy, imagination are all the beginning tools of creative thinking. Invention begins with a sense of "playing" with what's available—searching for a brand-new way of looking at the situation or problem at hand. Without such moments, we naturally return to what we know to be true and appropriate.

10. *Unconventional Thinking Is Important!* Creative thinking often means breaking with traditional ways of viewing something to develop a new strategy, a new product, a new concept. Sometimes students need to question old ways of doing things, rituals and traditions that have outlived their usefulness, rules that were made for another group of people, conventions that served a very different point in time. What will work today? How can we break conceptual boundaries which limit perspective and force old solutions or totally new problems? Students can learn to value the past and traditional approaches without being bound by inappropriate conventionality.

Implementing these guidelines will not always be easy; teaching through the metaphoric method for the first time takes a moment of courage, a leap of faith. From Gilgamesh to the present, our left brains have dominated and defined the contexts of learning while the right brain has been responsible for the major breakthroughs, the great conceptual advances. Creativity can now be more than the province of the poet, artist, or musician; it can also be the province of the student who regularly experiences the spontaneous right-brain insight, the metaphoric conceptual consolidation or coalescence that is as real as the left-brain factual knowledge which is so often so singularly valued. Research on hemispheric processing has brought creativity to the level of a teachable skill. We now have a choice.

# INDEX

Advance organizer
  designing of for concept
      formation, 132–135
  use of, 59, 130–135, 145, 150
  See also Experiential learning
Alford, Henry, 88
Allegories
  of the cave (Plato), 20–22
  teaching role of, 97
Analogies
  as defined by Gordon, W. J. J.
      compressed conflict, 99–100, 106
      direct, 97–99
      personal, 98–99
      improbable, 68–69
  of the "Poison Arrow," 22
Aquinas, Saint Thomas, 8
Archimedes, 37
Argument
  definition of, 117–118
Aristotle, 127
Asimov, Isaac, 198
Attitude
  change of, 115, 119–120
Ausabel, D., 130

"Back to basics" movement, 107
Beethoven, Ludwig van, 307
Bible passages, 21, 50, 78, 88, 89, 91,
      93, 94, 96–97, 100, 127
"Big picture," 51, 104, 118
Bismark, Otto von, 127
Brahms, Johannes, 37
Brain
  development of, 45
  duality of, 7–8, 23, 109
  functions of, 10–11, 14, 18, 36
  graphics of, 6, 9, 15, 18
  hemispheric specialization of, 8–9,
      11, 13–18, 36, 61, 97, 135, 198
  left hemisphere of, 4, 8, 10, 18, 19,
      23, 45, 91, 116, 119, 151
  mapping of, 14
  processes of, 51
  right hemisphere of, 8, 10, 19

surgery on, 5–6
  waves of, 16
Brain research
  educational implication of, 17–20
  epileptics and, 5, 6, 11–13
Brainstorming, 69
Brink, Carol R., 43
Bronowski, Jacob, 101
Bruner, Jerome, 25, 51–52

Capra, Fritzof, 8
Career education, 129, 132
Caxton, William, 93
Chesterton, G. K., 8
Closure metaphor, 152. See also
      Metaphor
Coleridge, William, 31
Columbus, Christopher, 59, 82, 84
Concept
  assimilation of information in,
      100
  attributes of, 113, 122–126
  attainment of, 24, 89, 106,
      113–126, 151
  bonding of with image, 264
  of change, 55, 57–69, 177–194
  common referents of, 95
  definition of, 113, 122–126
  development of, 4, 40, 109, 118
  formation of, 59
  identification of cultural imagery
      in, 122–126
  imagination's role in, 4
  learning of, 23
  mastery of, 51, 145
  metaphoric images in, 56, 106
  teaching of, 19, 39, 50–56, 60,
      122–126, 135, 141–142, 147,
      150, 155
  use of pictures in, 122
Conceptual ability, 17, 19, 51, 143
Conceptual blocks, 105
Conceptual breakthroughs, 312
Conceptual bridges, 144
Conceptual imagery, 4

Conceptual insight, 31, 86, 88
Conceptual leap, 25, 46, 54–55, 97, 105
Conceptual linking, 128
Conceptual system, 117
Conceptual tool, 7
Conceptual understanding, 11, 24, 106, 129, 135, 165
Conflicting values, 289–292
Confucius, 21, 73, 88
Conrad, Joseph, 8
Constructive feedback, 310
Conventional definition, 60, 116, 118, 135
Cook, Thomas D., 42
Cooptation
    concept of, 39, 95, 147–149
*Corpus callosum*, 5–6, 11–12, 14, 26
Courtesy, 39, 147–148
Cousteau, Jacques, 137
Creativity
    attributes of, 17, 23–40
    atmosphere inducive to, 36–39
    as brain process, 35–40
    classroom application of, 308–312
        concept mastery and, 102, 194
        incubation period and, 26–28
        measurement and, 34
        nature of, 6, 203
        preparation for, 26
        process awareness and, 23, 28, 32
        teaching process of, 36, 109
        verification of, 26–28
    definition of, 24–36
    and metaphoric brain, 36–40
    television's role in, 40–46
    Wallas's model of, 26–34
Creative approach
    attitude needed for, 30–36
    process of, 32, 36, 100
Creative breakthroughs, 31–32
Creative connection, 7, 39, 86, 99, 206
Creative historical moments, 27–32
Creative imagery, 99, 127
Creative individuals, 24–26, 28–30, 37–38
Creative insight, 20, 85, 111, 156
Creative juxtaposition, 77, 97
Creative leap, 52, 105
Creative outcomes, 164
Creative perception, 72, 105
Creative perspective, 100, 105, 309

Creative problem-solving, 38, 98
Creative skills, 33–35
Creative solution, 32
Creative thinking process, 33, 52, 149
Creative thoughts, 45
Crookes, William, 29, 32
Cultural definition, 55, 56, 72, 121, 125, 150
Cultural diversity, 147
Cultural history, 92
Cultural image, 119
Cultural lesson, 91, 126
Curiosity, 29, 30, 144, 148
Cyclical natural system, 229

Dali, Salvador, 84
da Vinci, Leonardo, 92, 93
Daydreaming, 10–11
Debriefing process, 3, 65, 67, 82, 11, 138–143
Democratic classroom, 311
Deutsch, George, 16
Diamantes, 203, 204
Directed dyads, 174
Disney, Walt, 131
Diversity, 281–287, 311

Edison, Thomas, 277, 307
Einstein, Albert, 17, 38
Electroencephalogram (EEG), 14, 16
Ellison, Robert, 108
Emerson, Ralph Waldo, 53
Empathy characteristics, 39, 105, 209, 217
Essential concept attribute, 275
Expansion question, 141, 310
Experiential learning
    and assessment, 138–139
    concept of, 4, 138, 144–145
    and experience, 53–55, 132, 142
    and lesson design, 128
    models of, 49, 102, 126–145
Experiential Learning Model
    components of
        focus, 130–135
        experience, 135–138
        assessment, 138–143
        integration, 143–145

Fables, 92–93
    of Aesop, 50
    of Africa, 94
    of Berechiah, 93, 103

of Japan, 93
  use of, 88, 91, 94, 97, 103
Faraday, Michael, 38
Faulkner, William, 70, 277
Ferguson, E. S., 37, 45
Finn, Huckleberry, 289, 310
Fleming, Alexander, 30
Focus metaphor, 145, 148, 169. *See*
  also Metaphor
Focus moment, 130. *See* also
  Advance organizer
Ford, Henry, 277
Folk tale, 7, 88–89, 93, 97
Formative evaluation, 311
Franklin, Benjamin, 50, 289

Galin, David, 16
Gallagher, James, 141
Generic instructional strategy,
  98
Gestalt psychology, 63, 126
Ghiselin, Brewster, 31
Glock, Marvin, 44
Goal-setting. *See* Metaphoric lesson;
  Metaphoric teaching
Gordon, W. J. J., 98–101
Gowan, John Curtis, 307
Guatania, Sakyamuni (Bhudda), 22
Guided fantasy
  experiential learning and, 104,
    137
  guidelines for, 209–210
  imagery design for, 2
  experience of, 3, 63, 78, 105
  preparation for, 208
  teaching strategies for, 110–111,
    138, 149, 174, 185, 209–210
Guilford, J. P., 26, 33, 34

Han Fei Tzu, 93
Hare, Julius Charles, 88
Hemispheric interaction, 24, 109.
  *See* also Brain
Hemispheric specialization, 4, 7, 45,
  49. *See* also Brain
Henry, Marguerite, 43
Heraclitus, 115
Hesoid, 93
Hippocampus, 49, 110
Historical truth, 263
Hitler, Adolf, 82–84
Holistic learning
  conceptual understanding of, 19,
    24, 55

Hooker, Richard, 115
Huxley, Thomas Henry, 50

I Ching, 8
Illumination, 27–28, 30–32, 32–38,
  143
Image
  creation of, 41
  definition of, 113, 121–122, 145
  as focus of metaphoric lesson, 168
  and logic, 149
  message by, 38
  processing of, 102
  use of, 35, 44, 55, 60–61, 126, 151
Image "clues," 105–106
Image retention, 89
Imagery
  development of, 41, 44
  formation of, 44–46
  role of television and, 40–46
  use of, 29, 36, 40–44, 51–52, 62,
    118
Imagination, 25, 41, 45, 129
Information assimilation, 19
Information-processing, 17, 101
Inquiry lessons, 46, 144
Insight, 4, 17, 27–28, 39, 59, 62, 76,
  77, 94, 96, 109, 113, 127, 134,
  138, 141–143, 151
Insight analogy, 86
Insight modeling, 222–223
Insight moment, 57, 59, 68–69, 97
Insight question, 85, 157
Insight statement, 189
Instructional concepts
  metaphoric examples of, 39, 40,
    48–49, 95–96, 108, 136–137,
    155–156, 169
  *See* also Subject content areas
Instructional design, 36, 72, 122,
  128–129, 142, 155–161, 163,
  177–178, 189
Internal imagery, 42, 45, 105
Internal reverie, 10
Intuition, 7–8, 11, 19, 23, 45, 113,
  151
Intuitive approach, 50–52
Intuitive perception, 30
Irving, Washington, 115

Jesus (of Nazareth), 21, 50, 88, 93,
  96, 97, 127
Johnson, Mark, 75, 117
Joseph, James, 147

Kafka, Franz, 310
Kantakona (Japanese phonetic
    alphabet), 102
Kanzi (Japanese pictographic
    alphabet), 102
Kekule, 27–29, 32
Kennedy, John F., 51
King, Martin Luther, 127, 216
Knapp, Mark L., 35
Koestler, Arthur, 25, 27
Kolb, David, 128–130
Krylov, Ivan, 93
Kuslan, Louis, 31–32

Lakoff, George, 55, 75, 117
Language development, 40, 72
Latham, Jean Lee, 43
Leadership, 48, 133
Learning-disabled, 11
Learning domains, 163
L'Engle, Madeline, 43
Lesson context, 57, 59, 72–73, 197
Lewin, Kurt, 128
Linguistic metaphor, 55, 72–73,
    116–124. *See* also Metaphor
Literal definition, 120–126
Lincoln, Abraham, 50, 289
Lombardi, Vince, 277
Love, 95–96
    Ulster's definition of, 95

*Macbeth*, 289, 310
Mainstreaming, 217
Management system, 39, 133
Maslow, Abraham, 26, 261
Math
    definition of, 121
    images of, 122
    instructional concept for, 121–122
    lesson design for, 153
Maxwell, James Clark, 38
McLeod, Alan, 44
Medawer, Peter, 5
Melville, Herman, 31
Mendel, Gregor, 28–32
Mendeleev, Dmitri, 27–32
Metamorphosis, 54, 60, 144, 180,
    182, 189
Metaphor
    Aristotle's definition of, 127
    attitude impact of, 119–120
    bridge, 3, 19, 49, 93, 150
    great masters of, 20, 21, 88, 93

of great teachers, 45
as historical teaching tool, 88
instructional role of, 51
and link to creativity, 20
as measuring tool, 307
as model for learning, 19
modern masters of, 106
role of, 53, 95, 106, 117, 127,
    149–150, 197
as teaching tool, 19, 49
types of, 95, 150
*See* also Allegories; Analogies;
    Fables; Folk tales; Parables;
    Storytelling; Sufi stories
Metaphoric approach
    and advance organizer, 133
    and allusions, 88
    and brain, 122
    comparison level of, 61–63, 69,
        171, 199, 233
    and concept mastery
    definition of, 120–121
    design format for, 190
    development of, 155
    examples of, 133
    exercises for, 24, 72
    experience of, 54
    focus for, 135, 170, 180
    levels of, 190
    modes of, 190
Metaphoric brain, 36
Metaphoric combination, 52
Metaphoric image, 59, 60, 62, 68, 73,
    88, 93, 108, 118, 127, 130, 145,
    148–149, 156
Metaphoric insight, 54
Metaphoric instructional design
    process, 195
Metaphoric interaction, 57, 59, 63,
    78
Metaphoric lesson, 54–59, 61, 70–73,
    77–85, 101, 107, 112, 122–124,
    138–145, 150–156
    design of, 113, 149, 154, 156,
        191–192, 196–202, 202–208
    example of
        change/butterfly, 57–69,
            177–194
        diversity/leaf, 281–287
        ecological food chains/chain,
            155–176
        empathy/shoe, 213–227
        goal-setting/balloon, 241–260

insight/rainbow, 229–240
perfect day, 288–292
perspective/time movie, 70–87
photography/film, 293–298
relationships/plamets, 299–305
security/rocks, 261–279
types of
abbreviated, 195
advanced, 70
condensed design, 192, 194–195
design format, 150
first lessom, 196, 202
instant lesson, 154
long form, 156, 176–177, 278
short form, 306
warm-up, 150
teaching strategies of
closure metaphor, 150
guided fantasy, 149
interpersonal exercises, 150
open-ended questions, 150
personal growth metaphors, 54
quick association, 54
Metaphoric teaching
basic strategy of, 45, 118, 138, 150
concept attributes of, 122–126
focus of lesson for, 179
four modes of, 102
method of, 17, 45–51, 87, 126, 130, 149
process of, 154
strategies for, 54, 97, 100, 149–150
Metaphoric linguistics, 97
Metaphoric method, 59–69, 76, 97–106, 108–112, 149
Metaphoric perception, 13
Metaphoric resources library, 154
Metaphoric thought, 4, 54, 113, 147
*Metaphorikan linai,* 127
Michelangelo, 37, 73, 307
Moustakas, Clark, 26
Movies, 248, 302
Mozart, Wolfgang, 31
Multi-cultural awareness, 216
Munro, Hector Hugo "Saki," 95

N. G. experiment, 12–13
Nageli, Karl, 28
Napoleon, 144, 277, 289
Natural metaphor, 136. *See* also Metaphor
Newton, Sir Isaac, 37
Nicolle, Charles, 31–32

Nonverbal behavior, 35, 37, 45, 185
Nonverbal reinforcement, 62, 79
Nonverbal walk, 223

Ocean, 142, 145
Ornstein, Robert, 16
Orwell, George, 73
Osmosis, 148

Paivio, Allen, 89
Pantomine, 124, 176
Parables, 20–23, 88, 91, 94, 97, 103
Paragraph
as instructional unit, 109–112
revision of, 111
Parnes, S. J., 25
Pasteur, Louis, 28
Patterns, 10, 30, 39, 60, 91, 133, 135. *See* also Image
Peer sanction, 309
Perception, 17–18, 22, 30, 32, 148, 181
patterns of, 99
simultaneity of, 35
Personalization
analogy of, 98–99
attitude toward, 63
awareness of, 105
comparison level of, 57–59, 76, 156, 171–173, 182
and dignity, 311
and goal-setting, 257
and insight, 173, 176, 193
and internalization, 63
and judgment, 108
metaphoric lesson for, 54
and motivation, 59
and stress, 289–292
and values, 289–292
Phaedrus, 299–305
Piaget, Jean, 25
Picasso, Pablo, 38
Pirsig, Robert, 40
Pitt, William, 127
Plateus, 190
Plato, 20–21
Postassessment
design of, 156, 175, 190
goal-setting and, 256
questions for, 190–193
Pre-assessment
and conventional definition, 165

Pre-assessment (*continued*)
  conceptual understanding of,
    166–167
  design for, 156, 164, 178
  questions for, 179
  subject matter of, 167
  types of, 165
Pressley G. Michael, 44
Prince, Goerge, 24–25
Protection, 167
Proverbs, 93–94
Procrastination, 39
Preparation, 26, 28, 30, 39. *See* also
  Creativity
Preconscious visions, 30
Psychomotor domain, 139, 163–164

Questions
  and debriefing, 140, 184
  and expansion, 141, 310
  open-ended, 310
Quick-association exercises, 54

*Rashomon,* 232
Rational thinking, 20, 32, 101, 106
Real life metaphors, 148. *See* also
  Metaphor
Relationship, 77, 149
Restak, Richard, 46
Rettie, James C., 78–79
Richter, Jean Paul, 95
Roentgen, Willhelm, 29, 30, 32
Rogers, Will, 52
Role-playing, 49, 104, 144
Roosevelt, Franklin D., 50
"Round-robin" sharing, 62

Sagan, Carl, 10, 26
Salk, Jonas, 105
Samples, Robert, 25, 101–106
Sawyer, Tom, 310
Scientific method, 50, 108, 121
Self-assessment, 145
Self-awareness, 22, 55, 143
Self-discipline, 140
Self-initiated learning, 309
Self-motivation, 51
Shah, Idries, 96–97
Shakespeare, William, 73, 115, 277,
  307
Shelley, Percy, 73–74
Simulations, 49, 104
Situational limits, 105

Social democracy, 56
Social metaphors, 117. *See* also
  Metaphor
Societal mores, 263
Socrates, 20
Speech, 14–15
Sperry, Roger, 11–12
Split brain patients, 12, 14–17. *See*
  also Brain
Spontaneity, 16, 32, 53, 76, 91
Springer, Sally, 16
Steingart, Sandra, 44
Storytelling, 1–2, 89, 93
Stroke patients, 11–15
Students
  background of, 158–160, 177
  career goals of, 134
  and cognition, 38, 139, 163
  enthusiasm of, 144
  deaf, 202–208
  motivation of, 135
Subject content areas
  art class, 215
  biology class, 213
  business class, 128–135, 144–145,
    274
  chemistry class, 229, 263
  English class, 68, 86, 109–112,
    114–115, 144, 214, 224–230,
    232, 243–244, 274, 276
  foreign language class, 114, 167,
    229, 275
  health class, 225
  history class, 68, 86, 114, 127, 144,
    167, 224, 229, 263, 274
  math class, 68, 114, 121–122, 148,
    214–215, 224, 241, 274
  music class, 215
  penmanship class, 225
  political science class, 39, 53, 92,
    95, 125, 275
  religion class, 275
  science class, 68, 70–87, 103, 114,
    155–176, 229–240, 243, 254,
    259, 299–305
  social studies class, 93–95, 103,
    107, 114, 117–118, 137–138,
    145, 148, 169–170, 215–216,
    224, 229–230, 243, 263, 273
  typing class, 114, 274
Sufi stories, 50, 93, 96–97
Super Sustained Silent Reading
  Time (SSSRT), 43

Synaptic interconnections, 5
Synetics, 49, 99–101, 106
Synergy, 97, 103–104, 143, 149

Tachistoscope, 12, 16
Taylor, Calvin, 108
Teacher
  and learner relationship, 54
  study of activities of, 18–19
Teaching strategies, 10, 39, 94, 113,
  150
Technical process, 293–298
Television, 36, 40–45
Texas Assessment of Basic Skills
  (TABS), 112
Time, 70–76, 86, 153
Tolerance, 122–126, 147–148, 312
Tolstoy, Leo, 30
Torrance, Paul, 18, 25
Truth, 22, 28, 53, 88, 93–97
Turner, Charles Hampden, 90

Unconventional thinking, 100, 312
Unsuspected connection, 51–54
Unusual connection, 30
Unusual idea, 311

Van der Post, Laurens, 1–3
Verification, 38. *See* also Creativity
Virchow, Rudolf, 105
Visual impact, 41, 45, 62, 76, 102
Voltaire, 53
Vulnerability, 166, 183

Wada test, 14–16
Wallas, Graham, 26–29, 32, 34
Washington, George, 277, 289
Wells, H. G., 144
Winn, Marie, 40, 42, 44
Wilder, Laura Ingalls, 43–44
Wilder, Thorton, 95
William, Augustus, 88
William, Garth, 43
Williams, Frank, 33–34
Wisdom, 2, 7, 53, 95, 105, 120,
  127
Words, 55–56, 95

Yeats, William, 52
Yukawa, Hideki, 7

X-rays, 29–30